THE

EVERYTHING

DESSERT
COOKBOOK

The Everything® Series:

The Everything® After College Book
The Everything® Astrology Book
The Everything® Baby Names Book
The Everything® Bartender's Book
The Everything® Beer Book
The Everything® Bicycle Book
The Everything® Bird Book
The Everything® Casino Gambling Book
The Everything® Cat Book
The Everything® Christmas Book
The Everything® College Survival Book
The Everything® Crossword and Puzzle Book
The Everything® Dreams Book
The Everything® Etiquette Book
The Everything® Family Tree Book
The Everything® Games Book
The Everything® Get Ready for Baby Book
The Everything® Golf Book
The Everything® Home Buying Book
The Everything® Home Improvement Book
The Everything® Internet Book
The Everything® Jewish Wedding Book
The Everything® Low-Fat High-Flavor Cookbook
The Everything® Pasta Cookbook
The Everything® Study Book
The Everything® Guide to Walt Disney World,
Universal Studios, and Greater Orlando
The Everything® Wedding Book
The Everything® Wedding Checklist
The Everything® Wedding Etiquette Book
The Everything® Wedding Organizer
The Everything® Wedding Vows Book
The Everything® Wine Book
The Everything® Dessert Book

THE EVERYTHING®

DESSERT COOKBOOK

300 fantastic desserts for every occasion and taste–
extravagant trifles, truffles, tarts, and more!

 Lisa Shaw

Adams Media Corporation
HOLBROOK, MASSACHUSETTS

For Miss Sugar Bombe, a cat who's sweeter than sugar

An Everything® Series Book.
Everything® is a registered trademark of Adams Media Corporation.

Published by Adams Media Corporation
260 Center Street, Holbrook, MA 02343

ISBN: 1-55850-717-5

Printed in the United States of America.

J I H G F E D C

Library of Congress Cataloging-in-Publication Data
Shaw, Lisa Angowski Rogak.
The everything dessert book / by Lisa Shaw.
p.   cm.
ISBN 1-55850-717-5
1. Desserts. I. Title.
TX773.S4274   1998
641.8'6—dc21   98-20078
                               CIP

Illustrations by Barry Littmann

This book is available at quantity discounts for bulk purchases.
For information, call 1-800-872-5627 (in Massachusetts, call 781-767-8100).

Visit our home page at www.adamsmedia.com

The Everything Dessert Cookbook

Introduction

People everywhere love their sweets. Words commonly associated with dessert—honey, sweetie, sugar, cookie—are regularly used as terms of endearment, and many believe that a meal is not complete without a sweet to finish it off.

Here, in *The Everything® Dessert Book*, you'll run out of days of the year before you run out of desserts to make. From the many recipes with variations to the cakes and pies that you personalize with your own thoughtful additions—a sprinkling of walnuts here, a splash of coffee liqueur there—you have in your hand a multitude of desserts to satisfy every specific craving that your sweet tooth may demand.

You may have heard the motto, "Eat dessert first; life is uncertain." In my house, this credo is taken seriously. In fact, many times when we go out for dinner and find there's a thirty-minute wait, we'll put our names on the list and head out for our real aim—dessert. We dash around the corner to the ice cream stand, order a double dip of anything, and then stroll around eating and talking. By the time we've reached the end of our cones, our table is ready. Now we can have a leisurely dinner, since the object of our affections—dessert—is already out of the way.

You should consider your dessert repertoire in the same fashion: sure, there are always people who will ooh and aah at your beef Wellington and lobster en croute. But if you go all out for an exquisitely rich and creamy chocolate mousse that everyone just takes a bit longer to devour than usual, you can get away with serving a box of spaghetti and a jar of sauce. Not really, of course, but we are a society that places enormous importance on dessert and all of its ramifications, despite the fact that our culture is supposedly so health conscious these days.

When I was growing up in the sixties and seventies, I would regularly have a piece of chocolate cake and a glass of milk for breakfast. Nobody was alarmed, and I made it all the way through to lunch without any unfortunate incidents. Perhaps the fact that we have created a system of branding "good" foods and "bad" foods (including dessert) has made us obsess even more about the sweet things we do and don't allow ourselves to eat.

Maybe it's time to welcome desserts back into your life with open arms. Prepare the recipes in *The Everything® Dessert Book* with lots of love, and respect each cake, pie, and candy as the treat and respite that it represents in our everyday lives.

A Dessert Dictionary

Angel Food Cake
If you thought only baking powder and baking soda were good for leavening, think again. Just look at any recipe for angel food cake and you'll find neither of these rising agents. In fact, in terms of simplification, angel food cake is as streamlined as it gets: the main ingredients are egg whites, sugar, and flour.

Baking Powder and Baking Soda
Baking powder and baking soda are leavening agents that cause batters and doughs to rise. Baking powder contains baking soda, cream of tartar (or other acid), and cornstarch (or other moisture absorber). When you add liquid to baking powder, it produces carbon dioxide, which causes the batter to rise. Baking soda is an alkaline substance that is used instead of—or in addition to—baking powder when a recipe calls for an acid ingredient, such as yogurt or buttermilk. Baking soda has a shelf life of about a year, but baking powder should be replaced at least twice a year.

Bavarian Cream
Bavarian cream is a thick, sweet dessert that has two opposing forces as ingredients: whipped heavy cream and powdered gelatin. It can be served by itself or used as a tasty filling for eclairs, cakes, or fruit desserts.

Butter
I use unsalted butter in all of my recipes because it is easier to figure out how much salt a recipe needs when the butter does not affect the measure. To soften butter to room temperature, you can either leave it on the counter for a few hours or put it in the microwave for 10 seconds. Do not soften the butter too much, however, or your batter or dough will be too liquid, which can affect the final result. If you don't want to wait or to microwave it, you can always cream the butter with an electric mixer for a few minutes to soften it before you add the other ingredients.

Butter Cakes
Also known as pound cakes, butter cakes are fine-textured, rich cakes made from butter, sugar, eggs, and flour. The butter is typically creamed with the sugar, and the eggs are added whole or separated.

Cocoa Butter
Cocoa butter is the solid fat extracted from cocoa beans during the manufacture of chocolate. It adds substance and flavor to chocolate and other foods and is also used in the making of cosmetics.

Cocoa Powder
When cocoa butter is separated from cocoa beans, the pastelike substance that remains is dried and ground to form cocoa powder. It is available as is or mixed with other ingredients, such as sugar. Dutch-process cocoa is

cocoa powder to which an alkali has been added to neutralize some of the product's natural acidity.

Chocolate

It seems that there are nearly as many different kinds of chocolate as there are chocolate lovers. Basically, however, two types of chocolate exist, sweetened, which contains some form of sucrose, and unsweetened, which does not. Semisweet and bittersweet are interchangeable, so feel free to use what you like best. The texture of the final dessert will not be affected.

Always look for an ingredient panel that contains chocolate or cocoa butter, which delivers a smooth texture. Products that list chocolate flavoring, a synthetic ingredient, can result in a grainy, uneven texture.

It's important to keep your baking chocolate stored in a cool, dry place. Use an airtight container so the chocolate cannot absorb flavors and odors from other foods. White and milk chocolates will keep for six months; dark and semisweet chocolates will keep for up to a year if stored properly. If your chocolate appears streaked with lighter brown, it's still good to eat. It just means that the cocoa butter has separated and risen to the top of the chocolate.

When a recipe calls for melted chocolate, it's best to heat it slowly in a double boiler over low heat and gently simmering water. First chop the chocolate into small bits and then place it in the top pan. It's important that the pan be clean and dry, since if even a drop of water touches the chocolate, it will become stiff and uneven in texture. Remove the chocolate from the heat before it is thoroughly melted. The remaining heat will melt the chocolate without overheating it.

Eggs

Always use the egg size that is specified in a recipe. When no size is indicated, large eggs are presumed. For the best result, allow the eggs to reach room temperature before using them for baking. To achieve this, you can either leave the eggs out on the counter for several hours or put them in a glass of warm water for 10 minutes.

If, however, you are separating eggs, it is easiest if they are cold. Try not to get any bit of the yolk in with the whites, or the volume of the white will reduce upon beating. To separate an egg, crack it and allow the white to drain into a bowl by quickly moving the yolk between the shell halves. Place the yolk in a separate bowl.

The mixing bowl and beaters should be clean, dry, and grease free when beating egg whites. Leftover eggs will keep for up to a week in a covered container in the refrigerator.

Flour

White all-purpose flour, either bleached or unbleached, is the most popular type of flour for baking. Always be sure to spoon flour into the measuring cup and then to level if off with a knife. Flour becomes compressed

during storage, so you should always sift it before using.

Cake flour, which is softer than all-purpose flour, is ideal for making cakes and light pastries.

Whole-grain flour adds texture and nutrients to sweet and savory breads, but should not be used as a substitute for all-purpose flour in cake and pastry recipes. Look for whole-grain recipes produced by companies that market whole-grain flour. Their recipes take the additional density and weight into consideration.

High-Altitude Baking

Baking calls for adjustments in altitudes over 2,500 feet. Liquids boil at lower temperatures and evaporate more quickly, and cooking times are longer because foods heat at lower temperatures. Generally speaking, pans should be greased more heavily, oven temperatures increased slightly, leaveners and sugar reduced, and liquids increased. The actual adjustments will depend on the altitude.

Baking at high altitudes requires chiefly two basic adjustments:

1. An increase in time for boiled foods.
2. A change in the proportions of ingredients used in leavened foods such as cakes and yeast breads. In some instances, a change in baking temperatures may also be necessary.

Changes in altitude do not affect oven temperatures; however, since atmospheric pressure decreases at the higher altitudes, leavened batters and doughs rise faster than they do at sea level. At elevations over 3,500 feet, the oven temperature for batters and doughs should be 25°F higher than the temperature used at sea level. Proofing time for yeast breads should be reduced.

Cake Baking at High Altitudes

Most cake recipes for sea level need no modification up to the altitude of 3,000 feet. Above that, it is often necessary to adjust recipes slightly. Usually, a decrease in leavening or sugar (or both) and an increase in liquid are needed.

Each or all of these adjustments may be required for every recipe is different in its balance of ingredients. Only repeated experiments with each recipe can give the most successful proportions to use.

The table below is intended as a helpful guide and may be all that is needed to adjust a sea level recipe to a higher altitude. Where two amounts appear in the table, the smaller adjustment should be tried first. Then if the cake still needs improvement, the larger adjustment can be used the next time.

Guide for Cake Baking at High Altitudes

Adjustment at 3,000 feet	Reduce baking powder: for each tsp., decrease $\frac{1}{8}$ tsp. Reduce sugar: for each cup, decrease 0 to 1 Tbsp. Increase liquid for each cup, add 1 to 2 Tbsp.
Adjustment at 5,000 feet	Reduce baking powder: for each tsp., decrease $\frac{1}{8}$ to $\frac{1}{4}$ tsp. Reduce sugar: for each cup, decrease 0 to 2 Tbsp. Increase liquid: for each cup, add 2 to 4 Tbsp.
Adjustment at 7,000 feet	Reduce baking powder: for each tsp., decrease $\frac{1}{4}$ tsp. Reduce sugar: for each cup, decrease 1 to 3 Tbsp. Increase liquid: for each cup, add 3 to 4 Tbsp.

Specific Altitude Adjustments for Cake Batters

Altitude Adjustment	*3,000 feet*	*5,000 feet*	*7,500 feet*	*10,000 feet*
Decrease baking powder: for each teaspoon called for, decrease by	$\frac{1}{8}$ teaspoon	$\frac{1}{8}$ to $\frac{1}{4}$ teaspoon	$\frac{1}{4}$ teaspoon	$\frac{1}{4}$ to $\frac{1}{2}$ teaspoon
Decrease sugar: for each cup called for, decrease by	0 to 1 tablespoon	0 to 2 tablespoons	1 to 3 tablespoons	2 to 3 tablespoons
Increase liquid: for each cup called for, add	1 to 2 tablespoons	2 to 4 tablespoons	3 to 4 tablespoons	3 to 4 tablespoons
*Increase flour: for each cup called for, add			1 to 2 tablespoons	1 to 2 tablespoons
Increase eggs				Add 1 egg

*Authorities do not agree on the wisdom of adding flour, except in foam cakes (sponge cakes, angel cakes, and chiffons), since additional flour has a drying effect that is unwelcome at altitudes where low humidity already makes for dry baked goods.

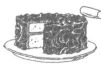

Meringue

Meringue is formed by whipping together egg whites and sugar. There are basically two types: soft and hard. The former is commonly used as a pie topping, while the latter is baked to a firm, airy shell of various sizes and then filled with fruit, chocolate, or cream, or formed into tiny mounds and eaten like a candy.

Nuts

If a recipe calls for toasted nuts, place them in a single layer on an ungreased baking sheet and bake in a preheated 350°F oven until lightly browned, stirring occasionally. Hazelnuts will take about 15 minutes, while most other nuts, including almonds, walnuts, and pecans, brown in about 10 minutes. Aroma, in addition to color, is a good indicator of when nuts are properly toasted: if they smell like freshly roasted nuts on the boardwalk, they're done.

Nuts can be frozen for more than a year with no loss in taste or quality. Some cooks believe freezing nuts with the shell on keeps them fresher.

Puff Pastry

Puff pastry is a multilayered pastry that is given loft by the presence of thin squares of butter between layers of dough. When baked, the trapped butter creates steam that causes the dough to separate into many layers. The result is pastry that is light and airy on the inside and golden and crisp outside. Napoleons and croissants are made from puff pastry.

Sugar

Granulated, or white, sugar is the most popular sugar in dessert making. It is inexpensive and adds both body and sweetness to a recipe.

Brown sugar, which is actually white sugar to which molasses has been added, can be dark brown or light brown and granulated or not. The differences in the color come from the amount of molasses, and the darker the color the stronger the taste. Store brown sugar in a tightly covered container in a cool, dry cupboard to avoid lumps.

Confectioners' sugar, also known as powdered sugar, is granulated sugar that has been ground to a powder. A little bit of cornstarch is added to prevent lumping.

Sugar substitutes aren't ideal for baking, so unless a recipe has been specially formulated for a sugar substitute, don't use one for baking.

Whipping Cream

Whenever a recipe specifies whipping cream, purchase containers labeled heavy whipping cream, whipping cream, or heavy cream. These products all have a high fat content, which causes them to increase dramatically in volume when whipped. If possible, choose pasteurized cream and not ultrapasteurized, as the latter has been heated to increase storage time, which, in turn, reduces whipping volume.

Always chill the mixing bowl and beaters before you whip the cream by placing them

in the freezer for about 15 minutes. This will help to increase the final volume.

Your Tools

Baking equipment that is high in quality and is in good shape is vital to ensuring your desserts turn out well. If you have two 8-inch and two 9-inch round cake pans and a 9-inch springform pan on hand, you'll be able to tackle most any cake. It's also a good idea to keep some 8- and 9-inch square pans on hand, along with a 9-by-12-inch pan. Three heavy-duty aluminum baking sheets are necessary, too. To frost your cakes, you'll need two stainless-steel flexible icing spatulas, one 8 inch and one 4 inch. The spatulas will help to ensure a smooth frosted surface for your cakes.

One way to streamline your work when decorating cakes (and to eliminate twisting and hurting your wrists) is to use a lazy Susan on a turntable. A turntable will also help you to frost more evenly and smoothly.

And if you regularly take your cakes traveling to parties, you'll need some corrugated cardboard rounds known as cake circles. They will help to support your cakes in transit.

A Brief History of Chocolate

Confectionery history is at least four thousand years old, dating back to when Egyptians recorded their interest on papyrus.

Sweetmeats were being sold in the Egyptian marketplace in 1566 B.C.

Yet chocolate didn't appear on the scene until the ancient Aztec and Mayan cultures discovered the value of the cacao tree, which is reputed to have originated in the Amazon or Orinoco basin.

In A.D. 600 the Mayans migrated into the northern regions of South America, establishing the earliest known cacao plantations in the Yucatán. It has been argued that the Mayans had been familiar with cacao, also known as cocoa, several centuries prior to this time, and had considered it a valuable commodity, used both as a means of payment and as units of calculation.

Mayans and Aztecs took beans from the cacao tree and made a drink they called *xocoatl*. Aztec legend held that cacao beans had been brought from Paradise, and that wisdom and power came from eating the fruit of the tree.

Aztecs, believing that the god Quetzalcoatl traveled to earth on a beam of the Morning Star with a cacao tree from Paradise, took his offering to the people. They learned from Quetzalcoatl how to roast and grind the cacao beans, making a nourishing paste that could be dissolved in water. They added spices and called this drink *chocolatl*, or bitter water, and believed it brought universal wisdom and knowledge.

The word *chocolate* is said to derive from the Mayan *xocoatl*; while cocoa comes from

the Aztec *cacahuatl*. The Mexican Indian word *chocolate* comes from a combination of the terms *choco* ("foam") and *atl* ("water"). Early chocolate was only consumed in beverage form. A mug of the frothy drink was ritually shared between the new husband and wife at twelfth-century Mesoamerican marriages.

Arthur W. Knapp, author of *The Cocoa and Chocolate Industry* (Pitman, 1923), points out that if we believe Mexican mythology, "chocolate was consumed by the Gods in Paradise, and the seed of cocoa was conveyed to man as a special blessing by the God of the Air."

The ancient Mexicans believed that Tonacatecutli, the goddess of food, and Calchiuhtlucue, the goddess of water, were guardians of cocoa. Each year the people performed human sacrifices to this pair, giving the victim cocoa at his last meal.

In another acknowledgment of its higher existence, Swedish naturalist Carolus Linnaeus (1707–78) was dissatisfied with the word *cocoa*, so renamed it *theobroma*, Greek for "food of the gods."

Upon returning from his fourth visit to the New World, Christopher Columbus is said to have delivered cocoa beans to King Ferdinand, but they were overlooked in favor of the many other treasures he had found.

In 1519, Spanish explorer Hernando Cortés visited the court of Emperor Montezuma of Mexico. In *History of the Conquest of Mexico* (1838), American historian William Hickling reports that Cortés observed that Montezuma "took no other beverage than the chocolatl, a potation of chocolate, flavored with vanilla and spices, and so prepared as to be reduced to a froth of the consistency of honey, which gradually dissolved in the mouth and was taken cold." The fact that Montezuma consumed his *chocolatl* in goblets before entering his harem led to the belief that it was an aphrodisiac.

In 1528, Cortés brought cocoa beans back from Mexico to the royal court of King Charles V. Monks, hidden away in Spanish monasteries, processed the beans and kept chocolate a secret for nearly a century. It made a profitable industry for Spain, which planted cocoa trees in its overseas colonies.

It took an Italian traveler, Antonio Carletti, to discover the chocolate treasure in 1606 and take it into other parts of Europe.

When the Spanish Princess Maria Theresa was betrothed to Louis XIV of France in 1615, she gave her fiancé an engagement gift of chocolate, packaged in an elegantly ornate chest. Their marriage was symbolic of the marriage of chocolate in the Spanish-Franco culture.

The first chocolate house was reputedly opened in London in 1657, by a Frenchman. Costing 10 to 15 shillings per pound, chocolate was considered a beverage for the elite class. Sixteenth-century Spanish historian Oviedo noted: "None but the rich and noble

could afford to drink chocolatl as it was literally drinking money. Cocoa passed currency as money among all nations; thus a rabbit in Nicaragua sold for 10 cocoa nibs, and 100 of these seeds could buy a tolerably good slave."

Chocolate also appears to have been used as a medicinal remedy by leading physicians of the day. Christopher Ludwig Hoffmann's treatise "Potus Chocolate" recommends chocolate for many diseases, citing it as a cure for Cardinal Richelieu's ills.

Chocolate traveled to the Low Countries with the Duke of Alba. By 1730, it had dropped in price from three dollars per pound to being within the financial reach of those other than the very wealthy. The invention of the cocoa press in 1828 helped further to cut prices and improve the quality of chocolate by squeezing out some of the cocoa butter and giving the beverage a smoother consistency.

With the Industrial Revolution came the mass production of chocolate, and thus the spread of its popularity among the citizenry.

Discussing the introduction of coffee, tea, and cocoa into Europe, Isaac Disraeli (1791–1834) wrote in his six-volume Curiosities of Literature: "Chocolate the Spaniards brought from Mexico, where it was denominated chocolatl. It was a coarse mixture of ground cacao and Indian corn with roucou; but the Spaniards, liking its nourishment, improved it into a richer compound with sugar, vanilla and other aromatics. We had Chocolate houses in London long after coffee houses; they seemed to have associated something more elegant and refined in their new form when the other had become common."

An 1891 publication, The Chocolate-Plant, by Walter Baker & Co., records that, "At the discovery of America, the natives of the narrower portion of the continent bordering on the Caribbean Sea were found in possession of two luxuries which have been everywhere recognized as worthy of extensive cultivation; namely, tobacco and chocolate."

Chocolate was introduced to the United States in 1765, when John Hanan brought cocoa beans from the West Indies into Dorchester, Massachusetts, to refine them with the help of Dr. James Baker. The first chocolate factory in the country was established there. Yet, chocolate wasn't really accepted by the American colonists until fishermen from Gloucester, Massachusetts, accepted cocoa beans as payment for cargo in tropical America.

Where chocolate was mostly considered a beverage for centuries, and predominantly for men, it became recognized as an appropriate drink for children in the seventeenth century. It had many different additions: milk, wine, beer, sweeteners, and spices. Drinking chocolate was considered a fashionable social event.

In 1747, Frederick the Great issued an edict forbidding the hawking of chocolate.

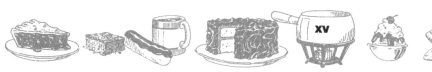

By 1795, Dr. Joseph Fry of Bristol, England, employed a steam engine for grinding cocoa beans, an invention that led to the manufacture of chocolate on a large scale. Around 1847, Fry & Sons sold a Chocolat Delicieux à Manger, which is thought to be the first chocolate bar for eating.

Nestlé declares that from 1800 to the present day, these four factors contributed to chocolate's "coming of age" as a worldwide food product: the introduction of cocoa powder in 1828; the reduction of excise duties; improvements in transportation facilities, from plantation to factory; and the invention of eating chocolate and improvements in manufacturing methods.

By the year 1810, Venezuela was producing half the world's requirements for cocoa, and one-third of all the cocoa produced in the world was being consumed by the Spaniards.

The invention of the cocoa press in 1828 by C.J. Van Houten, a Dutch chocolate master, helped reduce the price of chocolate and bring it to the masses. Van Houten squeezed out cocoa butter from the beans, an alkalizing, or "dutching," treatment that resulted in Dutch-process cocoa powder, which has deeper flavor and less acidity than regular cocoa powder.

Daniel Peter of Vevey, Switzerland, experimented for eight years before finally inventing a means of making milk chocolate for eating in 1876. He brought his creation to a Swiss firm that today is the world's largest producer of chocolate: Nestlé.

In 1879, Rodolphe Lindt of Berne, Switzerland, produced chocolate that melted on the tongue. He invented "conching," a means of heating and rolling chocolate to refine it. After chocolate had been conched for 72 hours and had more cocoa butter added to it, the original fondant was created.

Cadbury Brothers displayed eating chocolate in 1849 at an exhibition in Bingley Hall at Birmingham, England.

Prince Albert's Exposition in 1851 in London was the first time the United States was introduced to bonbons, chocolate creams, hand candies (called "boiled sweets"), and caramels.

Swiss chocolate maker Jules Sechaud of Montreux introduced a process for manufacturing filled chocolates in 1913.

The New York Cocoa Exchange, now located at the World Trade Center, was opened on October 1, 1925, so that buyers and sellers could get together for transactions.

Brazil and the Ivory Coast are leaders in the cocoa bean belt, accounting for nearly half of the world's cocoa.

While the United States leads the world in cocoa bean importation and chocolate production, Switzerland continues as the leader in per capita chocolate consumption.

In 1980, a story of chocolate espionage hit the world press when an apprentice of the Swiss company of Suchard-Tobler unsuccessfully attempted to sell secret chocolate recipes to Russia, China, Saudi Arabia, and other countries.

By the 1990s, chocolate had proven its popularity as a product, and its success as a big business. Annual world consumption of cocoa beans averages 600,000 tons, and per capita chocolate consumption is greatly on the rise. Chocolate manufacturing in the United States is a multibillion-dollar industry.

More about Chocolate

Melting Chocolate

Chocolate scorches easily, so always melt it over (not touching) hot (not boiling) water. It is best to use a double boiler, but you can improvise by using a heatproof bowl placed in the rim of a saucepan over gentle heat. The water must be kept below simmering to prevent steam from curling up and hitting the chocolate. If steam gets into melted chocolate, the mixture will thicken immediately to a stiff mass. To rescue the chocolate, soften it again: add 1 to 2 table-spoons vegetable shortening—never use butter, as it contains moisture that will cause the chocolate to stiffen further—to the chocolate and stir vigorously. You can also melt chocolate directly over very low heat in a heavy saucepan, but you must watch the mixture carefully.

Making Chocolate Curls

Use a vegetable peeler with a long, narrow blade and a chunk or bar of chocolate. Be sure your peeler is absolutely dry. Draw the peeler along the smooth surface of the chocolate.

Grating Chocolate

Be sure the block of chocolate is cool and firm. Grate on a handheld grater, cleaning the grater often so that the chocolate doesn't clog the surface of the blade. You can also use a blender, but be sure to cut the chocolate into small pieces first.

Storing Chocolate

Chocolate should be stored in a cool, dry place at a temperature of about 60°F. If the chocolate becomes too warm, the cocoa butter rises to the surface and forms a dusty gray film known as "bloom." This bloom is not harmful and disappears once the chocolate is melted. If you do store chocolate in the refrigerator or freezer, take it out and let it stand until it returns to room temperature before you use it in a recipe. Chocolate is sensitive to sudden changes of temperature, and you will not get the best results if you do not handle it properly.

Chocolate Substitutions

Unsweetened baking chocolate: Substitute 3 tablespoons unsweetened cocoa powder plus 1 tablespoon shortening or oil for each ounce of baking chocolate.

Premelted unsweetened chocolate: Substitute 3 tablespoons unsweetened cocoa powder plus 1 tablespoon oil or melted shortening for each ounce envelope of melted chocolate.

Semisweet chocolate: Substitute 6 tablespoons unsweetened cocoa powder, 7 tablespoons sugar, and $\frac{1}{4}$ cup shortening for 1 cup semisweet chocolate chips or 6 ounces semisweet baking chocolate. Or combine 1 ounce unsweetened chocolate and 1 tablespoon sugar or use 3 tablespoons semisweet chocolate for 1 ounce.

Semisweet chocolate chips (for melting): Substitute 3 ounces semisweet chocolate for $\frac{1}{2}$ cup.

Sweet baking chocolate: Substitute 3 tablespoons unsweetened cocoa powder, $4\frac{1}{2}$ tablespoons sugar, and 2 tablespoons plus 2 teaspoons shortening for 4 ounces sweet baking chocolate.

Chocolate Trivia
(Courtesy of Godiva Chocolates)

- There are 5 to 10 milligrams caffeine in 1 ounce of bittersweet chocolate, 5 milligrams in milk chocolate, and 10 milligrams in a 6-ounce cup of cocoa. By contrast, there are 100 to 150 milligrams caffeine in an 8-ounce cup of brewed coffee. You would have to eat more than a dozen Hershey Bars, for example, to get the amount of caffeine in one cup of coffee.

- Chocolate has long been heralded for its value as an energy source. Think of it this way: a single chocolate chip provides sufficient food energy for an adult to walk 150 feet. Hence, it takes about 35 chocolate chips to go a mile or 875,000 for an around-the-world hike.

- Although chocolate is not an aphrodisiac, as the ancient Aztecs believed, chocolate contains phenylethylamine (PEA), a natural substance that is reputed to stimulate the same reaction in the body as falling in love. Hence, heartbreak and loneliness are great excuses for chocolate gorging.

- It is reported that Napoleon carried chocolate with him on his military campaigns, and always ate it when he needed quick energy.

- While solid chocolate is definitely high in fat, only slightly over half the calories in bittersweet, semisweet, and milk chocolate come from fat. And even though the cocoa butter in chocolate is mostly saturated fat, studies have shown that it doesn't appear to raise blood cholesterol.

- It's a common myth that chocolate aggravates acne. Experiments conducted at the University of Pennsylvania and the US Naval Academy found that consumption of chocolate—even frequent daily dietary intake—had no effect on the incidence of acne. Professional dermatologists today do not link acne with diet.
- Ten percent of the US Recommended Daily Allowance of iron is found in 1 ounce of baking chocolate or cocoa.
- Lecithin is an emulsifier used to reduce the viscosity of chocolate. It serves to lessen the amount of cocoa butter required in the manufacturing process.
- Chocolate can be lethal to dogs. Theobromine, an ingredient that stimulates the cardiac muscle and the central nervous system, causes chocolate's toxicity. About 2 ounces of milk chocolate can be poisonous for a 10-pound puppy.
- Consumers spend more than $7 billion a year on chocolate.
- US consumers eat 2.8 billion pounds of chocolate annually, representing nearly half of the world's supply.
- US annual per capita consumption of chocolate is 12 pounds per person.
- American chocolate manufacturers use about 1.5 billion pounds of milk—surpassed only by the cheese and ice cream industries.
- Most Americans, some 92 percent of the population in fact, prefer milk chocolate, but dark chocolate's popularity is growing rapidly!

- Chocolate syrup was used for blood in the famous 45-second shower scene in Alfred Hitchcock's *Psycho*, which actually took seven days to shoot.
- Chocolate has over 500 flavor components, more than twice the amount found in strawberry and vanilla.

Not to Miss Baking Tips

Tips for Better Baking

- Practice, practice, practice.
- Be orderly: Do your planning before you start. Choose your recipe, read it through carefully, and understand it fully. Gather all the ingredients it calls for in their order. Assemble all the tools you will need for the job. Have a do-it-right attitude from the beginning and baking will become a joy instead of a job.
- Use the proper tools and pans: The proper tools will simplify baking, enabling you to do things more easily and more accurately. They speed up mixing and help you to achieve uniformly successful results. Always use the specified pan, or your cakes may be too flat and your pies may be spilling over the edges.
- Choose high-quality ingredients: You can't do first-rate work with second-rate ingredients. What you put in is what you get out. Make sure that your ingredients are fresh and are always of the highest quality.

- Measure accurately: Correct measuring is a *must*. The best ingredients, the highest skill level, and the best tools cannot overcome poor measuring. If the recipe tells you to sift your flour, do it. If you don't, the flour will be the wrong measure. Make sure that all your measuring cups and spoons are of the right kind to do the right job. For example, use a measuring cup with a pouring lip for measuring liquids instead of a measuring cup with an unbroken rim.

Tips for Better Cakes

- To prevent the topping for pineapple upside-down cake from darkening too much before the cake is done, set the cake pan on a baking sheet before it goes into the oven. This extra thickness keeps the brown sugar mixture and the pineapple a perfect color.
- If a buttercream frosting is too thick, use a little milk to thin it, or warm in the microwave for a few seconds. Icing a cake can sometimes be difficult, and it's important to use buttercream at a soft consistency.
- If cake layers seem particularly soft and crumbly, chill them before applying the frosting. Do not freeze them, however, because water can form on the outside of the finished frosting.

- Place a high-quality fruit preserve in your blender or food processor and mix until smooth. This only takes a few seconds. Use the mixture as a spread between the layers or on top of your cake. You may also add a little of the mixture to buttercream frosting to give it a fruit color and flavor.
- Mix cocoa powder with melted butter or margarine to make a thick, smooth paste. Use this paste to change white buttercream into chocolate buttercream frosting. Sometimes just adding cocoa powder to white buttercream will cause lumps of cocoa that cannot be broken up.
- Not all greased pans need a dusting of flour. Cakes that have a high sugar content must be coated, but many others do not. Use cocoa powder to coat a chocolate cake pan for a little more flavor and to eliminate the color of the flour.
- Butter or margarine can be used to coat cake pans, but shortening is economical and does not burn like butter or margarine. Non-stick cooking spray that contains flour is a perfect choice for most recipes. Lightly dust with flour or cocoa powder after using a spray that does not contain flour.
- Line the bottom of a cake pan with wax paper to help sheet cakes and large layers release without sticking.

Tips for Great Caramel Results

- Avoid making a dessert with caramel in humid weather. The caramel will attract moisture in the atmosphere and will not harden properly.
- Use a heavy, straight-sided saucepan for cooking the caramel to distribute the heat evenly and help prevent scorching. The best pans to use are heavy-gauge aluminum lined with stainless steel or a large, heavy nonstick skillet.
- Butter the sides of the pan before you begin making the caramel, which will prevent the caramel from becoming grainy. It also helps to sift the white sugar beforehand, as well as break up any lumps in brown sugar. Before the caramel comes to a boil, all the sugar crystals must be dissolved.
- Add a pinch of baking soda to the caramel when it first starts to boil. It will help to neutralize the excess acid in the mixture and prevent it from curdling.
- While the caramel is cooking, rinse the candy thermometer under hot water two or three times. This removes any clinging sugar crystals and is especially important if the thermometer is mounted on a metal frame where sugar crystals are likely to form.

Tips for the Perfect Cheesecake

- Before mixing, bring all ingredients to room temperature.
- Combine cream cheese and eggs before adding liquids or sour cream.
- Use the paddle attachment of an electric mixer if possible. This will cut down on the air that is incorporated into the batter. Standard beaters add too much air, which will lead to cracks. If you do use standard beaters, set them to very low speed. The more you beat, the more cracks you will have.
- Cheesecakes must cool very slowly without drafts. Extreme temperature changes cause surface cracks. If possible, cool in a turned-off oven with the door ajar.
- Always let a cheesecake "set" overnight before serving.
- If cracks do appear, cover them with fruit or a pie filling.
- Cheesecakes are sometimes difficult to cut cleanly. To cut one properly, use a thin-bladed knife that has been moistened with a warm, wet towel. Push the blade lengthwise into the cake and pull straight out from the bottom (do not lift up the blade). Clean and moisten the blade with the towel before each cut.

Tips for Better Cookies and Brownies

- Chill dough for 15 to 30 minutes before shaping cookies.
- Put only enough flour on your work surface and rolling pin to prevent sticking. Excess flour can cause cookies to turn out tough.
- Use an ice-cream scoop to drop cookies. Your cookies will all be the same size and will bake evenly. If the dough is sticky, dip the scoop into water between scoops.
- Cut cookies out of dough as close together as possible. Gently work the remaining dough back into the fresh dough.
- Use the thin edge of a drinking glass to cut out cookies. Use a widemouthed jar to cut out large cookies.
- Use a salt shaker for sprinkling sugar on the tops of cookies. The result looks better and is not as messy as using your hand.
- Drizzle a warm confectioners' sugar–milk glaze over cookies for extra sweetness. Color the glaze a bit and sprinkle on decorations while it's still wet to make cookies even prettier.
- Remove baked brownies from the pan and ice them upside down. They will cut into squares more neatly.

Tips for Better Custards

- Almost all custard failure is a result of cooking too long or cooking at too high a temperature.

- For baked custards, always pour custard into cups, set them in a baking pan, and pour water into the pan to reach halfway up the sides of the cups.
- To test a baked custard for doneness, insert a knife midway between the center and the outer edge of the custard. If it comes out clean, the custard is done. Immediately remove from the baking pan. To chill quickly, set the custard cups in ice water, but only if cups can take abrupt changes in temperature without breaking.
- When cooking custard on top of the stove, use a double boiler (or heatproof bowl placed over a saucepan) and medium heat only. If cooked too fast, the eggs will lump and will not hold the liquid in suspension as they should. Add about $1/2$ cup of the hot liquid to the eggs and stir in before adding the eggs to the mixture.
- To test a stirred custard for doneness, stir the custard until it leaves a thick, translucent, almost jellylike coating about the consistency of gravy on the back of a metal spoon. If you suspect that the custard is on the verge of curdling, plunge the pan into ice water to stop the cooking.
- If a baked custard curdles, turn it into a trifle by mixing it with small hunks of cake.
- If a stirred custard curdles, strain out the lumps and serve as a sauce over cake, fruit, or gelatin dessert.

- Continue to stir the custard after it has been removed from the heat in order to release the steam. For the best texture, set the pan in a bowl of ice water while stirring.
- Add bananas, coconut, fruit, or nuts after the custard has cooled.
- Use leftover custard to add moisture to your boxed cake mix. Add $1/4$ cup to the fully mixed cake batter. Heat the rest in a microwave and use it to frost the cake.

Tips for Better Dessert Sauces

- Melt chocolate chips and a little whipping cream together in your microwave or in a double boiler (or in a heatproof bowl placed over a saucepan). Add enough cream to thin the melted chocolate so it's pourable. Remove from the heat and gently stir in an egg yolk to give the mixture a glossy finish. If the mixture is too thick, add whipping cream a little at a time until it is right. The egg yolk must be at room temperature before adding or it will cause the chocolate to set (always use clean, uncracked eggs).
- Make a simple syrup of twice as much sugar as water (2 cups sugar plus 1 cup water) by just boiling them together. Add lots of chopped fresh fruit while the sauce is hot and make a delicious sauce for pouring over ice cream or for adding a little extra to your cake layers.
- Use sweetened whipping cream (unwhipped) as a sauce for pouring over

cake slices, brownies, or warm slices of pie. It's delicious.
- Substitute lemon juice for half of the water in a simple syrup to make a sauce that is extra tangy. It's excellent over pound cake.
- Substitute any fruit juice for the water when making a simple syrup and use for brushing over cake layers. The cake will be extra moist and have a hint of the fresh flavor of the juice.

Tips for Better Microwave Desserts

- Defrosting pies in the microwave is quick and easy. A frozen fruit pie will take 4 to 5 minutes on DEFROST, with an additional 5 minutes standing time. A frozen cream pie will take about $1 1/2$ minutes on DEFROST, with an additional 5 minutes standing time. Always remove the pie from its metal pan and place it in a glass or paper pan before putting it into the microwave. Using metal of any kind in a microwave is dangerous and may ruin your oven.
- A frozen layer cake will take about 2 minutes on SIMMER, with an additional 5 minutes standing time. Leave the cake in its package for defrosting unless there is metal in the package, in which case remove the metal and then defrost the cake.
- Defrost packages (boxes) of frozen fruit for 5 minutes on DEFROST, with an additional 1 minute standing time. Pouches of frozen fruit will defrost in about 3 minutes on

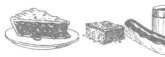

DEFROST, with about 1 minute standing time. These times are variable as is the power of your microwave.

- Always use round dishes instead of square dishes if possible in your microwave. Using round dishes will eliminate burned or dry corners.
- Sauces are easily prepared in the microwave. Use the microwave setting that seems best for each kind of sauce. Stir the sauce every few seconds and heat to a temperature of 140°F to 150°F. Use the microwave to heat up premade sauces just before serving, and don't worry about over cooking or scorching. Hot chocolate sauce poured over a dish of ice cream and sprinkled with chopped nuts is easy and delicious.
- You can easily toast coconut in the microwave. Spread the coconut thinly on a paper plate or towel and use the HIGH setting for 2 or 3 minutes. Watch it closely because it will brown quickly when it heats up.
- Microwave ovens vary in power output. Some recipes may have to be adjusted to come out right in your microwave.

Tips for Better Fudge

- Fudge is generally cooked to the soft-ball stage, 234°F to 238°F on a candy thermometer. (Use the lower temperature when the weather is clear and the higher temperature when the weather is damp.)

If you do not have a thermometer, pour about $1/2$ teaspoon of the hot candy into a cup nearly full of very cold water. If the candy can be shaped into a soft ball that flattens on removal from the water, it is ready.

- If your fudge turned to sugar, if it is stiffened in the saucepan, or if it crumbled when you cut portions (because you beat it too long), add 2 tablespoons cream and stir over very low heat, cutting up the fudge with a wooden spatula while you stir. Cook and stir only until warm and slightly softened but not until hot or thin. Remove from the heat, beat again until smooth and thick, and them turn it out of the saucepan again. (Some cooks think this twice-cooked fudge is creamier and smoother than once-cooked fudge.)
- If your fudge did not set, you didn't cook it long enough or you poured it too soon. If you think that you did not cook it long enough, add $1/4$ cup milk or cream, then cook and stir constantly until it reaches 236°F again. Let cool and beat again until smooth and thick. But if you think that you cooked it enough and simply poured it too soon, transfer the mixture to a marble, tile, or Formica countertop. Squeeze it between your hands and knead it as though it were bread dough until it is firm enough to hold a shape. Then roll it into a log or form it into a square about 1 inch thick. Let stand for just a few

moments and then slice the log or cut the square into portions.

- Unless someone wants to lick the pan, the fudge that remains can be scraped out, kneaded with your hands until smooth and creamy, and rolled into marble-sized balls.

Tips for Better Ingredients

- Salted butter can be used in most recipes that call for unsalted butter. There is very little salt in butter, and most people will not notice any difference in the taste of baked items. The salt taste is stronger if salted butter is brushed on a baked item.
- Hot water is defined as water very hot to the touch but not boiling.
- Cold water is defined as water very cold to the touch but not ice water.
- Ice water is defined as water from the refrigerator or water that has been cooled by adding ice to it.
- Tap water is defined as water at room temperature, not warm and not cold.
- Fruit may be fresh, frozen, or canned. The recipe will usually tell you which to use. All are different, so substitute carefully.
- Nuts are generally interchangeable, so use what you have on hand or what suits your taste.
- In general, always use the type of sugar specified in a recipe. Sometimes confectioners' sugar can be substituted for granulated sugar, such as in the case of a sponge cake. Brown sugar comes in light,

medium, and dark brown. The type of brown sugar you use will determine the characteristics of the baked item.

- In cookies and in some cakes, margarine or butter can be substituted for vegetable shortening to create a better flavor. Lard is generally a poor substitute for shortening. It makes a flaky pie crust but should not be used otherwise.
- Powdered milk may be used in place of whole milk, but it cannot be used to replace cream or condensed or sweetened condensed milk.
- Cake flour makes cakes with a particularly tender crumb. Bleached and unbleached flours are interchangeable in recipes.
- Using 2 egg yolks and 1 egg white as a substitute for 1 egg will make almost any baked item moister and richer. Using 2 whites instead of 1 yolk and 1 white will eliminate the fat and a cake will still bake fine.
- Almost all modern recipes call for double-acting baking powder. If you are using a very old recipe, however, single-acting baking powder is best. Make it yourself by sifting together 2 tablespoons cream of tartar, 1 tablespoon baking soda, and 1 tablespoon cornstarch. Use exactly what you need and keep the rest stored in a tightly sealed container.
- *Dust* is an ingredient term that is usually used to describe how flour should be applied to a work surface to prevent

something from sticking to it. It also is used to describe the coating of a greased pan with cocoa powder, cookie crumbs, flour, or sugar to prevent sticking.

- Coconut is easy to color for parties. Place a few drops of food coloring in 1/2 teaspoon milk and, using a fork, toss with 1 to 1 1/2 cups coconut. Toast the coconut in a 350°F oven, stirring often, for 7 to 10 minutes, or until lightly colored.

- Almond paste, or marzipan, makes a wonderful filling, topping or flavoring but is hard to find in stores. It is also very expensive. Ask your local bakery to sell you some.

- Raisins are best plumped by putting in hot apple juice for about 20 minutes. A pinch of ground clove in the apple juice makes them taste even better.

Tips for Better Meringue

- A simple soft meringue is made by whipping egg whites with a little granulated sugar (2 tablespoons sugar to 1 white), vanilla, and a bit of salt or cream of tartar. This slightly sweet topping is heaped over a cream pie and then lightly browned for a finishing touch. A perfect soft meringue will be light and airy with no signs of shrinking.

- A hard meringue contains more sugar and is baked at a low temperature (200°F) until it is firm (crispy). Meringue shells,

fruit cups, and cookies are made from hard meringue.

- Meringue will not tolerate even the smallest amount of fat. Since egg yolk contains fat, separating the whites from the yolks must be done carefully. The mixing bowl and the beaters must also be fat free. Wash them in hot soapy water, rinse in hot water, and dry well before using to make meringue.

- Plastic bowls will sometime hold fats even after machine washing. Always use glass or metal bowls for beating and holding meringues.

- The addition of the sugar to the egg whites as you beat them should be done very slowly so it will dissolve completely.

- Meringue is ready when the sugar is dissolved and the mixture stands up in stiff peaks when the beaters are lifted.

- Spread the meringue over the pie filling (be sure any hot filling has cooled completely) making certain it touches the pie crust all around. This will minimize shrinking and slipping.

- Brown meringue at a high temperature for only a few minutes (400°F to 425°F) until the peaks are lightly browned. If using a low temperature, the meringue will have a thick crust and be difficult to cut.

- Allow hard meringues to dry completely before adding the filling.

- Make little cups from hard meringue, fill them with fresh fruit, and top with whipped cream or whipped topping for something special. Be sure to fill the cups just before serving, because they will become soggy fast.
- Fold chopped pecans into hard meringue and spread it about $1/4$ inch thick on wax paper on which you have drawn five 8-inch circles. These flat meringues dry in a 200°F oven for about $2^1/2$ hours or until dry and crisp. Stack them with a thick filling of whipped topping between the layers, and then ice the outside with whipped topping and sprinkle with shaved chocolate. Freeze the cake, then cut it while it is still very cold. It is sweet beyond compare, but many people think it is the best dessert ever.
- If you fear salmonella, use meringue powder in recipes calling for egg whites. Two teaspoons of meringue powder dissolved in 2 tablespoons warm water equals 1 egg white. You can find meringue powder at your bakery- or restaurant-supply store or from popular mail-order houses.

Tips for Better Muffins and Quick Breads

- Almost any quick-bread batter can be also used to make muffins. Just put the batter into muffin cups and bake at a slightly higher temperature (about 10 degrees).

- Muffins freeze well; reheat in the microwave or oven as needed.
- When adding fresh fruit to muffin batter, either cut back on the liquid in the recipe or drain off excess fruit juice. Crushed strawberries are wonderful used in muffins but will make the batter too thin if you do not adjust for their extra juice.
- Use apple juice instead of water in your muffin recipe.
- Quick breads that contain nuts will almost always crack on the top during baking. Don't worry, as the taste will still be good.

Tips for Better Pie Crusts and Pies

- Have the butter, shortening, and water as cold as possible. Using a pastry blender, cut the butter into the flour until it becomes crumbly, then add the shortening, mixing only enough for moist crumbs to form. Add the water a drop at a time and mix until the dough just sticks together when you press it between your hands.
- Don't overwork the dough. Pat into a disk, wrap in plastic wrap, and chill until firm or for up to 2 hours. The chilling allows the gluten in the dough to rest before you start to roll it out.
- Place pie dough between sheets of wax paper when rolling it out to aid in transferring to pie pan. Once the dough is thoroughly chilled, you can begin rolling.

Remember to be gentle with the dough, and don't use too much flour at this stage, or the crust will be tough and hard when it is baked.

- Lightly dust the surface of the dough and the board with flour and start rolling the dough from the center out. Ideally, you should end up with a round that measures $\frac{1}{8}$ inch thick and about 2 inches larger in diameter than your pie pan.

- Carefully place the rolled-out dough in your pie pan. Do not stretch or pull the dough when fitting it to the pan, or it will shrink when baked. Prick the dough with fork tines and chill for an hour or longer while you prepare the filling. Chilling will help keep the crust from shrinking when baked.

- When adding eggs to a hot cooked pie filling, always add a little of the hot filling to the eggs first, then stir into the filling. Eggs cook quickly. If added to a boiling mixture, they can cook into tiny lumps rather than blend into the filling. Since they are used as a thickener, the filling will be lumpy and runny.

- If your pie crust takes too long to brown and the filling boils out, add a little milk powder and sugar to the dough recipe the next time you make it. The crust will taste better and will brown quickly.

- Cover the top of a fruit pie with an empty pie tin while baking to keep the top crust from browning too much before the bottom crust is done.

- Brush melted hot apple jelly or a honey-water glaze over the crust of a baked fruit pie to make it shine.

- Prebake pie crusts to be used for fruit or custard fillings to prevent them from becoming soggy. Paint a light coating of egg wash (egg beaten with a little water) on the bottom of the pie crust and bake at 375°F for about 10 minutes. The crust will still look raw, but it will be baked enough to seal it.

- When using graham crackers or vanilla wafers for a crumb crust, you'll need $1\frac{1}{2}$ cups of crumbs. That is about 20 graham cracker squares or about 45 vanilla wafers.

- Dip banana slices in lemon juice as you cut them. They will not turn dark as quickly.

- Stir cream filling while it is cooling to let the steam escape. The filling may break and become watery if you don't.

- Bake a graham cracker or cookie crust for about 4 to 6 minutes at 350°F. Let cool, then fill with a no-bake filling. The crust won't be as crumbly.

- Fold peanut butter (about 4 tablespoons) into canned or made-from-scratch vanilla pie filling to make a delicious peanut butter pie. Top with whipped cream and chopped peanuts.

Tips for Better Puddings

- The consistency of puddings depend upon the temperature at which they are served.

Some puddings must be served hot or else they are soggy. Other puddings must be chilled almost to the freezing point when served. Therefore, it is very important to follow a recipe's handling directions precisely.

- Keep puddings from forming a crust by covering them with plastic wrap pressed directly onto the hot surface.
- Grease molds well before adding the pudding mixture.
- To unmold a chilled pudding, dip the base of the mold in hot water for a few seconds or wrap the base in a hot towel for a few seconds.
- Add $\frac{1}{4}$ cup pudding to a fully mixed cake batter made from a box. Mix in the pudding just until incorporated. This will make the cake moister and add a little flavor. It is important to add the pudding last.

Tips for Better Recipes

- To prevent sticking, dip a cookie or biscuit cutter (or the rim of a glass) into flour.
- A glass bottle makes a perfect stand for holding an inverted angel food cake as it cools.
- There are two kinds of measuring cups. One is for measuring dry ingredients and has an even round. The other is for measuring liquids and has a lip for pouring. Be sure to use the correct cup for the job or else the measurement will be wrong.

- If you use glass or thin aluminum pans for baking, reduce the baking temperature by about 25°F.
- Use bowls, pans, glasses, or cups as molds for baked items or soft molded desserts. Always make sure they are oven or microwave safe.
- Use a tightly capped jar filled with water as a rolling pin.
- Punch holes in the lid of a jar and use it to shake sugar over cookies and cakes.
- Put crackers, cookies, and graham crackers between sheets of wax paper and crush with a rolling pin to make crumbs.
- To make crushed ice, place ice cubes in a cloth towel and rap with a hammer or meat mallet.
- Parchment paper is the best material to use for making a cone for decorating, but wax paper works, too.
- Wrap a hot towel around a molded dessert dish or cold cake pan for a few seconds to help the contents release easily.
- Use the microwave to heat small amounts of liquids quickly or to melt shortening, chocolate, or butter.
- Your food processor or blender will make fresh apple sauce in a few seconds. Add spices to create a delicious topping for ice cream or for eating plain.

Sweetened Condensed Milk

Yield: About 1⅓ cups or 1 can (10¾ ounces) sweetened condensed milk

> 1 cup powdered milk
> ⅓ cup boiling water
> ⅔ cup sugar
> 3 tablespoons butter

In a blender, combine all the ingredients and blend until the sugar dissolves. If the mixture is too thick for your purposes, add a few drops of water and blend.

- Use a piece of clean brown paper cut from a sack to cover the tops of breads or pies to prevent overbrowning.
- If you don't have cheesecloth on hand, strain liquids through a clean piece of cloth cut from old sheets or pillowcases.
- Oven thermometers are inexpensive and come in two types: one kind is used to measure the internal temperature of the baked item, and the other kind is used to measure the temperature of the oven. It is a good idea to use both types.
- Folded towels make excellent pot holders.
- Cake cooling racks come in all sizes and shapes. It is a good plan to have different sizes on hand for various baking projects.
- When baking cakes in your microwave, place a small juice glass greased or sprayed with nonstick cooking spray top up in the center of a large cake pan. Pour the cake batter around the glass and bake as usual. The cake will bake better.
- Clean copper bowls with a mixture of equal parts vinegar and table salt.
- If the dessert flops, send someone to the bakery to pick up something. It happens to us all.

Tips for Better Whipped Cream

- Whipping cream contains 30 percent fat and can be whipped until it doubles in volume. Each cup of cream will yield about 2 cups whipped cream.

- Be careful: overwhipped cream will turn into butter.
- Always use chilled cream and a chilled bowl and beater. Whipping cream may not whip if it is not cold.
- Do not attempt to whip more than 2 cups of cream at one time for the most successful result.
- Add 2 to 4 tablespoons sugar per cup of cream to sweeten. Add the sugar when the volume and stiffness is almost complete. If added too soon, the cream may not whip.
- Add 1 teaspoon vanilla extract per cup for extra flavor.
- Whipped cream freezes well (up to 3 months), but should be served or used while still very cold.

One Smart Cookie

Most cookie recipes are easy to make, but sometimes we can get lazy and miss some of the important details. A little extra thought and attention can ensure perfect cookies every time.

First, it's important to use only heavy-duty baking sheets to ensure even browning and baking. Some prefer a sheet with sides; others line the nonstick pans with wax paper, both to keep the bottoms of the cookies from over-browning and to speed clean up. The choice is yours.

If you're not sure if a cookie has finished baking, lean on the side of underbaking. To help keep tabs on the cookies, always check to see if the cookies are done at least 3 minutes before the suggested baking time is up. Ovens are unpredictable, so you'll need to pay close attention.

Preparing Cookies for Shipping

Materials needed:

your home-baked cookies
sturdy cardboard box, cookie tin, or empty coffee can
aluminum foil or plastic wrap
lock-top plastic bags
paper towels or bubble wrap
freezer, plastic, or masking tape
brown mailing paper

Bar, drop, or fruit cookies can best withstand mailing; tender, fragile cookies are apt to crumble in transit. Use a heavy cardboard box, cookie tin, or empty coffee can as a mailing container. Line the container with aluminum foil or plastic wrap. Wrap four to six cookies of the same size together in aluminum foil, plastic wrap, or plastic food bags and seal securely with tape; repeat until the container is full. Place the heaviest cookies at the bottom of the container, and layer the wrapped cookies with crumpled paper towels around them. Bubble wrap can be used to line the container and divide layers of cookies. Seal the container with tape. Wrap the container with an outer paper wrapping.

Brown mailing paper or a cut grocery sack works well. Print the mailing address and the return address on the package in waterproof ink; mark the package Perishable Food to encourage careful handling.

All about Spices

Allspice
These small, dark, reddish brown berries are so called because their aroma and flavor resemble a combination of cinnamon, cloves, and nutmeg. Use berries whole or ground for flavoring cakes, cookies, and pies.

Anise
Commonly called aniseed, these small, brown, oval seeds have the sweet, pungent flavor of licorice. Also available ground. Use whole seeds for sprinkling over sweet breads before baking and ground anise for flavoring pastries for fruit pies.

Caraway
Small, brown, crescent-shaped seeds with a strong licorice flavor. Used as a flavoring in cakes.

Cardamon
Small, triangular-shaped pods containing several small black seeds that deliver a warm, highly aromatic flavor. You can buy green or black cardamoms, although the smaller green type is more widely available. Great for flavoring cookies and spice cakes.

Cinnamon and Cassia
Shavings of bark from the cinnamon tree are processed and curled to form cinnamon sticks. Also available in ground form. Spicy, fragrant, and sweet, it is used widely in sweets. Cassia, from the dried bark of the cassia tree, is similar to cinnamon, but less delicate in flavor, with a slightly pungent bite.

Cloves
These dried, unopened flower buds have a distinctive aroma and pungency and must be added with care so as not to overpower what they flavor. Available in ground form. Cloves are added to apple pies and other pastries.

Coriander
Available in seed and ground form. These tiny, pale brown seeds have a mild, spicy flavor with a slight orange peel fragrance. Good in many cake and cookie recipes.

Ginger
Available in many forms. Invaluable for adding to many desserts and for baking gingerbread and brandy snaps. Fresh ginger looks like a knobby stem. It should be peeled and finely chopped or sliced before use. Dried ginger is very hard and light beige. To release flavor, "bruise" with a spoon or soak in hot water before using. This dried type is more often used in pickling, jam making, and preserving. Also available in ground form, as preserved stem ginger, and crystallized.

Mace and Nutmeg

Both spices are found on the same plant. The nutmeg is the inner kernel of the fruit. When ripe, the fruit splits open to reveal bright red arils that lie around the shell of the nutmeg. The arils, once dried, are known as mace blades. The flavor of both spices is similar—warm, sweet, and aromatic, although nutmeg is more delicate than mace. Both spices are also sold ground. Commonly sprinkled over puddings and custards and used as a flavoring in many desserts.

Poppy Seeds

These tiny, slate blue seeds add a nutty flavor to sweets. Used as a filling for a variety of pastries and cakes and as a topping for various baked goods.

Sesame Seeds

High in protein and oil, sesame seeds have a crisp texture and sweet, nutty flavor that combines well with cookies and pastries.

All spices should be stored in small, airtight jars in a cool, dark place, as heat, moisture and sunlight reduce their flavor.

Cookware Safety

Aluminum

Despite much talk to the contrary, there is no scientific proof that aluminum cookware is hazardous to health or is a cause of Alzheimer's disease. Do not, however, cook or store acid foods in aluminum cookware, as they can cause erosion of the aluminum finish.

Copper

Copper cookware is popular because it conducts heat evenly and efficiently. Most copper pots and pans are lined with tin or steel, so there is little chance of the migration of copper into the food. Unlined cookware that has lost its lining due to repeated use should not be used in food preparation, while antique copper cookware is often unlined and should not be used. Some new copper utensils have a protective coating that prevents discoloration. This coating must be removed before using to prepare food or before placing over heat. Refer to the manufacturer's directions for removal.

Ceramic Pottery

Use only pottery or ceramic cookware that has been made especially for food purposes, so that no lead is present in the glaze. Pottery or ceramic pieces not specifically manufactured for food purposes should be considered decorative pieces only. It is also wise not to store any acid foods in even properly manufactured pieces for any length of time.

Using Honey in Cooking

Honey may be substituted for sugar in recipes for custards, frostings, pie fillings, cobblers, and puddings. If honey is to be the main

sweetener in cakes and cookies, it is best to use recipes specifically developed with honey. Honey may replace part of the sugar, however, if these guidelines are followed:

Cakes: Replace up to half of the sugar. Reduce the total liquid by $\frac{1}{4}$ cup for every 1 cup sugar replaced.

Cookies and Brownies: Replace up to half the amount of sugar. Reduce the total liquid by $\frac{1}{4}$ cup for every 1 cup sugar replaced.

Fruit Bars: Replace up to two-thirds of the sugar. Reduce the total liquid by $\frac{1}{4}$ cup forevery 1 cup sugar replaced.

Gingersnaps: Replace no more than one-third of the sugar. Mix the honey with either the shortening or the liquid, blending it in thoroughly to avoid a soggy layer on top. Reduce the total liquid by $\frac{1}{4}$ cup for every 1 cup sugar replaced.

Products containing honey brown faster, so reduce the oven temperature by 25 degrees when baking with honey. Remember, too, honey should not be used in foods for infants under 12 months of age.

If honey crystallizes, remove the lid and place the jar in warm water until the crystals dissolve. Or microwave 2 cups honey in a microwave-safe container at HIGH for 2 to 3 minutes, or until the crystals dissolve; stir every 30 seconds. Do not boil or scorch.

Most Frequent Baking Bungles

- **Why is my cake dry?**
  The oven temperature may have been set too low, or the cake was cooled in a draft. Check the accuracy of your oven dial by placing an oven thermometer in the oven. Always cool your cakes in a draft-free environment.

- **Why do my chocolate chip cookies taste great when first baked but lose flavor when they cool?**
  Heat releases the flavor of chocolate and nutmeats. Try reheating chocolate chip cookies in your microwave or oven for a few seconds before serving.

- **Why are my muffins flat on top?**
  You need to bake muffins first at a high temperature and then at a lower temperature to get a peaked top. Start at 425° and bake for about 5 minutes. Turn down the heat to about 375° and finish the bake.

- **Why does the filling for my fruit pie recipe call for adding lemon juice?**
  Lemon juice restores the natural tartness of fruit that has been lost if canned or frozen. It also helps fruits retain their color.

- **Why are my biscuits heavy and hard?**
  A number of reasons are possible: You may be overmixing the dough. Your

baking powder may be old or ruined. You are not using a cold dough, and the baking powder is working before the biscuits go in the oven. You are baking at too low a temperature for too long a time. (Biscuits bake best at 375° to 400°.)

- **Why are my brownies gummy in the middle and hard around the edges?**

  Baking brownies at a temperature that is too high will cause the middle to rise quickly and then fall. This makes the center gummy and the outside edges hard. Baking brownies at a temperature that is too low will create the same result. Brownies are usually baked at about 350°F for about 30 minutes. They will usually rise in the middle and then fall. When they fall, they are done.

- **Sometimes when I place a baked pie in the refrigerator for storing, the crust sticks to the pan after I remove the refrigerated pie for serving. What can I do?**

  Set the pie on a warm towel for a few minutes and the cold shortening (which causes the crust to stick to the pan) will melt and the crust will release. This is also a good method of release with crumb-type pie crusts.

- **My meringue is soft and will not whip up correctly no matter how hard I beat it. It also gets watery after I put it on my pie. What's wrong?**

You may have a small amount of shortening or butter in your mixing bowl or on your beaters. Meringue must be mixed in a totally fat-free environment in order for the egg whites to fluff up properly. Plastic mixing bowls may hold fat even after machine washing. It's best to use glass or stainless-steel bowls. Add the sugar to the egg whites very slowly as you beat them. Brown meringue at a high temperature (375°F) for a few minutes; a lower temperature may cause the meringue to fall. The pie filling must be cool before it is topped with meringue.

Handy Substitutions

Allspice: 2 parts ground cinnamon to 1 part each ground nutmeg and ground cloves

Baking powder: For 1 teaspoon, combine $\frac{1}{4}$ teaspoon baking soda and $\frac{1}{2}$ teaspoon cream of tartar.

Buttermilk: For 1 cup, combine 1 tablespoon vinegar or lemon juice with enough milk to measure 1 cup.

Cake flour: For 1 cup, measure out 1 cup all-purpose flour, then remove 2 tablespoons.

Cinnamon Sugar: $\frac{7}{8}$ cup sugar plus 2 tablespoons ground cinnamon

Cornstarch: For 1 tablespoon, use 2 tablespoons flour.

Dried Currants: Chopped dark raisins

Flour (for thickening): Use $1\frac{1}{2}$ teaspoons cornstarch for 1 tablespoon flour.

Half-and-half: For 1 cup, combine $\frac{7}{8}$ cup ($\frac{3}{4}$ cup plus 2 tablespoons) milk and 3 tablespoons margarine or butter.

Honey: For 1 cup, combine $1\frac{1}{4}$ cups sugar plus $\frac{1}{4}$ cup liquid.

Lemon juice: Use 2 to 3 tablespoons bottled lemon juice in place of the juice of 1 medium lemon.

Orange juice: Each medium orange yields $\frac{1}{4}$ to $\frac{1}{3}$ cup juice.

Pumpkin Pie Spice: 4 parts ground cinnamon to 1 part each ground ginger, ground nutmeg, ground mace, and ground cloves

Self-rising flour: For 1 cup, combine 1 cup all-purpose flour, $1\frac{1}{2}$ teaspoons baking powder, and $\frac{1}{2}$ teaspoon salt.

Sour cream: Use 1 cup plain yogurt for 1 cup sour cream.

Vanilla extract: To make at home, finely chop several vanilla beans and place them in a jar with a tight-fitting lid. Cover with vodka or brandy and seal. Shake the jar well. Store the extract for about a month, or until it is nicely fragrant, shaking it every day, then strain it through a coffee filter. The finished product will probably not be as strong as purchased vanilla extract, so use more than the recipe states.

Freezing and Thawing Baked Goods

It's a good idea to have a pie, dessert, cookies, or cake stored in the freezer for your family or unexpected guests. Many baked goods freeze and thaw beautifully. Keep the following points in mind when freezing baked goods:

- The freezer temperature should be 0 degrees Fahrenheit or less.
- Use moistureproof, vaporproof wraps, or other airtight packaging such as plastic containers with tight-fitting lids, heavy-duty foil, and freezer bags.
- Be sure there is enough room for expansion when filling containers. Press out the air and seal tightly when wrapping foods.

Quick Breads, Muffins, and Coffee Cakes

Let cool completely; do not frost or decorate. Before freezing, place coffee cakes on foil-wrapped cardboard. Unwrap slightly and let thaw at room temperature for 2 to 3 hours. Serve at room temperature or reheat wrapped in foil at 350°F for 15 to 20 minutes.

Storage: Up to 1 month.

Frosted and Unfrosted Cakes

Let cakes cool completely and place frosted cakes in freezer to harden the frosting before covering. Place layer cakes in a container to prevent crushing. Angel and chiffon cakes are best left in the pan or placed in containers to avoid crushing them. Cakes may be filled or frosted with whipped cream or topping before freezing. Thaw unfrosted cakes covered for 2 to 3 hours at room temperature. Frost or serve according to the recipe. Thaw frosted cakes loosely covered overnight in the refrigerator.

Storage: Up to 6 months for unfrosted cakes, up to 3 months for frosted cakes.

Cheesecakes

If baked, let cool completely before wrapping. Thaw wrapped in the refrigerator for 4 to 6 hours.

Storage: Up to 5 months.

Cookies

Put cookies in containers with tight-fitting lids. If cookies are frosted before freezing, freeze them on a baking sheet, then put the frozen cookies between layers of wax paper in a container. Thaw in the container at room temperature. If the cookies should be crisp when thawed, remove from the container before thawing.

Storage: Up to 12 months for unfrosted cookies, up to 2 months for frosted.

Fruit Pies and Baked Pumpkin or Pecan Pies

Let baked pies cool quickly. For unbaked pies, brush the bottom pastry with egg white before filling to prevent it from becoming soggy, and do not slit the top pastry. Cover baked and unbaked pies with an inverted foil or paper plate and then wrap. To thaw baked pies, unwrap and heat at 325°F for 45 minutes, or until warm or at room temperature. To thaw unbaked pies, unwrap, cut slits in the top pastry, and bake at 425°F for 15 minutes, then bake at 375°F for 30 to 45 minutes, or until the center becomes bubbly.

Storage: Up to 4 months for baked pies, up to 3 months for unbaked pies.

Chiffon Pies

Do not top with whipped cream or topping. Refrigerate to set, then wrap as you would a fruit pie. Unwrap and thaw in the refrigerator for 2 to 3 hours, then top as desired. (Please note that custard pies, cream pies, and pies with meringue topping do not freeze well.)

Storage: Up to 2 months.

The Everything
Dessert Cookbook

Chapter 1: Dips and Sauces

As a kid growing up in the seventies, I have many fond memories of Saturday night pajama parties, where the highlight of the evening was the food, particularly the desserts. Chips and dip were popular as were the ubiquitous chocolate fondue and other sweet liquids bubbling in a Sterno-powered cauldron. Wielding a fondue fork that our mothers warned us not to run with, we'd stab strawberries, apple slices, and pound cake cubes and dip them into the thick sauce before popping them into our mouths.

Any one of the dips and sauces here could easily present a modern-day version of that pajama-party staple, or you could ladle them directly onto a dish of fruit or cake, thus rendering those "dangerous" fondue forks extinct.

Custard Sauce

Makes: About 1 cup

3 egg yolks
2 tablespoons sugar
pinch of salt
1 cup milk, scalded
$\frac{1}{4}$ teaspoon vanilla extract

In the top pan of a double boiler over gently simmering water, beat the yolks slightly with a fork. Beat in the sugar and salt. Add the milk gradually, stirring constantly. Place over (not touching) hot water and cook, stirring constantly, until the mixture coats the back of a spoon, about 10 minutes.

Remove from the heat, cover with plastic wrap pressed directly onto surface to prevent a skin from forming; let cool, and chill. Stir in the vanilla just before serving. The sauce will keep for up to 5 days.

Use to pour over fruit, ladyfingers, or to dip cookies.

Maple Orange Sauce

Makes: About $1\frac{1}{3}$ cups

1 cup maple syrup
$\frac{1}{3}$ cup orange juice
1 tablespoon grated orange rind

Mix together the maple syrup and orange juice and rind in a saucepan. Bring to a boil, stirring constantly. Serve hot or cold on pancakes or puddings.

Use to pour over pancakes or waffles, or fruit.

Fluffy Lemon Sauce

Makes: About 1 cup

$1/2$ cup sugar
1 tablespoon cornstarch
$1/8$ teaspoon ground nutmeg
1 cup boiling water
1 tablespoon butter
$1/4$ cup lemon juice
1 teaspoon grated lemon rind
1 egg, well beaten

Mix together the sugar, cornstarch, and nutmeg in a saucepan. Stir in the boiling water over high heat and boil for 1 minute, stirring. Add the butter, lemon juice, and orange rind. Stir. Gradually beat in the egg. Serve warm over fresh raspberries.

Fudge Sauce

Makes: About $1^3/4$ cups

1 can (13 ounces) sweetened condensed milk
2 cups sugar
3 squares (3 ounces) unsweetened chocolate
1 teaspoon vanilla extract

Combine the milk, sugar, chocolate, and vanilla in a saucepan and bring to a boil. Cook for 5 minutes, stirring constantly. Remove from the heat. Add the vanilla and beat until smooth. Serve hot or cold over ice cream.

Keeping Fruit Fresh

If your schedule dictates that you have to cut up fruit a few hours before serving, brush the cut surfaces with lemon or orange juice to prevent them from browning. If you don't want to bother, serve fruits that require no advance preparation besides washing.

Cherry Dessert Dip

Makes: Enough for 1 pound cherries

1 cup sour cream
2 tablespoons orange marmalade
¹/₃ cup flaked dried coconut, toasted
chopped nuts

Combine the sour cream, orange marmalade, and coconut in a small bowl, stirring well. Put the nuts in another small bowl. To serve, dip sweet cherries with stems first into the sour cream mixture, and then into the bowl of nuts.

Peanut Butter Dip for Fruit

Makes: 2 cups, enough for 4 cups prepared fruit

1 cup creamy peanut butter
1 cup light cream
¹/₂ cup honey
chopped peanuts or flaked coconut

Place the peanut butter in a fondue pot. Gradually stir in the light cream, and then mix in the honey. Heat over low heat, stirring constantly, until the mixture starts to boil. Remove from the heat and keep warm throughout serving by placing over a warmer. Place the peanuts or coconut in a small bowl. To serve, spear a piece of fruit—whole strawberries, pear or apple wedges—with a fondue fork or long bamboo skewer. Dip the fruit first into the peanut butter mixture, and then coat with chopped peanuts or flaked coconut.

Port Wine Sauce

Makes: About 3 cups

¹/₂ cup butter
1 cup brown or white sugar
2 eggs, well beaten
¹/₂ cup port wine
2 packages (8 ounces each) frozen
    strawberries, thawed
juice of 1 lemon

Melt the butter in a saucepan over low heat. Add the sugar, eggs, and wine and, using a whisk, beat until foamy and slightly thickened. Remove from the heat.

Drain off the juice from the strawberries and press the fruit through a sieve to make a purée. (Or whirl in blender for a few seconds.) Stir into the hot sauce along with the lemon juice. Let cool.

Pour into a jar, cover tightly, and refrigerate for up to a week. Serve cold over ice cream, or reheat over very low heat (do not allow to boil) and serve over pound cake.

The Everything
Dessert Cookbook

Chapter 2: Frozen Desserts

Nobody doesn't like ice cream. Truthfully, have you ever heard a kid—or an adult—say that they didn't like ice cream or another sweet frozen dessert?

Of course not. Frozen desserts have always been the hallmark of desserts in American society. And though we've long ago come to view any type of food—from burgers to cake to even tofu—as making some kind of statement about the person who chooses it, ice cream perhaps is the quietest, probably because everyone, no matter what nutritional canon they subscribe to, likes some kind of frozen dessert, whether it's no-fat orange juice frozen into ice cubes or who-cares-about-the-fat kitchen sink ice cream sundaes, with every topping imaginable heaped on top of countless scoops of ice cream.

Whether you choose one of the light sherbets or the rich chocolate ice cream, you are an active participant in one of the great American pastimes.

Pineapple Milk Sherbet

Serves: 6

1³⁄₄ cups milk
¹⁄₂ cup sugar
1 can (8 ounces) crushed pineapple, drained
2 tablespoons lemon juice
¹⁄₄ cup orange juice

Combine the milk and sugar in a medium sized bowl. Add the pineapple and the lemon and orange juices and stir until the sugar is dissolved. Pour into a loaf pan and place in a freezer for 1¹⁄₂ hours. Stir once with a spoon after 30 minutes to break up the ice crystals and again after another 30 minutes.

Cranberry Sherbet

Serves: 4

1¹⁄₂ teaspoons unflavored gelatin
2 cups cranberry juice
¹⁄₂ cup sugar
pinch of salt

2 tablespoons skim dry milk
$^{1}/_{2}$ cup light corn syrup
3 tablespoons lemon juice

In a small saucepan, sprinkle the gelatin over $^{1}/_{2}$ cup of the cranberry juice. Heat, stirring, until dissolved. Stir in the sugar and salt. In a bowl, sprinkle the dry milk over the remaining 1 $^{1}/_{2}$ cups juice and beat with a fork to dissolve. Add the gelatin mixture, corn syrup, and lemon juice to the milk mixture and mix well.

Pour into a metal ice-cube tray (if you have one—I found one at a garage sale, the old-fashioned kind where you remove the insert that divides the tray into cubes) or loaf pan and freeze for about 1 hour, or until almost solid. Remove from the freezer and, using a spoon, beat until fluffy. Return to the freezer and freeze until firm.

Lo-Cal Orange Sherbet

Serves: 3

1 cup skim dry milk mixed with cold
    water to normal strength
3 tablespoons frozen orange juice
    concentrate
1 envelope artificial sweetener

Combine all the ingredients in a blender and blend until smooth. Pour into a metal ice-cube tray and freeze for about an hour, or until almost solid. Turn out of the tray into a bowl and beat with a fork to break up the ice crystals. Return to the tray and refreeze until firm.

Applesauce Ice Cream

Serves: 4

1 cup applesauce
$^{1}/_{2}$ teaspoon ground cinnamon
$^{1}/_{4}$ teaspoon ground nutmeg
$^{1}/_{4}$ teaspoon ground ginger
1 teaspoon butter, melted
2 teaspoons lemon juice
$^{1}/_{2}$ cup whipping cream, whipped

In a bowl, mix together the applesauce, spices, butter, and lemon juice. Cover and chill thoroughly. Fold in the whipped cream. Turn into a metal ice-cube tray or loaf pan. Freeze for 2 to 4 hours, or until firm.

Maple Ice Cream

Serves: 6

2 egg yolks
$^{1}/_{4}$ cup sugar
few grains of salt
$^{3}/_{4}$ cup maple syrup
1 $^{1}/_{2}$ cups whipping cream
2 egg whites, lightly beaten

In a bowl, beat together the egg yolks, sugar, salt, and syrup until smooth and thick. Add the cream and mix well. Then add the egg whites. Beat until well blended. Pour into 2 metal ice-cube trays or loaf pans and place in the freezer. Stir after 30 minutes and again after 60 minutes to ensure a smooth mixture. Freeze for 1 hour longer, or until smooth and firm.

Ginger

One of the best ways to spice up any frozen dessert is to add a bit of grated fresh ginger. Of course, it's much easier to spoon the powdered stuff out of a spice tin, but the surprise of biting into a fresh bit of ginger when least expected is a surefire way to win accolades from friends and family. Sprinkle it on top of ice cream, too, instead of walnuts.

Banana Ice Cream

Makes: 1 quart

> 1 $\frac{1}{4}$ teaspoons ($\frac{1}{2}$ envelope) unflavored gelatin
> 2 tablespoons water
> $\frac{3}{4}$ cup light cream, scalded
> $\frac{3}{4}$ cup sugar
> $\frac{1}{4}$ teaspoon salt
> 1 cup mashed ripe bananas
> 2 egg yolks, well beaten
> 2 teaspoons lemon juice
> 1 teaspoon vanilla extract
> 2 cups whipping cream, whipped
> 2 egg whites

In a bowl, sprinkle the gelatin over the water to soften. Add the hot cream and stir to dissolve the gelatin. Stir in $\frac{1}{2}$ cup of the sugar and the salt. Cover and chill for about 30 minutes, or until partially set.

Whip the gelatin mixture with a whisk until smooth. Mix in the bananas, egg yolks, lemon juice, and vanilla. Fold in the whipped cream. Beat the egg whites until soft peaks form. Gradually add the remaining $\frac{1}{4}$ cup sugar, beating until stiff peaks form. Fold into the banana mixture. Pour into metal ice-cube trays and freeze for about 1 hour, or until firm. Serve plain or with a warm sauce of your choice.

Baked Alaska

Serves: 8

1 sponge, angel food, or loaf pound cake
¹/₄ cup (4) egg whites
¹/₈ teaspoon cream of tartar
¹/₈ teaspoon salt
¹/₂ cup sugar
¹/₂ teaspoon vanilla extract
1 quart ice cream (your favorite flavor),
*   softened for 15 minutes*

Cover two thicknesses of corrugated 8-by-6-inch cardboard with aluminum foil. Cut the cake into slices ¹/₂ inch thick and arrange the slices on the covered cardboard in a 7-by-5-inch rectangle (you may not need all of the cake). Place in a freezer and freeze solid.

Let the egg whites stand at room temperature for 1 hour, then beat until frothy with a handheld electric mixer. Add the cream of tartar and salt, and continue beating until soft peaks form when the beaters are slowly raised. Gradually beat in the sugar 2 tablespoons at a time, beating well after each addition. Continue beating for about 3 minutes until glossy. Mix in the vanilla.

Meanwhile, preheat an oven to 500°F.

Spoon the ice cream onto the frozen cake base. Quickly spread the ice cream evenly over the top and sides of the cake. Spoon the egg whites on top, spreading them over the top and down the sides onto the foil to seal completely. Make swirls in the egg whites on the top and sides. Place the Alaska on a baking sheet. Bake in the preheated oven for 3 minutes, or until the meringue is light brown. Remove to a chilled platter and serve at once.

NOTE: Alaska may be prepared ahead and frozen, unwrapped, for up to 2 days. Brown just before serving.

Cherries Jubilee

Serves: 6

1 can (16 ounces) pitted sweet cherries
¹/₃ cup sugar
2 tablespoons cornstarch
1 tablespoon lemon juice
¹/₃ cup brandy (optional)
ice cream or cake à la mode

Drain the cherries, reserving the juice in a measuring cup. Add enough water to the juice to make 1 cup liquid. In a small saucepan, mix together the sugar and cornstarch. Gradually stir in the diluted cherry juice until smooth. Bring to a boil over medium heat, stirring constantly. Boil for 1 minute. Add the cherries and lemon juice, remove from the heat, and keep warm.

Just before serving, add the brandy, if desired, and ignite. After the flame dies down, spoon the cherries over ice cream or cake à la mode.

Blueberry Ice Cream

Makes: 1 quart

1 jar (7 ounces) marshmallow creme
1 can (14 ounces) sweetened condensed
*   milk*
2 cups whipping cream
1 cup milk
1 tablespoon vanilla extract
1 pint blueberries, crushed (about 1 1/2 cups)

Spoon the marshmallow creme into a bowl and gradually add the condensed milk, beating until well blended. Stir in the whipping cream, milk, and vanilla. Pour the mixture into a 9-by-13-inch baking pan. Cover and freeze for about an hour, or until almost solid but still mushy in center.

Scrape the mixture into a large chilled bowl and beat with a handheld electric mixer until smooth. Return to the baking pan and refreeze again until almost solid. Repeat beating step, and then beat in the berries. Return to the baking pan and refreeze until firm.

Peach Ice Cream: Substitute 1 1/2 cups mashed peaches for the blueberries.

Peach Melba

Serves: 4

Melba Sauce:
1 package (10 ounces) frozen raspberries,
*   thawed*
1/2 cup currant jelly
1 1/2 teaspoons cornstarch

1 tablespoon water
1 pint vanilla ice cream
4 peach halves
sweetened whipped cream (optional)

To make the Melba sauce, combine the raspberries and jelly in a saucepan and bring to a boil. In a small cup, stir together the cornstarch and water, and then stir into the raspberry mixture. Cook for 15 minutes, or until thickened, stirring constantly. Strain, let cool, cover, and chill before serving.

Scoop out (or slice) one-fourth of the ice cream onto each of 4 dessert plates. Top each with a peach half, cut side down. Spoon the sauce over the peaches and top with whipped cream, if desired.

Bananas Royale à la Microwave

Serves: 6

6 tablespoons butter or margarine
1/3 cup plus 2 teaspoons packed light
*   brown sugar*
1/4 teaspoon ground cinnamon
1/4 cup whipping cream
4 firm bananas, peeled and cut into 1/4
*   inch-thick slices*
6 scoops vanilla ice cream, prescooped
*   and frozen*
1/4 cup brandy or rum

Place the butter in a 9-inch round glass baking dish in a microwave oven and melt on

HIGH for about 30 seconds. Stir in the brown sugar, cinnamon, and cream. Microwave on HIGH for $1\frac{1}{2}$ to 2 minutes, or until slightly thickened. Set aside.

At serving time, reheat the sugar mixture on HIGH for about 1 minute. Add the bananas, stirring to coat. Microwave on HIGH for about 30 seconds. Put the ice cream on 6 dessert plates. Heat the brandy in a glass measure for about 30 seconds and pour over the bananas. Ignite with a long match. Spoon over the ice cream and serve.

Chocolate Date Pecan Sundae

Serves: 4

$\frac{3}{4}$ cup maple syrup
$\frac{1}{2}$ cup pitted dates, coarsely chopped
$\frac{1}{2}$ cup maraschino cherry halves
$\frac{1}{2}$ cinnamon stick
$\frac{1}{2}$ cup pecan halves
$\frac{1}{4}$ cup brandy
1 quart chocolate ice cream

Combine the maple syrup, dates, cherry halves, cinnamon stick, and pecans in a saucepan. Place over medium heat and simmer for 2 to 3 minutes, or until well blended. Stir in the brandy. Remove from the heat and let cool. Serve over the ice cream.

Marshmallow Creme

Today, the manufacturers of marshmallow creme produce a variety of flavored cremes. They can add a subtle undertone to everything from this easy recipe for blueberry or peach ice cream to the crisp rice cereal treats that many of us grew up with. Raspberry marshmallow creme goes best with peach ice cream.

Flavored Liqueurs

Even people who don't like alcoholic beverages will like this cappuccino dessert. Try it with a variety of flavored liqueurs: Amaretto is a popular favorite, but any kind of coffee dessert—hot or cold—will be greatly enhanced by frangelico (hazelnut), framboise (raspberry) Vandermint (mint), or Baileys (Irish whiskey).

Frosty Cappuccino Supreme

Serves: 6

6 squares (6 ounces) semisweet chocolate
2 tablespoons Kahlúa liqueur
1 tablespoon orange juice
$1/2$ teaspoon grated orange rind
2 whole eggs
2 egg yolks
1 teaspoon brandy extract
1 cup ricotta cheese
$1/4$ cup sugar
1 cup whipping cream

In a saucepan, melt the chocolate in Kahlúa and orange juice over low heat. Remove from the heat and set aside to cool. Put the orange rind, whole eggs, egg yolks, brandy flavoring, ricotta, and sugar in a blender. Blend for 2 minutes. Add the cream and blend for 30 seconds. Add the chocolate mixture and blend until smooth. Pour into parfait glasses and freeze for 1 hour before serving.

Coffee Delight

Serves: 4

2 egg whites
$1/4$ cup sugar
1 cup cold brewed coffee
1 pint coffee ice cream
$1/4$ cup almonds, toasted and coarsely
    chopped

In a bowl, beat the egg whites until frothy. Add the sugar and continue to beat until soft peaks form. Pour $1/4$ cup of the coffee into each of 4 glasses. Carefully spoon the egg whites on top, touching the sides of the glass all around. Spoon the ice cream on top, dividing it evenly. Sprinkle with almonds. Serve at once.

Frozen Espresso

Serves: 4

$3/4$ cup sugar
1 cup water
*3 tablespoons instant espresso coffee
    powder*
2 cups water
1 cup whipping cream
2 tablespoons confectioners' sugar
$1/4$ teaspoon ground ginger

In a saucepan, combine the sugar and water and bring to a boil. Reduce the heat to low and simmer, uncovered, for 5 minutes. Remove from the heat. Add the espresso powder a little at a time, stirring until dissolved. Stir in the water. Pour the mixture into a metal ice-cube tray and place in the freezer for 2 hours. Remove from the freezer, stir with a fork, and return to the freezer for another hour, stirring after 30 minutes. Stir again just before serving.

In a bowl, whip the cream with the sugar and ginger until soft peaks form. Spoon the coffee mixture and whipped cream into

chilled sherbet dishes in alternating layers. Serve at once.

Chocolate Tortoni

Makes: 24 tortoni

*2 squares (2 ounces) unsweetened
    chocolate*
6 squares (6 ounces) semisweet chocolate
$1/2$ cup chopped almonds
4 egg whites
$1/8$ teaspoon cream of tartar
$1/8$ teaspoon salt
$1/4$ cup plus 2 teaspoons sugar
$2 1/2$ cups whipping cream
1 tablespoon vanilla extract
*$1/2$ cup candied red cherries, chopped, plus
    24 whole candied cherries*

Line 24 muffin-tin cups with paper liners.

In the top of a double boiler or in a heat-proof bowl, melt the unsweetened and semi-sweet chocolates over gently simmering water. Set aside to cool. In a large bowl, using an electric mixer set on high speed, beat together the egg whites, cream of tartar, and salt until foamy. Gradually beat in the $1/4$ cup sugar, 1 tablespoon at a time, until soft peaks form.

In another bowl, beat 2 cups of the cream until stiff peaks form. Beat in the 2 teaspoons sugar, the vanilla, and the melted chocolate, mixing well. Fold the beaten egg whites, chopped cherries, almonds, and melted chocolate into the whipped cream mixture. Small chunks of chocolate may remain.

(continued)

Spoon the mixture into the paper-lined muffin cups, dividing evenly. Freeze until firm, about 4 hours or as long as overnight.

Just before serving, in a bowl, beat the remaining $1/2$ cup cream until stiff peaks form. Pack into a pastry bag fitted with a star tip and pipe a rosette of cream onto each tortoni, then top with the whole cherries. Serve at once.

Chunky Caramel Chocolate Banana Split
(Courtesy of Godiva Chocolates)

Serves: 6

Caramel nut ice cream:
6 egg yolks
1 cup sugar
Pinch of salt
2 cups half-and-half
1 cup whipping cream
2 teaspoons lemon juice
2 teaspoons vanilla extract
$1/2$ cup toasted almonds, coarsely chopped

Vanilla–white chocolate chunk ice cream:
1 pint vanilla ice cream
2 tablespoons kirsch (cherry brandy)
3 squares (3 ounces) white chocolate, coarsely chopped

Double–chocolate cookie ice cream:
1 pint chocolate ice cream
12 chocolate wafers, coarsely broken

Caramel rum sauce:
1 cup sugar
3 tablespoons water
2 tablespoons light corn syrup
$1/4$ teaspoon lemon juice
$2/3$ cup whipping cream
5 tablespoons unsalted butter, cut into $1/2$-inch cubes
1 tablespoon dark rum
1 teaspoon vanilla extract

Chocolate sauce:
8 squares (8 ounces) semisweet chocolate, coarsely chopped
$3/4$ cup plus 2 tablespoons whipping cream
Pinch of salt
3 tablespoons light corn syrup
1 tablespoon vanilla extract
1 tablespoon coffee-flavored liqueur (optional)

Strawberry sauce:
1 bag (20 ounces) unsweetened frozen strawberries
$2/3$ cup sugar
2 teaspoons arrowroot
1 tablespoon kirsch (cherry brandy)
2 cups whipping cream
$2^1/2$ tablespoons sugar
1 teaspoon vanilla extract
1 to $1^1/2$ quarts vegetable oil
9 bananas, slightly underripe
2 cups fresh white bread crumbs
1 cup finely ground blanched almonds
2 eggs

2 tablespoons milk
$1/3$ cup almond brickle chips
Sliced fresh strawberries for garnish

To make the caramel nut ice cream, in a bowl, whisk together the egg yolks, 1 tablespoon of the sugar, and the salt until blended. Set aside. In a saucepan, bring the half-and-half and whipping cream to a gentle boil. Remove the pan from the heat. In a heavy, large saucepan, using a wooden spoon, stir together the remaining sugar and the lemon juice. Place over medium heat and cook, stirring frequently, for 3 to 5 minutes, or until the sugar liquefies and the mixture then turns to an amber-colored caramel. Remove from the heat and stir in the half-and-half mixture. Return the pan to the heat and cook, stirring constantly, to help dissolve any caramel that may have hardened. Bring the caramel mixture to a gentle boil and remove from the heat.

Gradually whisk about 1 cup of the hot caramel mixture into the beaten egg yolks until blended. Return this mixture to the saucepan. Continue cooking over medium-low heat, stirring constantly with a wooden spoon, for 2 to 4 minutes, or until the custard has thickened slightly. It is done when you can run your finger down the back of the custard-coated spoon and a path remains. Do not let the custard boil.

Remove from the heat and immediately strain the custard through a fine-mesh sieve into a stainless-steel bowl. Nest the bowl over a larger bowl of ice water and stir the custard

(continued)

Coffee Almond Float

Serves: 1

$1/4$ cup freshly brewed hot
    coffee
1 teaspoon brown sugar
splash of orgeat (almond)
    syrup
ice
milk
1 scoop coffee or chocolate ice cream

In a parfait glass, dissolve the sugar in the coffee. Add the syrup and stir well. Add ice and milk to fill the glass. Stir well again. Top with ice cream.

for 5 to 10 minutes, or until cool. Stir in the vanilla. Remove the bowl of custard from the bowl of ice water. Cover with plastic wrap, pressing it directly onto the surface, and refrigerate until very cold, at least 6 hours or as long as overnight.

Scrape the chilled custard into the container of an ice cream maker and freeze according to the manufacturer's instructions, adding the chopped almonds during the last 2 minutes of freezing. Transfer the ice cream to a bowl. Cover the surface of the ice cream with plastic wrap and cover the bowl tightly with aluminum foil. Freeze overnight.

To mix the vanilla–white chocolate chunk and double–chocolate cookie ice creams: Let the vanilla ice cream soften at room temperature for 10 to 15 minutes, or until soft enough to scrape out of the container. Scrape the ice cream into the chilled $4^1/_2$ quart bowl of a heavy-duty electric mixer fitted with the paddle attachment. At low speed, beat the ice cream for about 5 seconds, or until evenly softened. Quickly add the kirsch and white chocolate pieces and mix a few more seconds until the liqueur and chips are incorporated. Scrape the ice cream into a small bowl and cover the surface with

plastic wrap and freeze for 6 hours or as long as overnight. Repeat the softening and mixing process with the chocolate ice cream and cookie pieces.

To make the caramel-rum sauce, in a small, heavy saucepan, combine the sugar, water, corn syrup, and lemon juice. Cook over medium-low heat, stirring constantly with a wooden spoon, until the sugar dissolves. Increase the heat to medium-high and bring the syrup to a boil without stirring for 4 to 7 minutes, or until the syrup caramelizes and turns dark amber in color. Remove from the heat and add the cream. When the mixture stops bubbling, stir the mixture until smooth. Stir in the butter until melted. Stir in the rum and vanilla. If not serving the sauce immediately, store in an airtight jar in the refrigerator. Reheat the sauce over low heat, stirring constantly, just before serving.

To make the chocolate sauce, place the chocolate in a medium bowl. In a small saucepan over medium heat, bring the cream, salt, and corn syrup to a gentle boil. Pour the hot cream mixture over the chocolate and let stand for 30 seconds to melt the chocolate. Whisk until smooth. Whisk in the vanilla and the coffee-flavored liqueur, if using. Let the sauce cool until tepid. If not serving the sauce immediately, store in an airtight jar in the refrigerator. Reheat the sauce over low heat, stirring constantly, just before serving.

To make the strawberry sauce, in a nonreactive saucepan, combine the frozen strawberries and sugar. Place over medium heat and cook, stirring constantly with a wooden spoon, until the sugar dissolves completely. Continue to cook for 10 to 15 minutes, stirring frequently, until the berries are soft. Do not let the mixture boil.

Press the berry mixture through a sieve into a bowl. Return the strained sauce to the saucepan. Place the arrowroot in a small cup. Slowly stir in 2 tablespoons of strawberry purée until completely smooth. Pour the mixture back into the saucepan with the remaining purée. Cook over medium heat, stirring constantly, until the sauce comes to a boil and thickens. Remove from the heat. Let cool completely and stir in the kirsch, if using. Pour the sauce into a small bowl, cover, and refrigerate until chilled.

To assemble the banana split, in the chilled $4^{1}/_{2}$-quart bowl of the heavy-duty electric mixer fitted with the wire whip attachment, beat together the cream, sugar, and vanilla at medium-high speed until soft peaks begin to form. Fill a pastry bag fitted with a star tip with the whipped cream. Refrigerate until ready to use.

In a large, high-sided skillet or electric frying pan, heat the oil to 375°F. Peel the bananas and split each one in half lengthwise. In a shallow dish or pie plate, combine the bread crumbs and ground almonds. In another shallow dish, whisk together the eggs and milk until well blended. Line a baking sheet with 3 layers of paper towel.

Coat 2 of the banana halves in the egg mixture. Immediately coat the banana halves with the bread crumb–almond mixture, patting the bananas so that the coating adheres well. Slip 2 coated banana halves into the oil and fry, turning once, for 2 to 3 minutes, or until golden brown. Carefully transfer the fried bananas to the paper towel–lined baking sheet. Repeat with the remaining banana halves, frying 2 halves at a time.

For each banana split place 1 scoop of each flavor ice cream in a large dish, place them in a row. Lay 3 fried banana halves on each side of the ice cream. Spoon some of each flavor sauce onto the ice cream, as desired. Pipe rosettes of whipped cream around the edges of the dish and between the ice cream scoops. Garnish generously with strawberry slices and almond brickle chips. Repeat with the remaining ingredients to make 6 banana splits in all. Serve immediately.

The Everything
Dessert Cookbook

Chapter 3: Sweet Pancakes from Around the World

P ancakes, blintzes, etc., are not just for breakfast anymore. On the contrary, many people for whom breakfast is not their favorite meal favor dessert crêpes at the end of a meal.

And what a wealth of choices! Strawberries, blueberries and bananas provide a burst of flavor to the recipes offered here. In fact, they can be interchanged in most recipes as well. But beware: if you count yourself among the non-breakfast-eaters fraternity, once you start creating these masterpieces for dessert, the thought that they're equally at home for the first meal in the morning might motivate you to get up earlier in the morning to create these sweet treats.

Cottage Cheese Blintzes with Strawberry Sauce

Serves: 8

Blintzes:
3 eggs
$^3/_4$ cup flour
$^1/_2$ teaspoon salt
$1^1/_2$ cups milk
melted butter

Filling:
$1^1/_4$ cups small curd cottage cheese
2 teaspoons grated lemon rind
1 egg, lightly beaten
$^1/_4$ cup sugar
3 tablespoons butter, softened
2 teaspoons vanilla extract
$1^3/_4$ cup sour cream
1 tablespoon butter

Strawberry Sauce:
$^3/_4$ cup strawberry preserves
1 tablespoon sherry

To make the blintzes, beat the eggs in a bowl until blended. Combine the flour and salt in a separate bowl. Alternately add the flour mixture and the milk to the eggs in batches, beating with a handheld electric mixer at low speed only until smooth.

Preheat a skillet over medium heat; brush with melted butter. To make each blintz, pour about 3 tablespoons batter into the skillet and immediately rotate the pan to form a thin sheet about 6 inches in diameter. Cook on one side only for about 30 seconds, or until the bottom is golden brown. Place, cooked side up, on paper towels.

To make the filling, in a small bowl, stir together the cottage cheese, lemon rind, egg,

sugar, butter, and vanilla until well mixed. Fold in the sour cream.

Spoon about 2 tablespoons filling onto the cooked side of each blintz. Fold opposite edges of the blintz toward the center, and then roll crosswise with ends tucked in.

In a large, heavy skillet, melt the 1 table-spoon butter over low heat. Place 8 blintzes, folded side down, in the skillet. Cook, turning once, for about 5 to 7 minutes, or until golden on both sides. Place on a heated platter; keep warm.

To make the sauce, add the preserves to the skillet and heat just until melted. Remove from the heat and stir in the sherry. Serve with the blintzes.

Banana Fritters

Serves: 6

3 firm bananas
2 tablespoons orange juice
1 tablespoon sugar
1 cup sifted flour
$^1/_2$ teaspoon baking powder
$^1/_2$ teaspoon salt
1 egg, lightly beaten
$^1/_2$ cup milk
2 tablespoons butter, melted
$^1/_2$ teaspoon vanilla extract
1 teaspoon grated orange rind
vegetable oil for deep-frying

Orange-Lemon Sauce:

$^1/_2$ cup sugar
1$^1/_2$ tablespoons cornstarch
pinch of salt
$^3/_4$ cup water
2 tablespoons butter
$^1/_4$ cup orange juice
1 tablespoon lemon juice

whipped cream

Peel the bananas, cut in half crosswise, and then lengthwise. Combine the orange juice and sugar in a shallow bowl, stir well, and place the banana pieces in the bowl. Sift together the sifted flour, baking powder, and salt into a bowl. In another bowl, stir together the egg, milk, butter, vanilla, and orange rind. Add the egg mixture to the flour mixture, stirring only until moistened.

In a deep-fat fryer or a deep skillet, heat oil for deep-frying to 375°F. Meanwhile, make the sauce: In a small saucepan, combine the sugar, cornstarch, and salt. Add the water and bring to a boil over medium heat, stirring constantly. Cook, stirring, for about 10 minutes, or until thick and clear. Remove from the heat and add the butter and the orange and lemon juices. Keep warm.

Drain the bananas. Dip them into the batter, coating evenly, and slip into the hot oil. Do not crowd the pan. Cook for 2 to 3 minutes, or until golden brown. Transfer to paper towels to drain. Serve hot with whipped cream. Pass the Orange-Lemon Sauce.

The Best Bananas for Fritters and Pancakes

For any recipe in which you want bananas to retain their shape, select fruits that are light yellow and tipped with a bit of green. This advice is the opposite of what is best to use for making banana bread, where the bananas need to be slightly overripe so they can be smoothly incorporated into the batter.

Apple Fritters

Serves: 6

1 $1/3$ cups sifted flour
1 tablespoon granulated sugar
2 teaspoons baking powder
$1/2$ teaspoon salt
2 eggs, lightly beaten
$2/3$ cup milk
1 tablespoon vegetable oil or melted vegetable shortening
3 cups small apple strips (see note)
vegetable oil for deep-frying
confectioners' sugar for dusting

Sift together the sifted flour, granulated sugar, baking powder, and salt. In another bowl, stir together the eggs, milk, and oil. Add the flour mixture to the egg mixture all at once and mix just until moistened. Stir in the apple strips.

Preheat an oven to 250°F. In a deep-fat fryer or a deep skillet, heat oil for deep-frying to 375°F. Drop the apple mixture by tablespoonfuls into the hot oil and fry, turning once, for 3 to 4 minutes, or until puffy and golden. Transfer to paper towels to drain briefly. Place in the preheated oven to keep warm while you fry the remaining fritters.

Place the fritters on a warmed platter, sprinkle with confectioners' sugar, and serve at once.

Note: Peel and core 3 or 4 tart apples; cut crosswise into $1/8$-inch-thick slices. Stack several slices and cut into $1/8$-inch-wide strips.

Cinnamon Apple Ring Fritters

Serves: 6

> 4 medium-sized tart apples
> 1³/₄ cups sifted flour
> 6 tablespoons granulated sugar
> ¼ teaspoon salt
> 2 eggs, separated
> ½ cup milk
> 1 teaspoon ground cinnamon
> vegetable oil for deep-frying
> confectioners' sugar for dusting

Peel and core the whole apples, then cut crosswise into rings ¼ to ⅓ inch thick. Set aside. Sift together the sifted flour, 2 table-spoons of the granulated sugar, and the salt into a bowl. In another bowl, beat together the egg yolks and milk. In yet another bowl, beat the egg whites until stiff peaks form. Stir the egg yolk mixture into the dry ingredients, mixing until smooth. Fold the egg whites into mixture.

In a deep-fat fryer or deep skillet, heat oil for deep-frying to 360°F. Meanwhile, combine the remaining 4 tablespoons granulated sugar with the cinnamon in a shallow dish. Coat the apple slices with the cinnamon sugar and then dip into the batter, coating thoroughly. Slip the apple rings into the hot oil a few at a time, and fry for 2 minutes, or until golden brown. Do not crowd the pan. Transfer to paper towels to drain. Arrange on a warmed platter and sprinkle with confectioners' sugar. Serve hot.

Golden Pineapple Fritters

Serves: 6

> 1 can (16 ounces) pineapple spears
> 1½ cups sifted flour
> ⅓ cup sugar
> 1 tablespoon baking powder
> 1½ teaspoons salt
> 2 eggs, lightly beaten
> 1 tablespoon vegetable oil
> vegetable oil for deep-frying
> flour for coating
> sweetened whipped cream
> ground nutmeg

Drain the pineapple, reserving ⅓ cup of the syrup. Place the spears on paper towels to dry.

Sift together the sifted flour, sugar, baking powder, and salt. In another bowl, combine the eggs, the ⅓ cup syrup, and the 1 table-spoon oil. Add the egg mixture to the flour mixture, stirring just until smooth.

Preheat an oven to 250°F. In a deep-fat fryer or deep skillet, heat the oil for deep-frying to 375°F. Roll the pineapple spears in flour, covering all sides, and spread with the batter, coating evenly. Slip the pineapple spears into the hot oil a few at a time, and fry for about 1 minute on each side, or until golden brown. Transfer to paper towels to drain. Place in the preheated oven to keep warm while you fry the remaining fritters. (The fritters will stay crisp for 15 to 20 minutes.) Arrange on a warmed platter and

(continued)

serve topped with sweetened whipped cream sprinkled with nutmeg.

Note: For easier handling, insert a skewer lengthwise into a pineapple spear before spreading it with the batter. Push the pineapple spear off the skewer into hot oil.

Apple Pancake

Serves: 4

> 2 tablespoons butter
> 2 medium-sized apples, peeled, cored, and sliced
> $\frac{1}{4}$ cup packed brown sugar
> $\frac{3}{4}$ teaspoon ground cinnamon
> 3 eggs
> $\frac{1}{2}$ cup milk
> $\frac{1}{4}$ cup flour
> $\frac{1}{2}$ teaspoon salt
> sweetened whipped cream (optional)

Preheat an oven to 450°F.

Melt the butter in a 9- or 10-inch skillet with an ovenproof handle. (To make a handle ovenproof, wrap aluminum foil securely around it.) Arrange the apples in a single layer in the butter. Combine 2 tablespoons of the brown sugar and the cinnamon, and sprinkle over the apples. Cook over medium-high heat, stirring frequently, for 5 to 6 minutes, or until the apples are slightly soft.

Meanwhile, beat together the eggs, milk, flour, and salt in a small bowl. When the apples are ready, remove from the heat and pour the egg mixture over them.

Bake in the preheated oven for 8 minutes. Remove from the oven and sprinkle the remaining 2 tablespoons sugar over the pancake. Return to the oven, reduce the heat to 375°F, and bake for 8 to 10 minutes, or until evenly browned. Remove from the oven, loosen the pancake around the edges with a knife, and cut into wedges. Serve plain or with sweetened whipped cream.

Dutch Baby

Serves: 6

> 2 large or 3 small eggs
> $1\frac{1}{2}$ cups sifted flour
> $\frac{1}{2}$ teaspoon salt
> $\frac{1}{2}$ cup milk
> 2 tablespoons butter, melted and cooled
> 1 tablespoon lemon juice
> confectioners' sugar
> $1\frac{1}{2}$ pints strawberries, sliced, or an equal amount of other cut-up fruit
> sour cream
> brown sugar
> ground cinnamon

Preheat an oven to 450°F. Grease a 9-inch round cake pan.

In a large bowl, beat the eggs until well blended. Sift together the sifted flour and salt into another bowl. Add the flour mixture and milk to the eggs and beat until smooth. Stir in the butter. Pour into the prepared pan.

Bake for 20 minutes. Reduce the heat to 350°F, prick the shell with the tines of a fork,

and bake for 20 minutes more, or until fork comes out clean. Remove from the oven and sprinkle with the lemon juice and confectioners' sugar. Fill with the fruit. Top with a large dollop of sour cream and sprinkle with brown sugar and cinnamon. Serve at once.

Flapjacks Soufflé

Serves: 4

> 6 eggs, separated
> $1/2$ cup buttermilk pancake mix
> $1/2$ teaspoon salt
> $1/2$ cup sour cream
> melted butter

In a bowl, beat the egg yolks until thickened and lemon colored. Add the pancake mix, salt, and sour cream and stir to combine. In another bowl, beat the egg whites until stiff peaks form. Fold into the yolk mixture.

Preheat a griddle or skillet over medium-hot heat. When hot, brush lightly with the melted butter. Pour about $1/3$ cup of the batter onto the hot griddle or pan for each flapjack and cook each side until golden brown. Serve hot.

A Hot Griddle Is Best

Whenever you're cooking pancakes or fritters, make sure that the pan or griddle is hot before you pour in the batter. Sprinkle a few drops of water on the cooking surface when you think it is adequately preheated. If the drops dance and skitter around for a few seconds, the surface is ready.

Pancake Batter

You probably learned this in home economics back in high school, but whenever you mix up batter for pancakes or other griddle cakes, it's important to mix the ingredients together until the dry ingredients are just barely moistened. The natural inclination is to make sure the batter is nice and smooth before you pour it onto the griddle, but overmixing will result in a dry, tough pancake. Mix with quick, steady strokes, fifteen to start, and then adding a few more if the batter seems like it needs it.

Blueberry Pancakes

Serves: 6

$2^1/_2$ cups flour
1 teaspoon baking soda
$^1/_2$ teaspoon salt
$1^1/_2$ tablespoons sugar
1 egg, well beaten
2 cups buttermilk
$1^1/_2$ tablespoons butter, melted and cooled
1 pint blueberries

Sift together the flour, baking soda, salt, and sugar into a bowl. Combine the egg and milk in another bowl and beat to combine well. Add the milk mixture slowly to the flour mixture, beating until smooth. Stir in the butter and berries.

Preheat a griddle or skillet over medium-high heat. Pour the batter by the tablespoonful onto the hot griddle or pan and cook for about 2 to 3 minutes, or until browned. Do not crowd the pan. Flip the pancakes and cook on the second side until browned, about 2 minutes longer. Serve hot, dusted with confectioners' sugar and sprinkled with blueberry syrup, if desired.

26

Crêpes Suzette

Serves: 8

Orange Rind:
1 large orange
¹/₃ cup sugar
¹/₃ cup water
1 teaspoon corn syrup

Orange Butter Sauce:
1 large orange
1¹/₂ teaspoons fresh lemon juice
1 cup unsalted butter, softened
¹/₄ cup sugar
*3 tablespoons Grand Marnier or other
    orange-flavored liqueur*

Crêpes:
3 eggs
1 cup milk
1 teaspoon vanilla extract
3 tablespoons unsalted butter, melted
1 tablespoon Grand Marnier
³/₄ cup cornstarch
¹/₈ teaspoon salt
1 tablespoon sugar

To Flambé:
3 tablespoons confectioners' sugar
¹/₃ cup Grand Marnier
¹/₃ cup brandy

To prepare the orange rind, peel the orange with a vegetable peeler. Remove only the orange portion, not the white pith. Cut into ¹/₄-inch-wide strips. Squeeze the juice from the orange and set aside to use for the sauce. Bring a saucepan filled with water to a boil, add the strips, and reduce the heat to medium-low. Simmer for 15 minutes. Drain and rinse under cold water.

In a small saucepan, combine the sugar, water, and corn syrup. Bring to a boil, stirring constantly. Add the orange strips, reduce the heat to low, and cover tightly. Simmer for 15 minutes. Let cool completely, covered.

To make the orange butter sauce, peel the orange with a vegetable peeler. Remove only the orange portion, not the white pith. Chop the zest finely. Squeeze the juice from the orange and add it to the juice reserved from preparing the rind. Strain out any seeds and pour into a measuring cup. You should have almost ²/₃ cup. Stir in the lemon juice.

In a large bowl, using an electric mixer set on low speed, cream together the butter and sugar until smooth, about 1 minute. Gradually mix in the juice, chopped zest, and the Grand Marnier. Refrigerate.

To make the crêpes, in a blender, combine the eggs, milk, vanilla, butter, Grand Marnier, flour, salt, and sugar. Blend at high speed for 10 seconds.

Spray an 8-inch crêpe pan with nonstick cooking spray and heat over medium heat until a drop of water sizzles. Pour in enough of the batter to form a thin sheet in the bottom of the pan (about 2 tablespoons). Cook for 15 to 20 seconds, until the top starts

(continued)

to dry out and the edges of the crêpe begin to turn brown. Using a small metal spatula, lift an edge of the crêpe to check if it's golden brown. Flip the crêpe over and cook for 10 more seconds, or until lightly browned. Remove the crêpe from the pan and repeat with the rest of the batter.

Place 1 crêpe on a plate and spread lightly with the orange butter. Fold in half and spread with more orange butter. Fold in half again. You'll use about 1 tablespoon of orange butter for each crêpe. Repeat with the remaining crêpes.

Place the rest of the orange butter in a large crêpe pan and heat until melted over medium heat. Place the folded crêpes and candied orange rind in the pan. Heat for 2 minutes, spooning the orange butter over the crêpes. Remove from the heat and sprinkle with the confectioners' sugar.

Place the liqueur in a large saucepan. Heat over high heat, then ignite with a match. Pour over the crêpes and allow the flame to die out. Serve the crêpes garnished with the orange rind.

Creamy Strawberry Crêpes

Serves: 6

> 2 pints strawberries, stemmed and sliced, plus 12 whole strawberries with stems
> 2 tablespoons sugar

> 1 can (14 ounces) sweetened condensed milk
> $^{1}/_{2}$ cup whipping cream, whipped, plus whipped cream for serving
> $^{1}/_{4}$ cup lemon juice
> 12 ready-made dessert crêpes

In a bowl, sprinkle the sliced strawberries with the sugar; set aside. In another bowl, using a whisk, beat together the milk and lemon juice until thick. Fold in the sliced strawberries and the whipped cream.

Divide the berry mixture evenly among the crêpes; fold in half. Place 2 crêpes on each plate and garnish each crêpe with additional whipped cream. Place a whole strawberry in the center of each mound of cream.

Chocolate Raspberry Cream Crêpes

Serves: 6

Crêpes:
3 eggs
$^{1}/_{4}$ cup sugar
1 cup flour
1 cup milk
1 tablespoon unsweetened cocoa powder
1 tablespoon unsalted butter, melted
1 tablespoon vanilla extract

White Chocolate Sauce:
6 squares (6 ounces) white chocolate
5 tablespoons whipping cream
2 tablespoons light corn syrup

1½ tablespoons raspberry liqueur
½ teaspoon vanilla extract

Raspberry Cream:

1 cup whipping cream
1 tablespoon raspberry liqueur
1 tablespoon sugar
2 pints raspberries
fresh mint sprigs for garnish

To make the crêpes, in a blender or food processor, combine all the ingredients and process until smooth. Heat a small skillet over medium heat and spray with nonstick cooking spray. Pour 3 tablespoons of the batter into the pan, and swirl to form a crêpe. Cook, turning once, for 1 minute on each side, or until golden. Transfer to a flat surface. Repeat with the remaining batter. Once the crêpes have cooled, they can be stacked and frozen. You should have 14 crêpes.

To prepare the sauce, in a small saucepan, melt the chocolate over low heat, stirring occasionally. Remove from the heat. Place the cream in another small saucepan and bring to a boil. Add the corn syrup, stirring until blended. Gradually add the cream mixture to the melted chocolate, stirring until smooth. Stir in the liqueur and vanilla. Keep warm.

To make the raspberry cream, in a bowl, using an electric mixer set on high speed, whip together the cream, raspberry liqueur, and sugar until soft peaks form. Fold in ½ cup of the raspberries.

To assemble, spoon some of the chocolate sauce in the middle of 4 dessert plates. To fill the crêpes, spoon a generous 2 tablespoons raspberry cream down the center of each crêpe. Fold two of the sides over and place the crêpe seam side down on the chocolate sauce. Sprinkle with the remaining raspberries and garnish with mint sprigs. Serve immediately.

Chocolate Crêpes
(Courtesy of Godiva Chocolates)

Serves: 6

Crêpes:
⅔ cup flour
½ cup unsweetened cocoa powder
2 tablespoons granulated sugar
⅛ teaspoon salt
3 eggs
1¼ cups skim milk
2 tablespoons unsalted butter, melted

Fruit filling:
2 pints strawberries, stemmed and quartered
½ pint raspberries
1 tablespoon Grand Marnier
rind of 1 orange, cut in narrow 1-inch-long strips

confectioners' sugar for dusting

To make the crêpes, in a food processor, combine the flour, cocoa powder, granulated sugar, and salt and pulse to mix. Add the eggs, skim milk, and melted butter and

(continued)

process for 30 seconds until well blended. Using a rubber spatula, scrape down the sides of the bowl and process for 15 seconds longer. Transfer the batter to a bowl and let stand for 15 minutes.

Lightly spray a 6- to 7-inch crêpe pan or small skillet with nonstick cooking spray. Place the pan over medium-low heat and heat for about 30 seconds (a drop of water should sizzle on contact). Pour about 2 tablespoons of the batter into the pan (a coffee measure is ideal). Quickly tilt the pan to coat the bottom evenly with the batter, and return to the heat. Cook the crêpe until small bubbles form on the surface and the bottom is set, 45 seconds to 1 minute. Using a wide spatula, flip the crêpe over and cook until cooked through, about 30 seconds longer. Transfer the crêpe to a plate. Repeat with the remaining batter, stacking the cooked crêpes one on top of the other.

To make the fruit filling, in a bowl, combine the strawberries, raspberries, liqueur, and orange rind; mix well. Place an equal amount of the fruit filling on each of the crêpes. Fold the crêpes in a cone shape around the filling. Arrange 2 filled crêpes on each dessert plate. Dust with confectioners' sugar and serve.

Raspberry Ricotta Soufflé

Serves: 4

1/4 cup plus 1 tablespoon granulated sugar
1 1/2 cup part-skim ricotta cheese
2 tablespoons flour
1/2 teaspoon grated lemon rind
1/2 teaspoon vanilla extract
1 teaspoon ground cinnamon
1 egg yolk
2 egg whites
1/4 teaspoon salt
1/2 pint raspberries
2 teaspoons confectioners' sugar

Preheat an oven to 350°F.

Spray four 3/4-cup individual soufflé dishes with nonstick cooking spray.

In a food processor, combine the 1/4 cup granulated sugar, the cheese, flour, lemon rind, vanilla, cinnamon, and egg yolk. Process for 1 minute, or until smooth, stopping and scraping down the sides of the bowl once. Spoon the mixture into a large bowl; set aside.

In a separate bowl, using an electric mixer set on high speed, beat together the egg whites and salt until foamy. Gradually add the remaining 1 tablespoon granulated sugar, beating until soft peaks form. Gently fold the egg white mixture into the cheese mixture, then fold in the raspberries.

Spoon the mixture into the prepared soufflé dishes. Place the soufflé dishes in a 9-by-13-inch baking pan and add hot water to the pan to a depth of 1 inch. Bake for 30 minutes, or until puffed and golden. Remove the dishes from the baking pan. Sprinkle each soufflé with 1/2 teaspoon of the confectioners' sugar and serve immediately.

Chapter 4:
Fudge and Really Sweet Desserts

A staple of church crafts fairs, excursions to the boardwalk, and an almost mandatory food group of family vacations, fudge and the other rich desserts created here provide us with an instant association with leisure time. This is as good a reason as any to try one of the recipes in this section.

The good thing about fudge is that you can customize it any way you want without compromising the integrity of the recipe. The basics—sugar, butter, milk—will remain the same, but if you're crazy for coconut, go ahead and use as much as you'd like. The same goes for nuts, chocolate chips and marshmallows. So go ahead and have a mini-vacation: Cook (And Eat) Fudge.

Peanut Butter Fudge

Makes: 2 pounds fudge

4$\frac{1}{2}$ cups packed brown sugar
4 cups granulated sugar
2 cups milk
3 cups creamy peanut butter
2 cups marshmallow creme

Butter an 8-inch square pan and a 9$\frac{1}{2}$-by-13-inch pan. In a saucepan, mix together the sugars. Add the milk and mix until smooth. Place on the stove and bring to a boil. Boil for about 10 to 15 minutes, or until the mixture registers 240°F on a candy thermometer. Remove from the heat and stir in the peanut butter and marshmallow creme, mixing until smooth. Do this step quickly. Pour into the prepared pans and let set. Cut into small squares while still warm.

Kahlúa Creamy Fudge

Makes: 1 pound fudge

1$\frac{1}{3}$ cups sugar
$\frac{2}{3}$ cup evaporated milk
1 jar (7 ounces) marshmallow creme
$\frac{1}{4}$ cup butter
$\frac{1}{4}$ cup Kahlúa liqueur
2 cups semisweet chocolate morsels
1 cup milk chocolate morsels
$\frac{2}{3}$ cup chopped walnuts
1 teaspoon vanilla extract

Line an 8-inch square pan with aluminum foil. In a 2-quart saucepan, combine the sugar, evaporated milk, marshmallow creme, butter, and Kahlúa. Bring to a rapid boil, stirring constantly, and boil for 5 minutes. Remove from the heat, add all the chocolate, and stir until melted. Add the nuts and

vanilla. Turn into the prepared pan. Refrigerate until firm, then cut into squares.

Fudge Caramels

Makes: 1 pound candy

$^2/_3$ cup unsweetened cocoa powder
2 cups sugar
1 cup light corn syrup
$^1/_8$ teaspoon salt
1 cup evaporated milk
$^1/_2$ cup water
$^1/_4$ cup butter
1 teaspoon vanilla extract

Butter a 9-inch square pan. Combine the cocoa, sugar, corn syrup, and salt in a heavy 3-quart saucepan. Add the evaporated milk and water, stir well, and bring to a boil over medium heat, stirring constantly. Cook, stirring frequently, for about 10 minutes, or until the mixture registers 245°F on a candy thermometer. Alternatively, test by dropping a nugget of the mixture into cold water; it should form a firm ball.

Remove from the heat, drop in the butter and vanilla, and stir to blend in the butter completely. Pour into the prepared pan, and let cool. Cut into squares (scissors are helpful) and wrap in wax paper.

New Orleans Pralines

Makes: 1 pound pralines

$1^1/_2$ cups packed light brown sugar
$^1/_2$ cup granulated sugar
$^1/_2$ cup evaporated milk
$^1/_4$ cup light corn syrup
1 tablespoon margarine
1 teaspoon vanilla extract
$1^1/_2$ cups pecans or walnuts, coarsely
    broken

Line baking sheets with wax paper. Stir together the sugars, evaporated milk, and corn syrup in a heavy 3-quart saucepan. Cook over very low heat, stirring frequently, for about 1 hour, or until the mixture registers 236°F on a candy thermometer. Alternatively, test by dropping a nugget of the mixture into cold water; it should form a soft ball that flattens upon removal from the water.

Remove from the heat. Add the margarine and vanilla and beat for about 1 minute, or until well blended. Add the nuts and stir until coated. Quickly drop by tablespoonfuls onto the wax paper–lined baking sheets. When cool and set, remove from the paper.

NOTE: The mixture will curdle if cooked too rapidly.

Chocolate Log Cabin Rolls

Makes: 20 slices

> 1 cup packed light brown sugar
> $^3/_4$ cup granulated sugar
> $^1/_2$ cup maple syrup
> 1 cup light cream
> 2 tablespoons butter
> few grains salt
> $1^1/_2$ squares ($1^1/_2$ ounces) baking
>   chocolate, broken into small pieces
> 1 egg white, lightly beaten
> 1 cup pecans, coarsely broken

Combine the sugars, maple syrup, cream, butter, salt, and baking chocolate in a heavy 3-quart saucepan. Bring slowly to a boil, stirring constantly. Cover and cook for 5 minutes. Remove the cover and cook, stirring occasionally, for about 10 minutes, or until the mixture registers 236°F on a candy thermometer. Alternatively, test by dropping a nugget of the mixture into cold water; it should form a soft ball that flattens upon removal from the water. Remove from the heat and let cool until the bottom of the pan feels lukewarm.

Butter a large work surface. Beat the chocolate mixture vigorously until it begins to lose its gloss and begins to hold its shape. Turn out onto the buttered surface. Using buttered hands, knead the fudge until it can be shaped. Form into two 9-inch-long rolls. Brush with the egg white and roll immediately in the pecans, pressing the nuts into the rolls to coat evenly. Wrap and chill well, then cut into $^1/_2$-inch-thick slices.

Round Krispies

Makes: 24 krispies

> 1 cup confectioners' sugar
> 1 cup creamy peanut butter
> 1 tablespoon butter
> $^1/_2$ cup walnuts, chopped
> 1 cup crisped rice cereal
> confectioners' sugar for coating
> $^1/_2$ cup flaked dried coconut

Line a baking sheet with wax paper. Mix together the confectioners' sugar, peanut butter, and butter in a bowl. Add the nuts, and then stir in the cereal. Dampen your hands and shape the mixture into small balls. Coat each ball with confectioners' sugar and then with the coconut. Place on the wax paper–lined baking sheet and chill well before serving.

Chocolate Coconut Krispies

Makes: 20 cookies

> $^1/_2$ cup butter or margarine
> $1^1/_2$ cups (18 squares) graham cracker
>   crumbs
> 1 cup walnuts, chopped
> 1 package (6 ounces) semisweet chocolate
>   morsels
> $1^1/_3$ cups flaked dried coconut
> $1^1/_3$ cups sweetened condensed milk

Preheat an oven to 350°F.

Melt the butter in a 7-by-11-inch baking dish. Add the remaining ingredients layer by layer, in the order listed. Bake, uncovered, for about 8 minutes, or until the mixture just begins to show brown areas, rotating the pan twice during cooking. Remove from the oven, let cool, and cut into bars.

Chocolate Yummies

Makes: 12 squares

> 1 can (12 ounces) sweetened condensed milk
> 1 package (6 ounces) semisweet chocolate morsels
> 1 1/2 cups (18 squares) graham cracker crumbs

Preheat an oven to 350°F. Butter an 8-inch square cake pan.

Place the crumbs in the prepared pan and add the milk. Mix until the crumbs are moist. Add the chocolate morsels. Spread evenly in the pan. Bake for 30 minutes, or until firm. Remove from the oven; let cool.

Variation: If you want, add 1/2 cup chopped nuts with the chocolate chips.

Nutty Chocolate Nut Clusters

Makes: 24 clusters

> 1 package (6 ounces) milk chocolate morsels
> 1 teaspoon vegetable shortening

Chocolate Chip Substitutes

Nestle's and other companies that make chocolate chips and other add-ins for baking are coming out with a wide variety of deliciously different products to add zip to recipes that would normally use chocolate chips. Of course, peanut butter chips have been around for a while, but what about chocolate-covered raisins, toffee bits, or white chocolate chips? Combine two different "chips" for even more fun.

(continued)

Candy Thermometers

You should make sure that your candy thermometer gives accurate readings before you use it. To test its accuracy, place it in a pan of warm water and bring the water to the boiling point. The boiling point for water is 212° Fahrenheit. After 5 minutes, check the temperature reading on the thermometer. If it reads higher or lower than 212°F, figure out the exact number of degrees that it's off, and then use that number as your "boiling point" for future recipes.

$\frac{1}{2}$ cup each of cashews, peanuts, pecan halves, walnut halves, or miniature marshmallows

Line a baking sheet with wax paper.

Melt the chocolate morsels with the shortening in the top pan of a double boiler placed over (not touching) hot (not boiling) water. Throw in $\frac{1}{2}$ cup of the nuts at a time, stirring them into the melted chocolate. Take out the nuts with a fork and place in little piles on the prepared baking sheet. Refrigerate until set.

Crazy Crunch

Makes: 3 quarts candy

2 quarts popcorn
$2\frac{1}{4}$ cups dry-roasted mixed nuts
$\frac{2}{3}$ cup toasted almonds
$\frac{2}{3}$ cup toasted pecans
$1\frac{1}{3}$ cups sugar
1 cup margarine (2 sticks)
$\frac{1}{2}$ cup light corn syrup
1 teaspoon vanilla extract

Mix together the popcorn and all the nuts in a shallow roasting pan, spread evenly in the pan, and set aside. Mix together the sugar, margarine, and corn syrup in a 2-quart saucepan. Cook over medium heat, stirring constantly, until the mixture boils. Continue boiling, stirring occasionally, for about 15 minutes, or until the temperature registers 290°F on a candy thermometer. Alternatively,

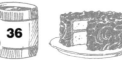

test by dropping a small amount of the mixture into cold water; it should separate into threads that are hard but not brittle.

Remove from the heat and stir in the vanilla. Pour over the popcorn mixture, stirring to coat well. Spread out to cool on wax paper. Break into pieces and store in a tightly covered container.

Almond Crunch

Makes: 1 pound candy

$1\frac{1}{2}$ *cups mini chocolate morsels*
$1\frac{3}{4}$ *cups almonds, chopped*
$1\frac{1}{2}$ *cups butter or margarine*
$1\frac{3}{4}$ *cups sugar*
3 tablespoons light corn syrup
3 tablespoons water

Preheat an oven to 350°F. Lightly grease a 9-by-13-by-2-inch pan.

Spread 1 cup of the chocolate morsels evenly over the bottom and set aside. Spread the almonds in a shallow pan or on a baking sheet. Toast in the preheated oven, shaking occasionally, for 7 to 8 minutes, or until golden brown. Remove from the oven and set aside.

Melt the butter in a $2\frac{1}{2}$-quart saucepan. Stir in the sugar, corn syrup, and water. Cook over medium heat, stirring constantly, for about 15 minutes, or until the mixture registers 300°F on a candy thermometer (hard-crack stage). Remove from the heat and stir in $1\frac{1}{2}$ cups of the toasted almonds.

Immediately spread the mixture evenly over the chocolate morsels in the pan, being careful not to disturb the morsels. Quickly sprinkle with the remaining $\frac{1}{4}$ cup almonds and $\frac{1}{2}$ cup chocolate morsels. Score into $1\frac{1}{2}$-inch squares, if desired. Let cool.

Cover the pan and store overnight. Remove from the pan, break into pieces, and store in a tightly covered container.

Butter-Almond Crunch

Makes: 1 pound candy

$1\frac{1}{2}$ *cups mini chocolate morsels*
$1\frac{3}{4}$ *cups almonds, chopped*
$1\frac{1}{2}$ *cups butter or margarine*
$1\frac{3}{4}$ *cups sugar*
3 tablespoons light corn syrup
3 tablespoons water

Preheat an oven to 350°F. Lightly butter a 9-by-13-inch pan. Spread 1 cup of the chocolate morsels evenly over the bottom of the prepared pan. Spread the almonds on a baking sheet and toast, stirring occasionally, for 7 or 8 minutes, or until golden brown. Remove from the oven and set aside.

Melt the butter in a saucepan and blend in the sugar, corn syrup, and water. Cook over medium heat, stirring constantly, for about 15 minutes, or until the mixture registers 300°F on a candy thermometer (hard-crack stage). Remove from the heat and stir in $1\frac{1}{2}$ cups toasted almonds. Immediately spread the mixture evenly over the chocolate

(continued)

morsels in the pan. Do not disturb the morsels. Sprinkle with the remaining $^1/_4$ cup almonds and $^1/_2$ cup chocolate morsels. Score into 1 $^1/_2$-inch squares, if desired. Let cool. Cover the pan and store overnight. Remove from the pan, break into pieces, and store in a tightly covered container.

Rum Balls

Makes: About 24 rum balls

> 1 $^1/_4$ cups finely crushed vanilla wafers
> $^1/_2$ cup sugar
> $^1/_4$ cups walnuts, finely chopped
> 1 tablespoon unsweetened cocoa powder
> 1 $^1/_2$ tablespoons dark corn syrup
> 2 tablespoons light rum
> confectioners' sugar for coating

In a bowl, mix together the wafer crumbs, sugar, walnuts, and cocoa. Add the corn syrup and rum and mix well. Using a spoon, shape into 1-inch balls. Roll the balls in confectioners' sugar, coating evenly. Store in tightly covered tin.

Chocolate Rum Balls

Makes: About 24 rum balls

> 1 package (12 ounces) vanilla wafers, crushed
> $^3/_4$ cup confectioners' sugar
> $^1/_4$ cup unsweetened cocoa powder
> 1 $^1/_2$ cups walnuts, chopped
> 3 tablespoons light corn syrup

> $^1/_2$ cup rum, or $^1/_2$ cup orange juice plus 1 teaspoon grated orange rind
> confectioners' sugar for coating

In a bowl, combine the crushed vanilla wafers, confectioners' sugar, cocoa, and nuts. Add the corn syrup and rum and mix well. Using a spoon, shape into 1-inch balls. Roll the balls in confectioners' sugar, coating evenly. Store in an airtight container for several days to develop the flavor before eating. Roll again in confectioners' sugar just before serving.

Peach Leather

Makes: 1 pound leather

> 10 ripe peaches or apricots (2 $^1/_2$ to 3 pounds)
> 1 cup sugar

Bring a saucepan filled with water to a boil. Add the peaches, in batches, blanch for 30 seconds, then transfer to cold water with a slotted spoon. Remove from the water, slip off the skins, and slice the peaches, discarding the pits. You should have about 10 cups.

Mix the peaches and sugar together in a large saucepan. Bring to a boil, stirring until the sugar is dissolved. Boil for 3 minutes, then pour into a blender. Whirl until smooth. Let cool to lukewarm.

Meanwhile, prepare a smooth, level drying surface in full sunlight. Cover baking sheets with sides with plastic wrap. Spread the purée

$^1/_4$ inch thick on the prepared surfaces. You can make 4 sheets each 12 by 15 inches. Let dry outdoors in the sunlight. Drying may take up to 3 days depending on the temperature and humidity. Bring the pans inside at the end of each day. The fruit is fully dry when the purée can easily be peeled off the plastic wrap.

For storing, roll up the "leather" in the plastic wrap. Wrap in more plastic wrap and seal tightly. (The leather will keep at room temperature for up to 1 month, in the refrigerator for up to 4 months, or in the freezer for up to 1 year.)

Peanut Butter Cups

Makes: 24 cups

> 2 cups milk chocolate chips
> 2 tablespoons shortening
> $^3/_4$ cup creamy peanut butter
> $^3/_4$ cup confectioners' sugar
> 1 tablespoon unsalted butter, melted

In the top of a double boiler or in a heat-proof bowl, combine the chocolate chips and shortening. Place over simmering water and stir until the chocolate is melted and the mixture is smooth. Remove from the heat but keep warm over hot water.

Using about 1 teaspoon of the chocolate mixture for each cup, coat the inside of 24 1-inch round paper candy cups. To do so, place each cup in the palm of your hand and rotate it gently, using the back of a spoon to

(continued)

Fast Fruit Leather

If you're impatient to eat your fruit leather, or want to make this treat in bad weather, you can dry it indoors. Let the prepared fruit sit under a lamp or in the sun for 2 hours, then place the baking sheets in an oven set at 140°. Leave the oven door ajar a few inches. The leather will be completely dried in 4 to 5 hours.

push the chocolate up the sides. Chill until firm, 15 to 20 minutes.

To make the filling, combine in a bowl, the peanut butter, confectioners' sugar, and butter; mix until well blended. Using slightly rounded teaspoonfuls, shape the filling into balls. Place 1 ball into each chilled cup and press lightly with fingers to flatten.

Spoon 1 teaspoon of the melted chocolate mixture on top of each filled cup and smooth over to seal. Chill until firm, about 45 minutes. Store in an airtight container in the refrigerator.

Fudgy Fudge

Makes: 40 pieces

$4^1/_2$ cups sugar
$^1/_3$ cup unsalted butter
1 can (8 ounces) evaporated milk
1 jar (7 ounces) marshmallow creme
2 cups semisweet chocolate chips
2 cups milk chocolate chips
2 teaspoons vanilla extract
2 cups pecans, chopped

Lightly grease a 9-by-13-inch pan.
In a large saucepan over medium heat, combine the sugar, butter, and milk. Bring to a boil and boil for 5 minutes, stirring constantly. Remove from the heat and add all the remaining ingredients except the nuts. Beat with an electric mixer set on medium speed until smooth, about 8 minutes. Stir in the nuts.

Pour into the prepared pan. Let cool completely before cutting.

Chocolate Pâté

Serves: 12

2 pounds dark chocolate
$1^1/_2$ cup unsalted butter
4 egg yolks
1 cup water
fruity red wine to taste

Line a large loaf pan with plastic wrap.
In the top of a double boiler or in a heatproof bowl over gently simmering water, combine the chocolate and butter with the water. Remove from the heat and stir in the egg yolks. Pour the chocolate mixture into the loaf pan. Cover with plastic wrap and chill for 3 hours. Unmold, slice and cut into desired shapes, such as triangles, for serving.

Quick Chocolate Pecan Fudge
(Courtesy of Godiva Chocolates)

Makes: 25 pieces

6 squares (6 ounces) semisweet chocolate, finely chopped
2 squares (2 ounces) unsweetened chocolate, finely chopped
2 tablespoons unsalted butter, cut into $^1/_2$-inch cubes
$1^1/_2$ cups sugar
$^1/_2$ cup plus 2 tablespoons whipping cream

3/4 cup marshmallow creme
2 teaspoons vanilla extract
25 pecan halves

Line an 8-inch square baking pan with aluminum foil, leaving a 2-inch overhang on two opposite sides. Lightly butter the bottom of the foil-lined pan.

Place the chocolates and butter in a large heatproof bowl. Set aside. Butter the sides of a heavy, nonreactive 2-quart saucepan. Add the sugar and cream. Stirring constantly with a wooden spoon, cook the mixture over medium-low heat for 10 to 15 minutes, or until the sugar crystals are completely dissolved. Using a pastry brush dipped in warm water, dissolve any crystals clinging to the sides of the pan.

Bring the syrup to a full boil without stirring. (Bubbles should appear all over the entire surface of the syrup.) Boil without stirring for 5 minutes. Pour the hot syrup over the chocolates and butter. Let stand for 30 seconds to melt the chocolate. Using a rubber spatula, stir until smooth. Stir in the marshmallow creme and vanilla. Scrape the fudge into the prepared pan. Arrange the pecan halves, evenly spaced, over the top of the fudge. (Eventually each square of fudge will have a pecan at its center.) Refrigerate for 1 hour, or until set.

Using the two foil ends as handles, lift the fudge out of the pan. Invert the fudge onto a cutting board and carefully peel off the foil. Invert again onto a smooth cutting surface. Using a large knife, score the fudge into 25 pieces. Cut the fudge, rinsing the knife with hot water and wiping dry between each cut. Store in an airtight container at room temperature.

Old-Fashioned Rocky Road Fudge
(Courtesy of Godiva Chocolates)

Makes: 18 pieces

2 cups sugar
3/4 cup plus 2 tablespoons half-and-half
3 tablespoons light corn syrup
a pinch of salt
4 squares (4 ounces) unsweetened chocolate, very finely chopped
2 tablespoons unsalted butter, cut into 1-inch cubes
2 teaspoons vanilla extract
1/3 cup chopped walnuts
1/3 cup semisweet chocolate chips
1/3 cup miniature marshmallows

Line a 9-by-5-inch loaf pan with aluminum foil, leaving a 2-inch overhang on two opposite sides of the pan. Lightly butter the bottom and sides of the foil-lined pan. Place a large glass of cold water in the refrigerator. Have a small glass cup handy. Fill the sink with water to a depth of 1 inch.

Butter the sides of a heavy, nonreactive 2-quart saucepan. Add the sugar, half-and-half, corn syrup, and salt. Stirring constantly with a wooden spoon, cook the mixture over

(continued)

medium-low heat for 5 to 10 minutes, or until the sugar crystals are completely dissolved.

Remove from the heat. Using a pastry brush dipped in warm water, dissolve any crystals clinging to the sides of the pan. Add the chocolate and gently stir until completely melted. (Place over heat if necessary.)

Return the pan to the heat and insert a candy thermometer into the syrup. Bring the syrup to a boil over medium-low heat. Cook the syrup without stirring for 20 minutes, or until the thermometer registers 232°F. Test the fudge to see if it will form a "soft ball": Fill the small glass cup about two-thirds full with some of the chilled water. Dip a clean, dry wooden spoon into the simmering fudge and drizzle about $1/2$ teaspoon fudge mixture into the chilled water. Try and gather up the drippings of fudge on the bottom of the cup into a ball. If they disintegrate in the water as you try, continue cooking and test the fudge again when the thermometer registers 234°F. (Wash and dry the wooden spoon; rinse out the glass cup and refill with fresh chilled water when you are ready to test again.) The fudge is ready when it will form a ball that holds its shape both in the water and when lifted out of the water between your thumb and forefinger (soft ball stage can be reached anywhere from 234°F to 238°F). Immediately remove the thermometer and place it in warm water. Place the pan of fudge in the water in the sink to stop the cooking process.

To cool the fudge, distribute the cubes of butter over the fudge, but don't stir them in. Remove the pan from the water, insert a clean thermometer into the fudge, and set the pan on a wire rack. If necessary, prop one side of the pan with a folded dish towel so that the thermometer is submerged in the fudge. Continue cooling the fudge without disturbing for 1 hour or until tepid (110°F).

Next, add the vanilla. Using a wooden spoon, stir the fudge until the butter and vanilla are incorporated. Continue stirring and working the fudge until it begins to thicken, lose its shine, and get lighter-colored streaks in it, 20 to 30 minutes. (Do not overmix or the fudge will set in the saucepan.) Immediately stir in the nuts, chocolate chips, and marshmallows. Scrape the fudge into the prepared pan. (Do not scrape the sides of the saucepan.) Spread in an even layer with a small flexible metal spatula. Place the pan on the wire rack and let the fudge set for 1 to 2 hours at room temperature until firm.

Using the two ends of aluminum foil as handles, lift the fudge out of the pan. Invert the fudge onto a cutting board and carefully peel off the foil. Invert again onto a smooth cutting surface. Using a large knife, score the fudge into 18 pieces. Cut the fudge, rinsing the knife with hot water and wiping dry between each cut. Store in an airtight container at room temperature.

The Everything
Dessert Cookbook

Chapter 5: Cakes and Frostings

R ecently, I read a magazine article about a woman who collected cake carriers that were made in the 1950s. She had over 200 cake carriers on display in her tiny apartment, and whenever she visited a friend, she baked a cake and toted it along in one of her carriers. Inevitably, her friends all became converts to cake carriers.

Today, people are more likely to buy cakes from the bakery or bake them from a mix than to create them from one of the great from-scratch recipes here. But in most cases, baking a cake from scratch requires no more time than using a mix, and the rewards are much more worth the effort.

In the midst of high-tech everything these days, there is a quiet yet significant movement towards creating foods and other items from nothing more than the basic ingredients. So the next time you bake one of the cakes in this section, tote it along in an old-fashioned carrier that you found at a garage sale. Your friends will be impressed.

CAKES

New England White Cake

Makes: 1 2-layer 8-inch cake

1 1/2 cups sifted cake flour
1/2 teaspoon salt
1 tablespoon baking powder
1/2 cup vegetable shortening
1 1/3 cups sugar
1 cup milk
1 teaspoon vanilla extract
3 egg whites, beaten stiff

Preheat an oven to 375°F. Butter two 8-inch round cake pans, then line the bottom with wax paper and butter the paper.

Sift together the sifted flour, salt, and baking powder into a bowl. In another bowl, cream the shortening until light and creamy. Add the sugar gradually, mixing well, and then add the vanilla. Add the flour mixture alternately with the milk to the shortening mixture, stirring just until blended. Fold in the beaten egg whites. Pour into the prepared pans.

Bake in the preheated oven for 25 minutes, or until a knife comes out clean.

Let cool completely before frosting.

Caramel Cake

Makes: 1 2-layer 9-inch cake

2$\frac{1}{2}$ cups sifted cake flour
1 tablespoon baking powder
$\frac{1}{2}$ teaspoon salt
$\frac{1}{2}$ cup vegetable shortening
1$\frac{1}{2}$ cups sugar
1 teaspoon vanilla extract
2 eggs
$\frac{3}{4}$ cup water
3 tablespoons Caramel Syrup (recipe follows)

Caramel Frosting:

1 cup sugar
1 cup water
1 tablespoon light corn syrup
2 egg whites
1$\frac{1}{2}$ teaspoons Caramel Syrup
1 teaspoon vanilla extract

Preheat an oven to 375°F. Grease two 9-inch cake pans with 1$\frac{1}{2}$-inch sides.

Sift together the sifted flour, baking powder, and salt into a bowl. In another bowl, cream the shortening with an electric mixer until light and creamy, then gradually add the sugar, creaming thoroughly. Add the vanilla, and then the eggs one at a time, beating for 1 minute after each addition. Add the flour mixture to the creamed mixture alternately with the water, a small amount at a time, beating until smooth after each addition. Add the Caramel Syrup. Beat the batter

(continued)

Plain Vanilla Alternatives

The next time a recipe calls for vanilla extract, reach for a different-flavored extract or flavoring. In the grocery store, you'll see almond, lemon, orange, mint, and even coconut extracts and flavorings. Vanilla is a great old standard, but there's a whole world of untapped flavors out there to help add some zip to your frostings, cakes, and cookies.

45

Creaming Butter

I know that whenever I've had to cream butter (or margarine) in the past and it's been too cold and hard, I've had to take quick walks around the kitchen to retrieve all of the stray butter chunks off the floor before the cats got to them. But whenever I've stuck the bowl in the microwave for 10 seconds, the butter usually goes too far in the other direction, resulting in a consistency that soaked up too much of the flour. So be patient. If it's hot out, place the bowl in a larger bowl full of cool water. If the butter is too cold, drape a towel over the bowl to trap some heat.

very well for 4 minutes. Pour into the prepared pans.

Bake for about 20 minutes, or until a knife comes out clean. Let cool for 10 minutes in the pans, then turn out onto racks to cool completely.

Meanwhile, make the frosting: Combine the sugar, water, and corn syrup in a saucepan. Cover and bring quickly to a boil. Uncover. Boil until a candy thermometer registers 240°F. Alternatively, test by dropping a small amount from a spoon; it should fall in a 6- to 8-inch thread. Remove from the heat. In a bowl, beat the egg whites until stiff but not dry. Pour the hot syrup in a slow, thin stream into the egg whites, beating constantly. Add the Caramel Syrup and vanilla. Beat until stiff peaks form and the frosting can be spread, about 6 minutes.

Frost the cake layers with the frosting.

Caramel Syrup: In a heavy skillet, melt $^2/_3$ cup sugar over low heat, stirring constantly. When a dark brown syrup has formed, remove from the heat and slowly add $^2/_3$ cup boiling water. Return to the heat and stir until the syrup is completely incorporated, then boil to reduce to $^1/_2$ cup. Let cool.

Old-Fashioned Butter Cake

Serves: 12

1 $^1/_2$ cups butter or margarine, softened
2 $^1/_2$ cups granulated sugar

8 eggs
3/4 teaspoon salt
3 cups sifted cake flour
1 1/2 teaspoons vanilla extract
confectioners' sugar for dusting
2 teaspoons baking powder

Preheat an oven to 350°F. Butter and flour a 12-cup fluted tube pan.

In a bowl, cream the butter until smooth. Gradually add the granulated sugar, blending well. Add the eggs one at a time, beating well after each addition. Sift together the sifted flour and the salt into a bowl. Gradually add the flour mixture to the butter mixture along with the vanilla, beating well. Spoon into the prepared pan.

Bake for 50 to 60 minutes, or until the top springs back when lightly touched. Remove the pan to a rack and let cool for 10 minutes. Dust cooled cake with confectioners' sugar.

Glazed Almond Puff

Serves: 8

2 cups flour
1 cup butter or margarine, softened
2 tablespoons plus 1 cup water
1 teaspoon almond extract
3 eggs
chopped nuts

Sugar Glaze:
1/2 cup confectioners' sugar

2 tablespoons butter, softened
1 to 2 tablespoons warm water
1 1/2 teaspoons almond or vanilla extract

Preheat an oven to 350°F. Have ready an ungreased baking sheet.

Place 1 cup of the flour in a bowl. Add 1/2 cup of the butter and cut in with a pastry blender until it resembles coarse meal. Sprinkle the 2 tablespoons water over the flour mixture and mix with a fork until a rough mass forms. Gather into a ball and divide in half. On the ungreased baking sheet, pat each half into a strip 12 inches long and 3 inches wide, placing the strips about 3 inches apart.

In a saucepan, bring the remaining 1/2 cup butter and the 1 cup water to a rolling boil. Remove from the heat and quickly stir in the almond extract and the remaining 1 cup flour. Return to low heat and stir vigorously until the mixture forms a ball, about 1 minute. Remove from the heat. Add the eggs all at once and beat until smooth. Spread half of the mixture over each dough strip, covering completely.

Bake for about 1 hour, or until the topping is crisp and brown. Let cool on a rack; remove from pan. Glaze when puff is cool.

Meanwhile, make the Sugar Glaze: combine all the ingredients in a bowl and mix until smooth.

Frost the cooled almond puffs with the glaze and sprinkle generously with nuts.

Almond Honey Cake

Serves: 12

$\frac{1}{4}$ cup ground almonds
1 cup cold strong brewed coffee
1$\frac{3}{4}$ cups honey
$\frac{1}{2}$ cup dried currants
3 tablespoons brandy
$\frac{1}{4}$ cup corn oil
1$\frac{1}{4}$ cups packed light brown sugar
4 eggs
3$\frac{1}{2}$ cups flour
1 tablespoon baking powder
1 teaspoon baking soda
$\frac{1}{4}$ teaspoon salt
1 teaspoon ground cinnamon
$\frac{1}{4}$ teaspoon ground cloves
$\frac{1}{2}$ teaspoon ground ginger
$\frac{1}{4}$ teaspoon ground nutmeg
$\frac{1}{2}$ cup sliced almonds
1 tablespoon grated lemon rind

Preheat an oven to 300°F. Butter 2 standard loaf pans and coat the bottoms and sides with the ground almonds.

Combine the coffee and honey in a saucepan and bring to a boil. Set aside to cool. Combine the currants and brandy and set aside to plump. Stir together the oil, brown sugar, and eggs in a large bowl until thoroughly mixed. Combine the flour, baking powder, baking soda, salt, cinnamon, cloves, ginger, and nutmeg. Add the flour mixture and coffee mixture alternately to the egg

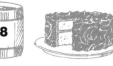

mixture, mixing well. Fold in the sliced almonds, currants and brandy, and lemon rind. Pour the batter into the prepared pans.

Bake for 1 hour, or until the cakes spring back to the touch. Let cool on a rack to room temperature, then turn out onto serving plates. This cake also freezes well; wrap in aluminum foil, then pack into a plastic bag.

Mardi Gras Cake

Serves: 8

1 can (30 ounces) fruit cocktail
¹/₂ cup margarine or butter
1 cup packed light brown sugar
1 package (18 ¹/₂ ounces) lemon cake mix
1 cup water
ice cream (optional)

Preheat an oven to 350°F.

Drain the fruit cocktail, reserving ¹/₃ cup of the syrup. Melt the margarine in a 9-by-13-inch cake pan or a 12-inch skillet. Add the sugar, spreading it evenly over the bottom of the pan. Arrange the fruit in the sugar mixture. Prepare the cake mix according to package directions, using 1 cup water and ¹/₃ cup reserved syrup for the liquid specified in the directions. Spread the batter over the fruit.

Bake for 45 to 50 minutes, or until a knife comes out clean. Let cool for 5 minutes in the pan, then invert onto a large serving dish. Serve warm or at room temperature with ice cream, if desired.

Blueberry Upside-Down Cake

Serves: 10

2 pints (4 cups) blueberries
1 tablespoon lemon juice
1¹/₄ cups sugar
1 teaspoon Angostura Bitters
4 tablespoons vegetable shortening
1 egg
1¹/₂ cups flour
dash of salt
1¹/₂ teaspoons baking powder
³/₄ cup milk
whipping cream, whipped stiff, if desired

Preheat an oven to 350°F. Generously butter an 8-inch square cake pan.

Place the blueberries in a bowl and squeeze the lemon juice over the top. Sprinkle with ³/₄ cup of the sugar and the Angostura Bitters. Set aside. In another bowl, cream together the shortening and the remaining ¹/₂ cup sugar until light and creamy. Add the egg, mixing well. Sift together the flour, salt, and baking powder into a bowl, and stir into the shortening mixture. Add milk and beat until smooth. Place the sweetened blueberries in the prepared pan, arranging them in an even layer. Smooth the cake dough over the berries.

Bake for 30 minutes, or until a knife comes out clean. Remove from the oven and immediately invert onto a platter. Cut into squares and serve warm with plain cream or whipped cream.

Pineapple Upside-Down Cake

Serves: 10

$^1/_2$ cup margarine, softened
$^1/_2$ cup packed light brown sugar
1 can ($8^1/_4$ ounces) sliced pineapple
12 maraschino cherries, halved
$^1/_2$ cup granulated sugar
1 egg
1 teaspoon vanilla extract
1 cup flour
$1^1/_2$ teaspoons baking powder
$^1/_4$ teaspoon salt
whipped cream (optional)

Preheat an oven to 350°F.

Melt $^1/_4$ cup of the margarine in an 8-inch square cake pan. Stir in the brown sugar, spreading it evenly over the bottom of the pan. Drain the pineapple, reserving the syrup; you should have about $^1/_2$ cup syrup. Arrange the pineapple slices in the pan. Place the cherries in the centers of the pineapple rings.

In a bowl, cream together the remaining $^1/_4$ cup margarine and the granulated sugar until light. Add the egg and vanilla. Combine the flour, baking powder, and salt. Alternately add the flour mixture and the reserved pineapple syrup to the margarine mixture, beating just until smooth. Pour the batter evenly over the fruit in the pan.

Bake for 40 minutes, or until a knife comes out clean. Cool in the pan for 5 minutes, then invert onto a serving plate. Serve warm, topped with whipped cream if desired.

Spice Cake

Serves: 6

1 tablespoon butter
1 cup sugar
2 eggs, well beaten
1 teaspoon baking soda
1 cup buttermilk
2 cups flour
1 teaspoon baking powder
pinch of salt
1 teaspoon ground nutmeg
1 teaspoon ground cinnamon
1 teaspoon ground allspice
1 teaspoon ground cloves
1 cup raisins

Preheat an oven to 350°F. Grease an 8-inch cake pan.

In a bowl, cream together the butter and sugar until well mixed. Add the eggs and mix thoroughly. In a small bowl, dissolve the baking soda in the buttermilk and stir into the sugar mixture. Sift together the flour, baking powder, salt, and all the spices directly onto the sugar mixture and mix well. Stir in the raisins and pour into the cake pan. Bake for about 1 hour, or until a knife comes out clean. Invert onto a rack and let cool.

Note: You can double this recipe and bake it in a 9-by-13-inch pan.

Spice Layer Cake

Serves: 10

$^3/_4$ cup vegetable shortening
$2^1/_4$ cups sifted cake flour
1 cup granulated sugar
1 teaspoon baking powder
1 teaspoon salt
$^3/_4$ teaspoon baking soda
$^3/_4$ to 1 teaspoon ground cinnamon
$^3/_4$ to 1 teaspoon ground cloves
$^3/_4$ cup packed brown sugar
1 cup buttermilk
3 eggs

Preheat an oven to 350°F. Grease two 9-inch cake pans.

In a large bowl, stir the shortening to soften. Sift together the flour, granulated sugar, baking powder, salt, baking soda, and spices directly onto the shortening. Add the brown sugar and buttermilk and mix until all the flour is moist. Beat vigorously for 2 minutes. Add the eggs and beat for 2 minutes more. Pour into the prepared pans.

Bake for 30 to 35 minutes, or until a knife comes out clean. Let cool on racks.

Cake Molds

For holidays or birthdays, many bakers like to make their cakes extra fancy by using a cake mold in the shape of a Christmas tree, sports car, or other personalized statement. Your local housewares store probably has a wide variety to choose from, or at least has a catalog so that you can place a special order. Some bakers even use molds they find in antique shops. Two hints: First, be liberal with greasing the mold; frosting can't cover up everything. Second, be sure to add certain identifying features, like nuts or dragées for eyes or headlights, after you've frosted the cake, and not before baking.

Carrot Cakes

Carrot cakes were a staple of my early baking experience, probably because there wasn't much of a chance to mess up the kitchen: two bowls, one pan, and a vegetable grater. And if I left the cake in the oven too long, that was okay because it was a moister cake than others I found in my mother's recipe books. But today, I would add some excitement to carrot cake by adding grated sweet potatoes and by substituting a cup of brown sugar for a cup of the white.

Carrot Cake

Serves: 10

3 cups flour
2 teaspoons baking powder
2 teaspoons salt
1 teaspoon baking soda
2 teaspoons ground cinnamon
1$\frac{1}{2}$ cups vegetable oil
2 cups sugar
3 cups grated carrots
4 eggs
$\frac{1}{2}$ cup walnuts, chopped
1 cup raisins

Preheat an oven to 350°F. Have ready an ungreased 9-inch tube pan.

Sift together the flour, baking powder, salt, baking soda, and cinnamon into a bowl. In another, larger bowl, mix together the oil, sugar, and carrots. Add the eggs one at a time, beating well after each addition. Gradually beat in the flour mixture, mixing well. Fold in the nuts and raisins. Pour into the tube pan.

Bake for 1 hour, or until a knife comes out clean. Let cool on a rack.

West Coast Carrot Cake

Makes: 1 9-by-13-inch cake

2 cups flour
1$\frac{1}{2}$ cups packed brown sugar
2 teaspoons baking soda
2 teaspoons ground cinnamon

1 teaspoon ground nutmeg
1 cup vegetable oil
3 eggs, well beaten
2 teaspoons vanilla extract
1 1/2 cups grated carrots
1 cup chopped walnuts
1 cup shredded dried coconut
1 can (12 ounces) crushed pineapple,
    drained
1/2 cup raisins
Cream Cheese Frosting (Chapter 5)

Preheat an oven to 350°F. Line the bottom of a 9-by-13-inch cake pan with wax paper and butter the paper and sides.

In a bowl, combine all the ingredients and mix well. Pour into the prepared pan.

Bake for 1 hour, or until a knife comes out clean. Let cool on a rack. Frost with Cream Cheese Frosting or serve plain.

Country Gingerbread

Serves: 8

1/2 cup shortening
1/2 cup sugar
1 egg
1/2 cup light molasses
1 1/2 cups sifted flour
3/4 teaspoon salt
3/4 teaspoon baking soda
1/2 teaspoon ground ginger
1/2 teaspoon ground cinnamon
1/2 cup boiling water

Preheat an oven to 350°F. Grease an 8-inch round cake pan.

In a bowl, stir the shortening to soften. Gradually add the sugar, creaming until light and fluffy. Add the egg and molasses and beat thoroughly. Sift together the sifted flour, salt, baking soda, ginger, and cinnamon into another bowl. Add to the molasses mixture alternately with the boiling water, beating well after each addition. Pour into the prepared pan.

Bake for 35 to 40 minutes, or until a knife comes out clean. Remove from the oven and let cool on a rack. Serve warm.

Lemon Cake

Makes: 1 ring cake

3/4 cup butter or margarine, softened
1 1/4 cups granulated sugar
8 egg yolks
2 1/2 cups cake flour
1 tablespoon baking powder
1/4 teaspoon salt
3/4 cup milk
1 teaspoon vanilla extract
1 teaspoon grated lemon rind
1 teaspoon lemon juice
confectioners' sugar for dusting

Preheat an oven to 325°F. Grease and flour a bundt pan.

In a bowl, cream together the butter and granulated sugar until light and fluffy. In another bowl, beat the egg yolks until light and lemon colored. Beat the yolks into the

(continued)

creamed mixture. Sift together the cake flour, baking powder, and salt into a bowl, then resift 3 times. Add the sifted ingredients to the creamed mixture in three batches alternately with the milk, beating thoroughly after each addition. Add the vanilla, lemon rind, and lemon juice. Beat for 2 minutes. Pour into the prepared pan.

Bake for 1 hour, or until a knife comes out clean. Cool in the pan 10 to 15 minutes, then turn out onto a wire rack or serving plate to cool completely. Dust with confectioners' sugar, if desired.

Orange Cake

Serves: 12

3/4 cup butter or margarine, softened
1 1/4 cups granulated sugar
3 eggs
2 1/2 cups flour
1 1/2 teaspoon baking soda
1 1/4 cups orange juice
1 tablespoon grated orange rind

Orange Frosting:

1 1/4 cups confectioners' sugar, sifted
3 tablespoons orange juice

Preheat an oven to 350°F. Grease and flour a 9-by-13-inch cake pan.

In a bowl, beat together the butter, granulated sugar, eggs, flour, baking soda, orange juice, and the orange rind until blended. Beat for 3 minutes, scraping down the sides of the

bowl occasionally. Pour the batter into the prepared pan. Smooth the top.

Bake for 45 to 50 minutes, or until a knife comes out clean. Cool in the pan on a wire rack for 15 minutes.

Meanwhile, make the frosting: In a bowl, beat together the confectioners' sugar and the 3 tablespoons orange juice until smooth.

Spoon the frosting over the top of the warm cake in the pan. Cool the iced cake completely in the pan on the rack. Cut into squares to serve.

Sour Cream Orange Cake

Serves: 6

3/4 cup margarine, softened
2 1/4 cups sugar
2 eggs
2 cups sifted flour
1 teaspoon baking soda
1/2 teaspoon salt
1 cup sour evaporated milk (add 2 tablespoons distilled white vinegar to create sour milk)
1/2 teaspoon vanilla extract
grated rind of 1 orange
1/2 cup walnuts, finely chopped
1/2 cup pitted cherries, cut in small pieces
1/2 cup raisins (optional)
juice of 1 orange (about 1/3 cup)

Preheat an oven to 375°F. Grease and flour a 10-cup tube pan.

In a bowl, cream the margarine until light. Add $1\frac{1}{2}$ cups of the sugar and the eggs and beat until creamy and light. In another bowl, stir together the sifted flour, the baking soda, and salt. Add the flour mixture to the margarine mixture alternately with the sour milk. Add the vanilla and orange rind. Fold in the walnuts, cherries, and raisins. Pour into the prepared pan.

Bake for 1 hour, or until a knife comes out clean. Meanwhile, in a bowl stir together the orange juice and the remaining $\frac{3}{4}$ cup sugar. When the cake comes out of the oven, invert onto a rack and cool thoroughly. Pour the orange juice glaze over the cake when cool.

Fresh Apple Cake

Serves: 8

2 cups flour
2 cups sugar
$\frac{1}{2}$ teaspoon salt
2 teaspoons baking soda
1 teaspoon ground cinnamon
$\frac{1}{2}$ teaspoon ground nutmeg
4 cups peeled and diced apples
$\frac{3}{4}$ cup milk
2 eggs
$\frac{1}{2}$ cup vegetable shortening
$\frac{1}{2}$ cup chopped walnuts

Preheat an oven to 325°F. Grease a 9-by-12-inch pan.

Sift together flour, sugar, salt, baking soda, cinnamon, and nutmeg into a large bowl. Add

(continued)

Egg Whites & Yolks

Frequently, a recipe will call for a number of egg whites—or yolks—without using up the other part of the eggs. If you're stuck with extra egg whites, they can be whipped up with a bit of sugar for some meringue cookies, or, unwhipped, they make a great face mask. Stir extra yolks lightly and then freeze in ice cube trays, to be thawed later for brushing onto bread loaves before baking. Or you can always mix them into the dog's food to ensure a shiny coat.

the apples, eggs, and milk. Beat until well mixed. Cream the shortening in a separate bowl and add to the batter. Pour into the prepared pan.

Bake for 1 hour, or until a knife comes out clean. Turn onto a rack and cool.

Amaretto Cake

Serves: 10

1 package (regular) yellow cake mix

Pudding Mixture:
$^1/_2$ *cup cornstarch*
$^1/_2$ *cup sugar*
2 cups milk
2 eggs, well beaten
1 teaspoon vanilla extract
1 teaspoon rum extract
$^3/_4$ *cup Amaretto liqueur*
1 jar (10 ounces) apricot preserves

Frosting:
2 cups whipping cream
$^1/_4$ *cup Amaretto liqueur*

fresh strawberries

Bake the yellow cake according to the package directions and let cool completely (can be done a day ahead).

To make the pudding, combine all the ingredients in a saucepan over low heat and cook, stirring constantly, for 15 minutes, or until skin begins to form. Remove from the heat and let cool.

Using a serrated knife, cut each cake layer in half horizontally, to yield 4 layers. Place a layer on a serving plate. Spread $^1/_3$ preserves and top with $^1/_3$ pudding. Repeat with the remaining layers, pudding, and preserves.

Make the frosting: Whip together the cream and Amaretto until soft peaks form. Frost the top and sides of the cake with the cream. Arrange the strawberries on top.

Compromise Cake

Serves: 8

2 cups packed brown sugar
1 cup water
1 cup raisins
$^1/_4$ *cup vegetable shortening*
1 teaspoon ground cinnamon
$^1/_4$ *teaspoon ground nutmeg*
$^1/_4$ *teaspoon ground cloves*
3 cups flour
$^1/_2$ *teaspoon salt*
$^1/_2$ *teaspoon baking powder*
1 teaspoon baking soda
$^1/_2$ *cup walnuts, chopped*

Preheat an oven to 350°F. Grease and flour 2 standard loaf pans.

Place the brown sugar, water, raisins, shortening, cinnamon, nutmeg, and cloves in a heavy saucepan. Bring to a boil. Reduce the heat and cook gently for 5 minutes. Remove from the heat, turn into a large bowl, and let cool until the mixture is comfortably warm to the touch.

Sift together the flour, salt, baking powder, and baking soda into a bowl. Add to the cooled sugar mixture, beating until no drifts of flour are visible and the batter is smooth. Stir in the walnuts. Spread evenly in the 2 prepared pans.

Bake for 45 minutes, or until a knife comes out clean. Let cool in the pans for 10 minutes, then turn out onto racks to cool completely. Wrap the loaves in plastic wrap and they will keep for at least 2 weeks at room temperature. This cake, also known as war cake, was made during World War II when eggs were hard to get.

Hawaiian Coconut Cake

Serves: 10

$3/4$ cup butter or margarine, softened
$1^1/2$ cups sugar
3 eggs, separated
3 cups sifted cake flour
1 tablespoon baking powder
$1/2$ teaspoon salt
$3/4$ cup coconut milk, homemade (recipe follows) or canned
$1/2$ teaspoon vanilla extract
$1^3/4$ cups freshly grated coconut
2 cups sweetened whipped cream or store-bought whipped topping

Preheat an oven to 350°F. Grease and flour two 9-inch cake pans.

In a large bowl, cream the butter until light and fluffy. Gradually add the sugar and beat until very light. In another, small bowl, beat the egg yolks until lemon colored. Add the yolks to the butter mixture, blending well. Sift together the sifted flour, baking powder, and salt into yet another bowl. Add the flour mixture to the butter mixture in three batches alternately with the coconut milk, beginning and ending with the flour mixture. Add the vanilla and stir in $3/4$ cup of the grated coconut. Beat the egg whites until stiff peaks form. Gently fold them into the cake batter. Turn the batter into the prepared pans.

Bake for 25 minutes, or until a knife comes out clean. Let cool in the pans for 15 minutes. Loosen the cake edges with a knife and invert on racks to cool completely. Frost between the layers, the top, and the sides with whipped cream. Sprinkle the remaining $3/4$ cup coconut over the top and sides of the cake.

Coconut Milk: Combine $3/4$ milk and 3 tablespoons packed grated coconut in a saucepan. Place over medium heat, bring to just below a boil, remove from the heat, cover, and let steep for 30 minutes. Strain the milk, pressing out as much liquid as possible from the coconut.

Baking from Scratch with a Mix

Amaretto Cake is the perfect example of a cake you can make when you don't want to start from scratch, but you want to do more than just beat together cake mix and water and pour into the batter pans. It requires a little more effort and imagination than using a mix, and you can easily personalize the cake with the cream—not canned frosting—and fresh strawberries. Overall, an easy compromise when you want to put your mark on a cake but not spend all day doing it.

COFFEE CAKES

Irish Coffee Cake

Serves: 10

> 3 tablespoons instant coffee powder
> $1/4$ cup Irish whiskey
> 1 cup butter or margarine, softened
> 2 cups sugar
> 1 cup sour cream
> 3 eggs
> 1 teaspoon vanilla extract
> $2\frac{1}{4}$ cups flour
> $1/2$ teaspoon salt
> $1/2$ teaspoon baking soda

Preheat an oven to 325°F. Grease and flour a 10-cup tube pan.

In a small bowl, dissolve the coffee in the whiskey. In a large bowl, cream the butter until light. Add the sugar and beat until fluffy. Add the sour cream and then the eggs, one at a time, beating well after each addition. Add the vanilla, and coffee and whiskey. Beat until blended. In another bowl, stir together the flour, salt, and baking soda. Stir the flour mixture into the butter mixture, then beat for 3 minutes at medium speed. Pour into the prepared pan.

Bake for 1 hour, or until a knife comes out clean. Invert onto a rack and cool thoroughly.

Crumb Cake

Serves: 8

$^1/_2$ cup butter, softened
1 cup sugar
2 cups flour
pinch of salt
1 teaspoon baking soda
1 teaspoon ground cinnamon
$^1/_4$ teaspoon ground nutmeg
$^1/_2$ teaspoon ground cloves
1 egg
1 tablespoon dark molasses
1 cup buttermilk

Preheat an oven to 350°F. Grease and flour an 8-inch square pan.

Mix together the first 8 ingredients. Set aside $^1/_2$ cup of the mixture and, to the remainder, add the egg, molasses, and buttermilk. Beat well, pour into 8-inch pan. Sprinkle the reserved flour-butter mixture evenly over the top.

Bake for 40 minutes, or until a knife comes out clean. Cool in the pan.

Strawberry Jam Cake with Coconut Topping

Serves: 12

$^1/_2$ cup butter, softened
1$^1/_4$ cups sugar
1 package (8 ounces) cream cheese, softened
2 eggs
$^1/_4$ cup milk
1 teaspoon vanilla extract
2 cups sifted cake flour
1$^1/_2$ teaspoons baking powder
$^1/_4$ teaspoon salt
1 cup strawberry preserves

Coconut Topping:
2 cups shredded dried coconut
$^1/_2$ cup packed brown sugar
1 teaspoon ground cinnamon
$^1/_4$ cup butter, melted and cooled

Preheat an oven to 350°F. Grease and flour a 9-by-13-inch pan.

In a bowl, cream together the butter, sugar, and cream cheese. Beat in the eggs, milk, and vanilla. Combine the sifted flour, baking powder, and salt in a bowl. Stir the flour mixture into the butter mixture. Spoon half of the batter into the prepared pan, spreading evenly. Spread the surface with the preserves. Dollop the remaining batter over the preserves; carefully spread with a spatula to completely cover preserves.

Bake for 35 to 40 minutes, or until a knife comes out clean. Meanwhile, make the coconut topping: In a bowl, combine all the ingredients and stir until smooth. Remove the cake from the oven and spread the top with coconut topping. Broil for 2 to 3 minutes, or until golden brown. Let cool completely in the pan before serving.

Graham Streusel Cake

Serves: 12

2 cups graham cracker crumbs
3/4 cup chopped walnuts
3/4 cup packed brown sugar
1/4 teaspoon ground cinnamon
3/4 cup margarine or butter
1 package (regular) yellow cake mix
1 cup water
1/3 cup vegetable oil
3 eggs
confectioners' sugar for dusting (optional)

Preheat an oven to 350°F. Grease and flour a 9-by-13-inch pan.

In a bowl, mix together the cracker crumbs, walnuts, brown sugar, cinnamon, and margarine; reserve. In another bowl, beat together the cake mix, water, oil, and eggs. Pour about 2 1/3 cups of the batter into the prepared pan. Sprinkle about 2 cups of the reserved crumb mixture evenly over the top. Pour the remaining batter into the pan, and sprinkle with the remaining crumb mixture.

Bake for 45 to 50 minutes, or until a knife comes out clean. Let cool in pan. Dust with confectioners' sugar, if desired.

Cocoa Streusel Cake

Makes: 1 10-inch ring cake

1 cup butter or margarine, softened
2 1/4 cups granulated sugar
2 eggs
1 cup sour cream
1 teaspoon grated lemon rind
1 teaspoon lemon juice
2 cups flour
1 teaspoon baking powder
1/4 teaspoon salt
1 cup walnuts, chopped
1/2 cup shredded dried coconut
1/4 cup unsweetened cocoa powder
1 teaspoon ground cinnamon
3 tablespoons butter or margarine, melted
   and cooled
confectioners' sugar for dusting (optional)

Preheat an oven to 350°F. Grease and flour a 12-cup bundt pan or a 10-inch tube pan.

In a large bowl, cream together the softened butter, 2 cups of the granulated sugar, and the eggs until light and fluffy. Mix in the sour cream, lemon rind, and lemon juice. In another bowl, combine the flour, baking powder, and salt. Add the flour mixture to the creamed mixture, mixing well. Combine the nuts, coconut, cocoa, the remaining 1/4 cup sugar, and the cinnamon in a small bowl. Stir in the melted butter and set aside.

Spoon half of the batter into the prepared pan. Sprinkle with half of the nut mixture. Spoon in the remaining batter and top with the remaining nut mixture. Bake for 60 minutes, or until a knife comes out clean. Let cool for 10 minutes, then transfer to a rack and let cool completely. Dust with confectioners' sugar, if desired.

Sour Cream Cake with Topping

Makes: 1 9-inch cake

$1/2$ cup butter, softened
1 cup sugar
2 eggs
1 teaspoon vanilla extract
1 cup sour cream
$1 1/2$ cups flour
$3/4$ teaspoon baking soda
$1 1/2$ teaspoons baking powder

Topping:
$1/2$ cup sugar
1 cup walnuts, chopped
1 teaspoon ground cinnamon

Preheat an oven to 350°F. Grease a 9-inch round cake pan.

In a bowl, cream together the butter and sugar until light. Add the eggs, vanilla, and sour cream, and beat well. In another bowl, mix together the flour, baking soda, and baking powder. Add the flour mixture to the butter mixture and beat well. Pour into the prepared pan. In a small bowl, quickly stir together all the topping ingredients and scatter three-fourths of the mixture evenly over the batter.

Cut the topping into the batter. Sprinkle the remaining topping evenly over the surface. Bake for 45 minutes, or until a knife comes out clean. Cool on a rack.

Shake and Bake

When I was a teenager just learning to bake, I remember making a recipe for crumb cake that called for putting the crumb topping mixture in a brown paper lunch bag and shaking it for around 5 minutes. I don't remember if the topping turned out any differently from the mix-with-a-fork method that my mother favored, but it certainly was a lot of fun. It also turned me into a cookbook aficionado, probably so I could find other recipes that would be as much fun. If you'd like your kids to get interested in cooking and baking, keep an eye out for those recipes in this book that contain tasks that you could turn into a fun activity.

Blueberry Coffee Cake

Serves: 8

1 pint blueberries
$\frac{1}{2}$ cup water
1 tablespoon lemon juice
$1\frac{1}{4}$ cups sugar
3 tablespoons cornstarch
$1\frac{3}{4}$ cups flour
$1\frac{1}{2}$ teaspoons baking powder
$\frac{1}{4}$ teaspoon salt
$\frac{1}{2}$ teaspoon ground cinnamon
$\frac{1}{8}$ teaspoon ground mace
$\frac{1}{2}$ cup plus 2 tablespoons margarine
1 egg, lightly beaten
$\frac{1}{2}$ cup milk
$\frac{1}{2}$ teaspoon vanilla extract
$\frac{1}{4}$ cup chopped walnuts

Preheat an oven to 350°F. Grease a 9-inch round cake pan.

Combine the blueberries and water in a saucepan, bring to a simmer, cover, and simmer for 5 minutes, or until the berries are tender. Stir in the lemon juice. Mix $\frac{1}{2}$ cup of the sugar and the cornstarch in a small bowl and add to the berries. Cook, stirring frequently, until thickened. Let cool.

In a bowl, combine $1\frac{1}{2}$ cups of the flour, the baking powder, salt, cinnamon, mace, and $\frac{1}{2}$ cup of the sugar. Using a pastry blender, cut in the $\frac{1}{2}$ cup margarine until the mixture resembles fine crumbs.

In another bowl, combine the egg, milk, and vanilla, mixing well. Add the milk mixture to the flour mixture and again mix well. Spread half of the batter in the prepared pan. Spoon the cooled berries evenly over the batter and top with the remaining batter. Combine the remaining $\frac{1}{4}$ cup each sugar and flour in a small bowl. Add the 2 tablespoons margarine and cut in with a pastry blender until crumbly. Stir in the walnuts. Sprinkle the nut mixture evenly over the batter.

Bake for 40 to 45 minutes, or until a knife comes out clean. Let cool partially, then serve warm.

Cocoa Swirl Coffee Cake with Orange Glaze

Serves: 8

$1\frac{1}{2}$ cups flour
$\frac{3}{4}$ cup plus 2 tablespoons granulated sugar
$2\frac{1}{2}$ teaspoons baking powder
$\frac{3}{4}$ teaspoon salt
$\frac{1}{4}$ cup vegetable shortening
2 eggs, slightly beaten
$\frac{2}{3}$ cup orange juice
1 teaspoon grated orange rind
$\frac{3}{4}$ cup confectioners' sugar
$\frac{1}{2}$ cup walnuts, chopped
$\frac{1}{4}$ cup unsweetened cocoa powder
3 tablespoons butter, melted

Orange Glaze:
1 cup confectioners' sugar
2 tablespoons orange juice
$\frac{1}{4}$ teaspoon grated orange rind

Preheat an oven to 350°F. Grease an 8-inch square pan.

In a large bowl, combine the flour, granulated sugar, baking powder, and salt. Using a pastry blender, cut the shortening into the flour mixture until the mixture resembles coarse crumbs. Add the eggs, orange juice, and orange rind. Stir just until blended. Set aside.

In a small bowl, combine the confectioners' sugar, walnuts, and cocoa. Stir in the melted butter to form a crumb mixture. Spread $^3/_4$ cup of the batter evenly on the bottom of the prepared pan. Sprinkle half of the crumb mixture evenly over the batter. Spread 1 cup of the batter over the top and sprinkle with the remaining crumb mixture. Cover with the remaining batter.

Bake for 35 to 40 minutes, or until a knife comes out clean. Meanwhile, make the orange glaze: combine all the ingredients in a small bowl and mix until smooth. Remove the cake from the oven and let cool slightly. Spread with the glaze and serve warm.

Nutty Banana Cake

Serves: 10

$^2/_3$ cup shortening
$2^1/_2$ cups sifted cake flour
$1^1/_3$ cups sugar
$^1/_2$ teaspoon baking powder
1 teaspoon baking soda
1 teaspoon salt

$1^1/_2$ cups mashed ripe bananas
$1^1/_2$ cups buttermilk
2 eggs
$^1/_2$ cup walnuts, chopped

Cocoa Whipped Cream:

1 cup sugar
$^1/_2$ cup unsweetened cocoa powder
$^1/_2$ cup whipping cream

2 bananas, peeled and sliced

Preheat an oven to 350°F. Line two 9-inch round cake pans with wax paper, and grease the sides.

Stir the shortening to soften. Sift together the flour, sugar, baking powder, baking soda, and salt. Add the mashed bananas and half of the buttermilk. Mix until all the flour is moist, then beat vigorously for 2 minutes. Add the remaining buttermilk and the eggs. Beat for 2 minutes longer. Fold in the nuts. Pour into the prepared pans.

Bake for 35 minutes, or until a knife comes out clean.

Let cool for 10 minutes in the pans on wire racks, then turn out of the pans and let cool completely.

While the cake layers are baking, make the whipped cream: Combine the sugar, cocoa, and cream in a bowl. Cover and chill for at least 1 hour. Remove from the refrigerator and beat until stiff.

To assemble the cake, place 1 layer on a serving plate and top with about one-third of

(continued)

Pound Cakes

As you probably already know, in colonial times, bakers didn't need a recipe for pound cake. Cooks simply just took a pound of everything, mixed it together, slid it into the oven, and let it bake over the coals. That's how the cake got its name. Today, however, the thought of mixing a pound of butter with a pound of anything else is enough to add five pounds to each hip instantly. Even though contemporary pound-cake recipes talk in terms of cups and teaspoons, they're tasty and still make enough to feed a small crowd.

the whipped cream. Arrange the banana slices on top of the whipped cream and then cover with the second layer. Cover the top and sides with the remaining whipped cream.

Date Cake

Makes: 1 loaf

$1\frac{1}{2}$ cups pitted dates, chopped
1 cup boiling water
$\frac{1}{2}$ cup vegetable shortening
1 cup sugar
1 teaspoon vanilla extract
1 egg
$\frac{1}{2}$ cup sifted flour
1 teaspoon baking soda
$\frac{1}{4}$ teaspoon salt
$\frac{1}{2}$ cup walnuts, chopped

Preheat an oven to 350°F. Grease a 9-by-13-inch baking pan.

In a bowl, combine the dates and the boiling water and let cool to room temperature. In a large bowl, stir the shortening to soften. Gradually add the sugar, creaming thoroughly. Add the vanilla and egg and beat well. In another bowl, sift together the sifted flour, baking soda, and salt twice. Add the flour mixture to the creamed mixture alternately with the date mixture, beating well after each addition. Fold in the nuts. Pour into the prepared pan.

Bake for 25 to 30 minutes, or until a knife comes out clean. Let cool on a rack.

Choco-Date Cake Variation: Sift 2 table-spoons unsweetened cocoa powder with the flour mixture and omit the nuts from the batter. Pour into a greased 9-by-13-inch pan. Sprinkle with the nuts and $^1/_2$ to 1 cup semi-sweet chocolate morsels. Bake as directed.

POUND CAKES

Pound Cake

Serves: 6

> $^2/_3$ cup vegetable shortening
> $1^1/_4$ cups granulated sugar
> 1 teaspoon grated lemon rind
> 1 tablespoon lemon juice
> $^2/_3$ cup milk
> $2^1/_4$ cups sifted cake flour
> $1^1/_4$ teaspoons salt
> 1 teaspoon baking powder
> 3 eggs
> confectioners' sugar for dusting

Preheat an oven to 300°F. Grease a 9-by-5-by-3-inch loaf pan.

In a bowl, stir the shortening to soften. Gradually add the granulated sugar and cream together until light and fluffy. Add the lemon rind and juice and mix well. Then add the milk, and mix enough to break up the creamed mixture. Sift together the flour, salt, and baking powder into another bowl. Add to the creamed mixture, and mix until smooth. Add eggs one at a time, beating well after

each addition. Beat an additional 1 minute at the end. Pour into the prepared pan.

Bake for 1 hour and 20 minutes, or until top springs back lightly to the touch. Let cool on a rack. When thoroughly cool, dust the top with confectioners' sugar.

Note: If desired, butter may be substituted for the shortening. Reduce the milk to $^1/_2$ cup.

Mocha Pound Cake

Serves: 10

> $^2/_3$ cup vegetable shortening
> 2 cups sifted cake flour
> $1^1/_4$ cups sugar
> 1 tablespoon instant coffee crystals
> 1 teaspoon salt
> $^1/_2$ teaspoon cream of tartar
> $^1/_4$ teaspoon baking soda
> $^1/_2$ cup water
> 1 teaspoon vanilla extract
> 3 eggs
> 2 squares (2 ounces) unsweetened
>   chocolate, melted and cooled

Preheat an oven to 325°F. Line a 9-by-5-by-3-inch loaf pan with wax paper.

In a bowl, cream the shortening until light. Sift together the sifted cake flour, sugar, instant coffee, salt, cream of tartar, and baking soda directly onto the shortening. Add the water and vanilla and mix until the flour is moistened. Then beat vigorously for 2 minutes until smooth. Add the eggs and

(continued)

chocolate. Beat for 1 minute. Pour into the prepared pan.

Bake for 65 to 70 minutes, or until top springs back when touched lightly. Let cool in the pan for 10 minutes, then turn out onto a rack to cool completely.

Glazed Chocolate Pound Cake

Serves: 10

1 cup butter or margarine, softened
¹/₂ cup vegetable shortening
3 cups sugar
5 eggs
1 teaspoon vanilla extract
3 cups flour
¹/₂ teaspoon baking powder
¹/₂ teaspoon salt
¹/₂ cup unsweetened cocoa powder
1 cup milk

Glaze (optional):
1 tablespoon butter, softened
1 cup confectioners' sugar
2 tablespoons milk
¹/₂ teaspoon vanilla extract

whipped cream (optional)

Preheat an oven to 325°F. Grease and flour a 10-inch plain or fluted tube pan.

In a bowl, cream together the butter and shortening until smooth. Add the sugar and mix well. Add the eggs one at a time, beating

well after each addition. Stir in the vanilla. Sift together the flour, baking powder, salt, and cocoa into another bowl. Alternately add the flour mixture and the milk to the creamed mixture. Spread the batter in the prepared pan.

Bake for 1 hour and 20 minutes, or until a knife comes out clean. Let cool in the pan on a wire rack for 15 minutes, then turn out of the pan onto the rack and let cool completely.

To make the glaze, combine all the ingredients in a bowl and beat until smooth. Spoon the glaze on the cooled cake. Alternatively, omit the glaze and serve with whipped cream.

CHOCOLATE CAKES

Died and Went to Heaven Chocolate Cake

Serves: 12

1³/₄ cups flour
1 cup granulated sugar
³/₄ cup unsweetened cocoa powder
1¹/₂ teaspoons baking soda
1¹/₂ teaspoons baking powder
1 teaspoon salt
1¹/₄ cups buttermilk
1 cup packed brown sugar
2 eggs, lightly beaten
¹/₄ cup vegetable oil, preferably canola oil
2 teaspoons vanilla extract
1 cup hot strong brewed coffee

Frosting:

1 1/2 cups confectioners' sugar
1/2 teaspoon vanilla extract
1 to 2 tablespoons buttermilk or 1% milk

Preheat an oven to 350°F. Lightly oil a 12-cup bundt pan.

In a bowl, stir together the flour, granulated sugar, cocoa, baking soda, baking powder, and salt. Add the buttermilk, brown sugar, eggs, oil, and vanilla and beat for 2 minutes until well incorporated. Stir in the hot coffee until completely incorporated. (The batter will be thin.) Pour into the prepared bundt pan.

Bake for 35 to 40 minutes, or until a knife comes out clean. Let cool in the pan on a rack for 10 minutes, then turn out onto the rack and let cool completely.

To make the frosting, in a bowl, beat together the confectioners' sugar, vanilla, and enough buttermilk or milk to make a thick but pourable frosting. Drizzle the frosting evenly over the top of the cake.

Phantom Chocolate Cake

Serves: 8

3/4 cups sugar
1 cup flour
2 teaspoons baking powder
1/8 teaspoon salt
*1 square (1 ounce) chocolate, melted and
    cooled, or 2 tablespoons unsweetened
    cocoa powder*

(continued)

Recipes That Seem to Get It Wrong

I love recipes like the one for Phantom Chocolate Cake, because it's the kind that's sure to bring every anxiety you've ever had in the kitchen times ten. "*Do not mix?* Are they crazy?" If you're like me, the first time you make it is for yourself—forget about company—and every minute it's in the oven you're obsessing over it, convinced that it's going to turn out wrong. Of course, once you take your first bite, you're more than pleasantly surprised, but it's recipes like these that keep us on our toes in the kitchen.

2 tablespoons butter or margarine

1 teaspoon vanilla extract

1/2 cup milk

1/2 cup packed brown sugar

1/2 cup granulated sugar

4 teaspoons unsweetened cocoa powder

1 cup cold strong brewed coffee

ice cream or whipped cream

Preheat an oven to 350°F. Grease an 8- or 9-inch square cake pan.

Sift together the granulated sugar, the flour, baking powder, and salt into a bowl. Add the chocolate, butter, vanilla, and milk and mix well. Pour into the prepared pan. Sprinkle the brown sugar, the remaining 1/2 cup granulated sugar, and the cocoa over the batter. Finally, pour the cold coffee evenly over the top. *Do not mix.*

Bake for 30 to 35 minutes, or until a knife comes out clean.

This cake is best served hot. Serve the cake portion on the bottom. Accompany with ice cream or with whipped cream.

Crazy Chocolate Cake

Serves: 8

3 cups flour

2 cups sugar

2 teaspoons baking soda

6 tablespoons unsweetened cocoa powder

1 teaspoon salt

3/4 cup vegetable oil

2 teaspoons vanilla extract

2 tablespoons distilled white vinegar

2 cups water

vanilla ice cream or favorite frosting (optional)

Preheat an oven to 350°F. Grease a 9-inch square cake pan.

Sift together the flour, sugar, baking soda, cocoa, and salt into a large bowl. Make 3 "wells" in the mixture and put the oil in one, the vanilla in the second, and the vinegar in the third. Pour the water over all, then mix with a fork. Pour into the prepared pan.

Bake for 35 minutes, or until a knife comes out clean. Cool on rack. Serve plain or with vanilla ice cream or your favorite frosting.

Black Beauty Cake

Serves: 10

3/4 cup unsweetened cocoa powder

1 cup boiling water

3 cups flour

2 cups sugar

1 1/2 teaspoons salt

2 teaspoons baking soda

1/2 teaspoon baking powder

4 eggs

1 1/2 teaspoons vanilla extract

1/2 pound unsalted butter, at room temperature

Black Beauty Frosting:

1 1/2 cups butter
1 tablespoon cornstarch
1 tablespoon granulated sugar
5 tablespoons unsweetened cocoa powder
1/2 cup milk
1 1/3 cups confectioners' sugar, sifted

Preheat an oven to 350°F. Grease and flour two 9-inch round cake pans or one 9-by-13-inch pan. In a bowl, mix together the cocoa and boiling water. Let cool to room temperature. In a large bowl, using an electric mixer, mix together the flour, sugar, salt, baking soda, and baking powder on low speed for 1 minute. In a small bowl, lightly beat together the eggs and vanilla. Beat in 1/4 cup of the cocoa mixture. Add the butter and the remaining cocoa to the flour mixture and beat at medium speed for 1 1/2 minutes. Scrape the bowl occasionally. Add the egg-cocoa mixture in 3 batches, beating for 20 seconds after each addition. Scrape the bowl before each addition. Pour into the pan(s).

Bake for 35 to 45 minutes, or until a knife comes out clean. Cool on a rack.

To make the frosting, melt the butter over low heat. (A double boiler works best.) Sift together the cornstarch, granulated sugar, and cocoa into a bowl, then mix into the melted butter. Add the milk and stir until completely blended. Cook over medium heat, stirring constantly, until the mixture comes to a boil. Continue to stir and cook for 1 minute longer.

Remove from the heat and let cool. Add the confectioners' sugar and blend thoroughly. Frost cake.

Black Satin Cake

Serves: 10

1/2 cup butter or margarine
4 tablespoons unsweetened cocoa powder
1/2 cup vegetable oil
1 cup water
2 cups flour
2 cups sugar
1/2 cup buttermilk
2 eggs
1 teaspoon baking soda
1 teaspoon vanilla extract

Black Satin Frosting:

1/2 cup butter or margarine
1 1/2 cups buttermilk
2 tablespoons unsweetened cocoa powder
1 pound confectioners' sugar
1/2 teaspoon salt
1/2 teaspoon vanilla extract
1/2 cup chopped nuts (optional)

Preheat an oven to 400°F. Grease a 9-by-13-inch pan.

Put butter, cocoa, oil, and water in a saucepan and bring to a boil. Remove from the heat. Sift together the flour and sugar into a large bowl. Pour the chocolate sauce over the flour mixture and mix well. In another bowl, beat together the buttermilk, eggs,

(continued)

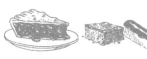

The Everything Dessert Buffet

If you're looking for a new way to entertain guests and you see a lot of recipes in *The Everything Dessert Book* that you can't wait to try, throw a dessert buffet party. Serve at least five different desserts from different chapters, and arrange all the choices on a long table. Try this for a Sunday afternoon get-together.

baking soda, and vanilla and add to the chocolate mixture. Pour into the prepared pan.

Bake for 20 minutes, or until a knife comes out clean. Meanwhile, make the frosting: Put the butter, cocoa, and buttermilk in a saucepan and bring to a boil. Remove from the heat and add the sugar, salt, vanilla, and nuts, mixing well.

Remove the cake from the oven and frost it immediately. Let the cake cool completely in the pan.

Chocolate Town Cake

Serves: 10

$^1\!/_2$ cup unsweetened cocoa powder
$^1\!/_2$ cup boiling water
1 tablespoon ground cinnamon (optional)
$^2\!/_3$ cup shortening
$1^3\!/_4$ cups sugar
1 teaspoon vanilla extract
2 eggs
$2^1\!/_2$ cups flour
$1^1\!/_2$ teaspoons baking soda
$^1\!/_2$ teaspoon salt
$1^1\!/_3$ cups buttermilk

Preheat an oven to 350°F. Grease three 8-inch or two 9-inch round cake pans.

In a small bowl, combine the cocoa and boiling water to form a paste; add the cinnamon to the paste, if desired. In a large bowl, cream together the shortening, sugar, vanilla, and eggs. In another bowl, stir together the flour, baking soda, and salt. Add

the flour mixture to the shortening mixture alternately with the buttermilk. Blend in the cocoa mixture. Pour into the prepared pans.

Bake for 30 to 35 minutes, or until a knife comes out clean. Cool on racks.

Chocolate Fudge Cake

Makes: 1 2-layer cake

1/2 cup butter or margarine, softened
1/2 cup shortening
2 cups sugar
2 eggs
1 teaspoon vanilla extract
1/2 cup unsweetened cocoa powder
2 1/4 cups flour
1 1/4 teaspoons baking soda
1/2 teaspoon salt
1 1/3 cups water

Preheat an oven to 350°F. Grease and flour two 9-inch round cake pans or 8-inch square cake pans.

In a large bowl, cream together the butter, shortening, and sugar until light. Add the eggs and vanilla and mix well. In another bowl, stir together the cocoa, flour, baking soda, and salt. Add the flour mixture to the butter mixture alternately with the water. Pour into the prepared pans.

Bake 35 to 40 minutes, or until a cake tester inserted into the center comes out clean. Let cool for 10 minutes in the pans, then turn out onto racks and cool completely. Stack and frost the layers as desired.

Rich Chocolate Fudge Cake

Serves: 10

3/4 cup butter, softened
1 1/2 cups sugar
1/2 cup unsweetened cocoa powder
1 teaspoon vanilla extract
3 eggs, separated
2 1/4 cups sifted cake flour
1 tablespoon baking powder
1 cup ice water
favorite chocolate frosting

Preheat an oven to 300°F. Line two 8-inch round cake pans with wax paper, and grease the sides.

In a large bowl, beat the butter with the cocoa. Gradually add the sugar, beating until fluffy and light. Add the vanilla. Beat in the egg yolks one at a time, beating well after each addition. Sift together the sifted flour and baking powder into another bowl. Add the flour mixture to the butter mixture alternately with the ice water, beginning and ending with the flour mixture, beating well after each addition. Beat the egg whites until stiff peaks form and fold into the batter. Pour into the prepared pans.

Bake for 30 to 35 minutes, or until a knife comes out clean. Let cool in the pans for 10 minutes, then turn out onto racks and let cool completely. Stack and frost the layers with your favorite chocolate frosting.

Midnight Cake

Makes: 1 2-layer, 9-inch cake

> $^1/_2$ cup vegetable shortening
> $1^3/_4$ cups sugar
>   1 teaspoon salt
>   1 teaspoon vanilla extract
> $1\,^2/_3$ cups water
> $^1/_2$ cup unsweetened cocoa powder
> $2^1/_2$ cups sifted cake flour
>   3 egg whites
> $1^1/_2$ teaspoons baking soda

Preheat an oven to 350°F. Line the bottom of two 9-inch round cake pans with wax paper and grease the sides.

In a large bowl, stir the shortening to soften. Gradually add 1 cup of the sugar, creaming together until light and fluffy. Add the salt and vanilla. In another bowl, combine $^1/_3$ cup of the water and the cocoa, mixing well. Beat into the creamed mixture. Add the sifted flour to the shortening mixture alternately with 1 cup of the water, beginning and ending with the flour, and beating well after each addition. Beat the egg whites until soft peaks form; gradually add the remaining $^3/_4$ cup sugar, beating until stiff peaks form. Fold into the batter. Dissolve the baking soda in the remaining $^1/_3$ cup water; stir into the batter, mixing thoroughly. Pour into the prepared pans.

Bake for about 30 minutes, or until a knife comes out clean. Cool on racks.

Best Chocolate Cake

Makes: 1 3-layer, 9-inch cake

>   1 cup vegetable shortening
>   2 cups sugar
>   2 teaspoons vanilla extract
>   1 square (1 ounce) unsweetened
>   chocolate, melted and cooled
>   5 eggs
> $2^1/_4$ cups sifted cake flour
>   1 teaspoon baking soda
>   1 teaspoon salt
>   1 cup buttermilk

Preheat an oven to 350°F. Line the bottom of three 9-inch round cake pans with wax paper and grease the sides.

In a large bowl, stir the shortening to soften. Gradually add the sugar, creaming until light and fluffy. Mix in the vanilla and chocolate. Add the eggs one at a time, beating well after each addition. In another bowl, sift together the flour, baking soda, and salt. Add the flour mixture to the creamed mixture alternately with the milk, beating well after each addition. Pour into the prepared pans.

Bake for 20 to 25 minutes, or until a knife comes out clean. Cool on racks.

72

Red Devil Chocolate Cake

Makes: 1 2-layer, 8-inch cake

> 2 cups packed brown sugar
> 1 cup milk
> 3 squares (3 ounces) unsweetened chocolate
> $\frac{1}{2}$ cup vegetable shortening
> 1 teaspoon vanilla extract
> $\frac{1}{2}$ teaspoon red food coloring
> 3 eggs
> 2 cups sifted flour
> 2 teaspoon baking soda
> $\frac{1}{2}$ teaspoon salt

Preheat an oven to 350°F. Line the bottom of two 8-inch round cake pans with wax paper and grease the sides.

In a saucepan, combine 1 cup of the brown sugar, $\frac{1}{2}$ cup of the milk, and the chocolate over very low heat until the chocolate melts. Remove from the heat and let cool. In a large bowl, stir the shortening to soften. Gradually add the remaining 1 cup brown sugar and cream until light and fluffy. Add the vanilla and red food coloring, mixing well. Beat in the eggs one at a time, beating well after each addition. Blend in the chocolate mixture. In another bowl, sift together the flour, baking soda, and salt. Add the flour mixture to the creamed mixture alternately with the remaining $\frac{1}{2}$ cup milk, beginning and ending with the flour mixture. Beat well after each addition. Pour into the prepared pans.

Bake for about 25 minutes, or until a knife comes out clean. Cool on racks.

Sweet Chocolate Layer Cake

Serves: 8

> 1 package (4 ounces) sweet chocolate
> $\frac{1}{3}$ cup water
> 1 cup sugar
> $2\frac{2}{3}$ cups butter or margarine, softened
> 3 egg yolks
> 1 teaspoon vanilla extract
> $1\frac{3}{4}$ cups sifted cake flour
> 1 teaspoon baking soda
> $\frac{1}{2}$ teaspoon salt
> $\frac{2}{3}$ cup buttermilk
> 3 egg whites
> favorite frosting

Preheat an oven to 350°F. Line the bottom of two 9-inch round cake pans with wax paper and grease the sides.

In a small saucepan, combine the chocolate with the water. Stir over low heat until the chocolate melts. Remove from the heat and let cool. In a large bowl, cream the butter. Gradually add the sugar, creaming until light and fluffy. Beat in the egg yolks one at a time, beating well after each addition. Mix in the vanilla and the chocolate. In another bowl, sift together the sifted flour, baking soda, and salt. Add the flour mixture to the creamed mixture alternately with the buttermilk, beating well after each addition. Beat the egg whites until stiff peaks form and fold into the batter. Pour into the prepared pans.

(continued)

Too Many Chocolate Cakes?

The number of chocolate cakes in this book just hints at the infinite number of variations of this much-loved dessert. There's no such thing as a standard chocolate cake. Even though chocolate is the favorite flavor of most Americans, many bakers feel they have to snazz up a chocolate cake in some way to make it their own. Some people do it on the outside with the frosting, while others love to hide subtle flavorings or surprises—adding a hint of cold espresso is my favorite—in the batter. Look over the chocolate cake recipes included here, and use them as inspiration for some new ways to add spice to your best recipe.

Bake for about 25 minutes, or until a knife comes out clean. Stack and frost the layers with your favorite frosting.

Black Forest Cake

Serves: 10

$^1/_2$ cup butter or margarine
$^1/_2$ cup sugar
3 eggs
$^1/_2$ cup almonds, finely chopped in a
   blender
1 package (6 ounces) semi-sweet chocolate
   morsels, finely chopped in a blender
1 teaspoon vanilla extract
$^3/_4$ cup cake flour
1 teaspoon baking powder
$^1/_2$ teaspoon salt
1 cup whipping cream
2 tablespoons honey
$^1/_4$ cup kirsch or other cherry brandy
1 can (1 pound) pitted, sour cherries,
   drained
well-drained maraschino cherries

Preheat an oven to 375°F. Grease two 8-inch round cake pans, line them with wax paper, and grease the paper.

In a large bowl, cream together the butter and sugar until light and fluffy. Add the eggs one at a time, beating well after each addition. Beat in the almonds, $^3/_4$ cup of the chopped chocolate, and the vanilla. In another bowl, sift together the flour, baking powder, and salt.

Stir the flour mixture into the butter mixture. Pour into the prepared pans.

Bake for 20 minutes, or until the cakes begin to pull away from the sides of the pans. Let cool in the pans on racks for 10 minutes, then turn out onto the racks and peel off the wax paper. Let cool completely. Cut a thin slice off the tops of the layers if necessary to flatten.

Whip the cream with the honey until stiff peaks form. Place a cake layer on a serving plate. Sprinkle half of the cherry liqueur over the layer. Spread with a layer of whipped cream and cover evenly with as many sour cherries as will comfortably fit. (Save the remainder for another use.) Place the second cake layer on top, pressing down lightly. Sprinkle with the remaining liqueur; cover the top and sides of the cake with the whipped cream. Decorate the top and sides of the cake with the remaining chocolate and the maraschino cherries. Chill well before serving.

Baileys Frozen Chocolate Mousse Cake
(Courtesy of Godiva Chocolates)

Serves: 8

$^1/_4$ cup ground espresso-roast coffee
$^1/_2$ cup water
1 cup cake flour
$^1/_2$ teaspoon baking soda
$^1/_4$ teaspoon salt
4 tablespoons unsalted butter
6 tablespoons granulated sugar
2 eggs
$^1/_2$ teaspoon vanilla extract
$^1/_4$ cup sour cream

Baileys frozen chocolate chunk mousse:

5 squares (5 ounces) bittersweet chocolate, coarsely chopped
6 tablespoons milk
$^1/_4$ cup granulated sugar
$^1/_8$ teaspoon salt
2 teaspoons vanilla extract
$^1/_2$ cup Baileys Irish Cream, divided
6 ounces ($^3/_4$ cup) mascarpone, at room temperature
1 cup whipping cream
$^1/_4$ cup hazelnuts, lightly toasted and coarsely chopped
4 squares (4 ounces) bittersweet chocolate, cut into $^1/_2$-inch chunks

Garnish:

$^3/_4$ cup whipping cream
2 tablespoons Baileys Irish Cream
1 tablespoon confectioners' sugar
2 squares (2 ounces) bittersweet chocolate, coarsely chopped
warm chocolate sauce (optional)

To make the espresso cake, position a rack in the lower third of the oven and preheat to 350°F. Lightly butter and flour an 8-inch square cake pan; tap out the excess flour.

(continued)

Place the ground espresso into a cup or small bowl. Heat the water to boiling and pour it over the ground espresso. Allow the grounds to steep for 5 minutes, then strain the coffee through a double thickness of cheesecloth. Measure out $1/4$ cup of the coffee and set aside.

In a large bowl, using a wire whisk, stir together the flour, baking soda, and salt. Sift the mixture onto a large piece of wax paper.

In the $4^1/2$-quart bowl of a heavy-duty electric mixer fitted with the paddle attachment, beat the butter on medium speed for 1 to 2 minutes until creamy. Gradually add the sugar, blending well between additions and scraping down the sides of the bowl when necessary.

Add the eggs one at a time and beat until combined. Add the vanilla and sour cream. Reduce the speed to low, add half of the flour mixture, and beat until combined. Add the $1/4$ cup espresso, and mix well. Add the remaining flour mixture and beat until combined. Scrape the batter into the prepared pan.

Bake for 25 to 30 minutes, or until the cake begins to pull away from the sides of the pan and a tester inserted into the center comes out clean. Let cool on a rack for 10 minutes. Invert the cake onto the rack and reinvert onto another rack. Let cool completely.

To make the Baileys frozen chocolate chunk mousse, put the 5 ounces of coarsely chopped bittersweet chocolate in a food processor. Process until finely ground, 20 to 30 seconds.

In a small saucepan over medium heat, combine the milk, sugar, and salt. Cook, stirring with a wooden spoon, until the sugar dissolves and the milk comes to a boil. Remove from the heat. Add the vanilla extract and $1/4$ cup of the Baileys.

With the motor of the food processor running, pour the hot milk through the feed tube. Process for 10 to 20 seconds, or until the chocolate is completely melted. Using a spatula, scrape the chocolate mixture into a large bowl and let cool until tepid, about 5 minutes.

In the $4^1/2$-quart bowl of the heavy-duty electric mixer fitted with the paddle attachment, beat the mascarpone at medium-low speed just until softened. Gradually add the rest of the Baileys, scraping down the side of the bowl as necessary. Switch to the wire whip attachment and, beating on medium speed, add the whipping cream. Increase the speed to medium-high and continue beating until soft peaks form when the whip is lifted, 2 to 3 minutes.

Using a large rubber spatula, fold one-third of the whipped cream mixture into the chocolate mixture to lighten it. Fold the remaining whipped cream into the chocolate mixture. Fold the toasted nuts and the

4 ounces chocolate chunks into the mousse.

To assemble the cake, line an 8-inch square pan with aluminum foil, leaving a 2-inch overhang on two opposite sides of the pan. Using a long serrated knife, slice the cake in half horizontally. Place the top layer, cut side up, in the bottom of the pan. Scrape the mousse onto the cake layer in the pan. Smooth the top with a small flexible metal spatula. Place the second layer, cut side down, on top of the mousse.

To prepare the garnish, in the 4 $\frac{1}{2}$-quart bowl of the heavy-duty electric mixer using the wire whip attachment, combine the whipping cream, Baileys, and confectioners' sugar and beat on medium-high speed until medium-stiff peaks form when the whip is lifted.

Using the small metal spatula, spread the top of the cake with the whipped cream. Sprinkle the chopped chocolate over the whipped cream. Cover and freeze for 6 hours or for up to overnight.

Remove the cake from the freezer. Lift it out of the pan, using the overhanging pieces of foil as handles, and set it on a cutting board to temper for 30 minutes. With a sharp knife, trim the four sides of the cake to even them, then cut into eight 4-by-2-inch bars. Serve on dessert plates with warm chocolate sauce, if desired.

Is It Done Yet?

To make sure that a cake is done before you take it out of the oven, insert a toothpick or cake tester into the middle of the cake. If it comes out clean, then it's done. Sometimes, however, it is hard to find a toothpick at my house, and forget about a cake tester. In that case, I either use a blunt knife—in the case of a loaf of carrot cake— or lightly touch the middle of the cake with a finger. If the cake springs back, it's done. If it retains your fingerprint, it needs another 5 or 10 minutes.

Blackout Cake with Banana Wafers and Café au Lait Sauce

(Courtesy of Godiva Chocolates)

Serves: 8

Blackout Chocolate Buttermilk Cake:

1 cup granulated sugar
$^3/_4$ cup flour
$^1/_2$ cup unsweetened cocoa powder
1 teaspoon baking soda
$^1/_2$ teaspoon baking powder
pinch of salt
1 whole egg, at room temperature
1 egg yolk, at room temperature
$^1/_2$ cup freshly brewed coffee, at room
    temperature
$^1/_2$ teaspoon vanilla extract
$^1/_4$ cup unsalted butter, melted
$^1/_2$ cup buttermilk

Banana wafer:

2 bananas, peeled and cut into 1-inch
    pieces

Café au Lait Sauce:

1 cup whipping cream
1 cup milk
$^1/_2$ cup granulated sugar
2 tablespoons ground coffee
5 egg yolks

Chocolate mousse filling:

$^2/_3$ cup whipping cream, chilled

9 squares (9 ounces) bittersweet chocolate
2 tablespoons unsalted butter
$^2/_3$ cup granulated sugar
$^1/_4$ cup water
7 egg yolks

Garnish:

Confectioners' sugar

To make the cake, preheat an oven to 350°F. Lightly butter a 17-by-11 $^1/_2$-inch baking pan. Line the bottom of the pan with wax paper.

In a large bowl, sift together the sugar, flour, cocoa powder, baking soda, baking powder, and salt. In a small bowl, whisk the whole egg and egg yolk until blended. Add the coffee and vanilla and whisk until combined. Add the melted butter and continue to beat. Add the buttermilk and whisk until smooth.

Pour the egg-buttermilk mixture into the flour mixture and whisk until smooth. Do not overmix. Scrape the batter into the prepared pan and spread evenly.

Bake for 18 to 22 minutes, or until the edge of the cake slightly pulls away from the sides of the pan. Let cool in the pan set on a rack for 15 minutes. Place a sheet of wax paper on the surface of the cake and invert onto the cake rack. Lift off the baking pan and allow the cake to cool completely.

To make the banana wafer, reduce the oven temperature to 200°F. Line a large, heavy baking sheet and set aside.

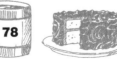

In a food processor, place the banana pieces. Process until smooth, 30 to 45 seconds. Scrape the banana purée onto the center of the lined baking sheet and, using a large flexible metal spatula, spread the purée evenly into a large rectangle about $\frac{1}{16}$ inch thick, almost completely covering the Magic sheet.

Bake for $2\frac{1}{2}$ to 3 hours, or until the banana wafer is completely dried and brown and the edges of the wafer lift slightly. Remove the baking sheet from the oven and remove the sheet with the dried banana wafer. While the wafer is still warm, peel it from the sheet. Leave to cool, uncovered, at room temperature for 1 hour. Break the banana wafer into 16 irregular-shaped pieces, and store in an airtight container until ready to serve the dessert. The wafer may be prepared up to 3 days ahead.

To make the café au lait sauce, in a heavy saucepan over medium heat, combine the cream, milk, and $\frac{1}{4}$ cup of the sugar. Bring to a gentle boil over medium heat. Remove from the heat, stir in the ground coffee, and let steep for 5 minutes.

In a bowl, whisk the egg yolks with the remaining $\frac{1}{4}$ cup sugar until blended. Gradually pour the hot cream mixture through a fine-mesh sieve into the egg yolk mixture, whisking until blended. Return the mixture to the saucepan and cook over medium-low heat, stirring constantly with a wooden spatula, for 3 to 5 minutes, or until the sauce has thickened slightly. Do not let the sauce

boil. The sauce is done when it coats the back of the spatula and if you run your finger down the back of the spatula, a path remains in the sauce for several seconds.

Remove from the heat and immediately strain the sauce through a fine-mesh sieve into a stainless-steel bowl set in a larger bowl filled with ice water. Stir the sauce for 10 to 15 minutes, or until cool. Remove the bowl of sauce from the bowl of ice water, cover with plastic wrap, and chill.

To make the chocolate mousse, in the chilled $4\frac{1}{2}$-quart bowl of a heavy-duty electric mixer fitted with the wire whip attachment, beat the cream just until soft mounds begin to form. Cover and refrigerate until ready to use.

In the top of a double boiler or a heat-proof bowl over gently simmering water, melt the chocolate. Add the butter and stir until melted. Transfer the chocolate to a large bowl and set aside to cool slightly.

In a small, heavy saucepan over medium-low heat, combine the sugar and water. Cook, stirring constantly with a wooden spoon, until the sugar dissolves. Stop stirring and reduce the heat to low.

In the $4\frac{1}{2}$-quart bowl of the heavy-duty electric mixer fitted with the wire whip attachment, beat the yolks at medium-high speed until thick and pale, about 3 minutes.

At this point, raise the heat under the sugar to medium-high and bring the mixture to a boil. Cook until the syrup registers 240°F on a candy thermometer. While

continuing to beat the yolks at medium speed, gradually pour the hot sugar syrup down the side of the bowl into the whipped yolks. Continue beating until the mixture is cool, about 8 minutes.

Scrape about 1 cup of the egg mixture over the melted chocolate and, using a rubber spatula, vigorously stir to combine. Scrape the remaining egg mixture over the lightened chocolate mixture and gently fold until the mixture is just combined.

Scrape the whipped cream over the chocolate-egg mixture and, using the rubber spatula, fold together, being careful not to overmix. Cover the bowl with plastic wrap and refrigerate while preparing the molds.

To assemble the cakes, line a baking sheet with wax paper. Evenly space eight 3-inch ring molds on the lined baking sheet.

Remove the sheet of wax paper from the surface of the cake, and invert the cake onto a large work area. Remove the second sheet of wax paper. Using a 3-inch biscuit cutter or one of the ring molds, cut out 16 rounds from the cake layer. Reserve the cake scraps. Place 1 cake round in the bottom of each of the ring molds.

Scrape $\frac{1}{4}$ cup of the chocolate mousse into each mold. Tap the baking sheet on the work surface several times to release any air bubbles and level the mousse. Place another cake round into each mousse-filled mold. Evenly press down on the cake round. Scrape another 2 tablespoons of chocolate mousse

onto each cake round, filling the mold to the top. Using a flexible metal spatula, scrape the top of each mold to level the mousse filling. Cover the tray with plastic wrap and place in the freezer until firm, about 3 hours.

To make the crumb garnish, preheat the oven to 375°F. Line a baking sheet with aluminum foil. Spread the reserved cake scraps in an even layer on the baking sheet. Bake for 6 to 8 minutes, or until the cake is dry. Allow the cake pieces to cool.

Place the dried cake pieces in a food processor and process until finely ground, 20 to 30 seconds. Transfer the crumbs to a shallow bowl and set aside.

To unmold and garnish the cakes, remove the baking sheet with the molds from the freezer. One by one, gently heat the outside of each mold using a portable hair dryer or a hot, damp towel. Carefully lift each ring mold, letting the cake slide onto the baking sheet.

Place one of the cakes in your open palm over the bowl of cake crumbs and, using your other hand, gently pat the dried cake crumbs evenly onto the side of the cake. Sprinkle the crumbs in an even layer over the top of the cake. Return the cake to the baking sheet and repeat with the remaining cakes. The cakes may be garnished up to 4 hours ahead, loosely covered with plastic wrap, and stored in the refrigerator.

To serve the cakes, place the shards of banana wafer in an even layer on a large work surface and dust with confectioners' sugar.

Place 1 cake in the center of a dessert plate. Stand 2 of the banana wafers on the plate by gently pressing them into the surface of the cake. Spoon 2 tablespoons of the café au lait sauce around the cake. Repeat with the remaining cakes. Serve at once.

ANGEL FOOD AND SPONGE CAKES

Angel Food Cake

Serves: 12

> 12 egg whites
> $^1/_2$ teaspoon cream of tartar
> $^3/_4$ cup granulated sugar
> $1^1/_2$ teaspoons vanilla extract
> $^1/_2$ teaspoon almond extract
> 1 cup sifted cake flour
> $1^1/_4$ cups confectioners' sugar
> $^1/_4$ teaspoon salt

Preheat an oven to 350°F. Have ready an ungreased 10-inch tube pan.

In a large mixing bowl, beat together the egg whites and cream of tartar on high speed until foamy. Add sugar one tablespoon at a time, beating constantly until the sugar is dissolved and whites are glossy and stand in soft peaks. Beat in the vanilla and almond extracts. In another bowl, sift together twice the flour, confectioners' sugar, and salt. Sift about $^1/_2$ cup of the flour mixture over the egg whites and gently fold in just until flour disappears. Repeat, folding in the remaining

Angel Cake Secrets

Angel cakes are leavened with air: no baking soda and no baking powder in sight. Whether or not you get a light, tender cake will depend on how much you beat the egg whites, the lightness with which you fold in the sugar-and-flour mixture, and the temperature at which you bake the cake. You should beat the egg whites until they are stiff enough to hold soft peaks but remain moist and glossy.

(continued)

Pitfalls of Angel Food Cake

If the crumb is tough, not tender?
- Oven too hot
- Not enough sugar
- Overmixing

If the texture is too coarse?
- Underbeaten egg whites
- Insufficient blending of ingredients
- Oven too cool

If the cake bottom is heavy and sticky?
- Underbeaten egg whites
- Insufficient mixing of whites with other ingredients

If there are cracks in the crust?
- Overbeaten egg whites
- Too much sugar
- Oven too hot

If the crust is sticky?
- Too much sugar
- Underbaking

If the cake looks like it has shrunk?
- Whites beaten too much or not enough
- Overmixing
- Pan too large
- Oven too hot

flour mixture ¹/₂ cup at a time. Turn into the ungreased tube pan. Gently cut through the batter with a metal spatula.

Bake for 30 to 40 minutes, or until the top springs back to the touch. Invert the cake in the pan onto a funnel or bottle neck and let cool completely.

Heavenly Angel Food Cake

Serves: 12

1 cup sifted cake flour
1 ¹/₄ cups sifted confectioners' sugar
1 ¹/₄ cups (12) egg whites
1 ¹/₂ teaspoons cream of tartar
¹/₄ teaspoon salt
1 ¹/₂ teaspoons vanilla extract
¹/₄ teaspoon almond extract
1 cup granulated sugar

Preheat an oven to 375°F. Have ready a 10-inch tube pan.

In a bowl, sift together the flour and confectioners' sugar three times. In another bowl, beat the egg whites with the cream of tartar, salt, vanilla, and almond extract until stiff enough to hold soft, moist, glossy peaks. Beat in the granulated sugar 2 tablespoons at a time, continuing to beat until the whites hold stiff peaks. Sift about one-fourth of the flour mixture over the whites; fold in lightly just until no white streaks remain. Fold in the remaining flour mixture in four batches. Turn into the tube pan.

Bake for about 30 minutes, or until the cake springs back to the touch. Invert the cake in the pan onto a funnel bottleneck and let cool completely.

Passionate Strawberry Angel Cake

Serves: 10

> 2 pints strawberries, stemmed and sliced
> 1 package (10 ounces) frozen passion fruit purée, thawed
> 2 cups sugar
> 2 tablespoons unflavored gelatin
> 10 egg whites
> 2 cups whipping cream, whipped to soft peaks
> 1 angel food cake (Chapter 5)

In a large saucepan over low heat, combine the strawberries, passion fruit, and 1 cup of the sugar. Heat until warm. Place the mixture in a food processor and add the gelatin while the mixture is still warm. Purée until smooth. Let cool for 15 minutes.

Meanwhile, place the egg whites in a mixing bowl. Using an electric mixer set on medium speed, beat the egg whites while gradually adding the remaining 1 cup sugar. When the whites hold soft peaks, increase the speed to high and whip until stiff peaks form.

Gently fold the egg whites into the purée. Follow with the whipped cream. Cut an angel food cake in half horizontally. Spread the mousse onto the bottom layer, top with the second layer, and freeze for 30 minutes before serving.

Strawberry Sparkle Cake

Serves: 10

> 1 package angel food cake mix
> 1 package (3 ounces) strawberry Jell-O
> 1 cup boiling water
> 1 package (1 pound) frozen strawberries
> 1 cup whipping cream
> 2 tablespoons sugar
> fresh strawberries (optional)

Bake the angel food cake as directed on the package. Let cool. In a large bowl, dissolve the Jell-O in the boiling water and add the frozen block of strawberries, stirring to break up and mix the berries.

Place the cake, widest side down, on a serving plate. Cut a 1-inch-thick layer from the top and set aside. Cut around the cake 1 inch from the outer edge to within 1 inch of the bottom. Then cut around the cake from the inner edge to within 1 inch of the bottom. Gently remove the section of cake between the cuts, and tear it into small pieces. Fold the pieces into the strawberry mixture and pour the mixture into the cake shell. Place the reserved cake layer on top. Whip the cream until thick and stir in the sugar. Spread over the top and sides of the cake. Decorate with fresh strawberries, if desired. Refrigerate for at least 1 hour before serving.

Orange Peach Angel Cake

Serves: 10

1 small angel food cake
1 can (8 ounces) sliced peaches
1 package (3 ounces) orange Jell-O
ice water
$\frac{1}{2}$ cup skim dry milk
2 tablespoons lemon juice
$\frac{1}{3}$ cup confectioners' sugar
1 can (10 ounces) mandarin oranges

Slice $\frac{1}{2}$ inch off the top of the cake and set aside. With the point of a knife, cut a circle $\frac{1}{2}$ inch in from the edge of the base and a second circle in from the center hole. Pull out the soft cake to form a trough $1\frac{1}{2}$ inches deep. Drain the peach juice into a measuring cup and add water as needed to measure $\frac{1}{2}$ cup. Heat to boiling and stir in the Jell-O. Chill until slightly thickened.

Mix ice water and the dry milk powder in a small bowl and beat until thick. Add the lemon juice. Beat until stiff. Fold in the sugar. Beat the thickened Jell-O until smooth and fold in the whipped milk. Divide the mixture in half. Add the peaches to half of the Jell-O and scrape into the cake shell. Spread evenly. Replace the top of the cake. Chill the remaining Jell-O mixture to spreading consistency, then frost top and sides of cake. Decorate with mandarin orange sections.

Hot-Milk Sponge Cake

Serves: 6

1 cup sifted flour
1 teaspoon baking powder
$\frac{1}{4}$ teaspoon salt
2 tablespoons butter or margarine
$\frac{1}{2}$ cup milk, scalded
2 eggs
1 cup sugar
1 teaspoon vanilla extract

Preheat an oven to 350°F. Line the bottom of a 9-inch round cake pan with wax paper and grease the sides.

Sift together the sifted flour, baking powder, and salt into a bowl. Add the butter to the milk and keep hot. In a large bowl, using an electric mixer, beat the eggs for about 3 minutes on high speed, or until thick and lemon colored. Gradually add the sugar, beating constantly at medium speed for 4 to 5 minutes. Quickly add the flour mixture to the egg mixture and stir just until blended. Stir in the hot milk mixture and the vanilla. Pour into the prepared pan.

Bake for about 25 minutes, or until top springs back when lightly touched. Let cool in the pan on a rack for 15 minutes, then turn out onto the rack to cool completely.

Chocolate Sponge Cake

Serves: 8

> 4 squares (4 ounces) unsweetened
>   chocolate
> 1 cup milk
> 1 cup sifted cake flour
> 1 teaspoon baking powder
> $1/2$ teaspoon salt
> 4 eggs, separated
> $1\,1/2$ cups sugar
> 1 teaspoon vanilla extract

Preheat an oven to 350°F. Have ready two ungreased 9-inch cake pans.

Break the chocolate squares in half and place in a small saucepan with the milk. Place over low heat and heat, stirring constantly, until the chocolate melts and the mixture is smooth. Remove from the heat and set aside. Sift together the sifted flour, baking powder, and salt into a bowl. Return the flour mixture to the sifter and set aside. Beat the egg whites until frothy. Beat in $1/2$ cup of the sugar 1 tablespoon at a time. Beat until stiff peaks form when the beaters are slowly withdrawn. Set aside. Without washing the beaters, beat the egg yolks until thickened and lemon colored. Gradually beat in the remaining 1 cup sugar and the vanilla until very thick and pale. Add the chocolate mixture and beat gently to blend. Gradually sift in the flour mixture, gently beating as you sift. Using a rubber spatula, fold in the egg

(continued)

Sponge Cake Secrets

Sponge cakes are delicate so they can be a bit temperamental. Follow these tips for a perfect cake: Be sure to prepare the pan according to the directions in the recipe; in other words, do not grease. Spread the mixed batter to the sides of the pan, filing all the corners. Angel and sponge cakes are done when they spring back to the touch, so you don't test with a toothpick. Then to cool, turn the pan upside down and cool thoroughly. If the cake falls away from the pan, it may be because pan was greased or because it wasn't baked long enough.

More Sponge Cake Secrets

Of course, the method for making a sponge cake varies from recipe to recipe, but the standard rules for making angel food cakes—beating egg whites and folding in sugar and flour—hold true for sponge cakes, too. It's also important to beat the egg yolks until they're as thick as whipped cream and lemon colored. You may beat some or all of the sugar with the yolks, but remember to add the sugar gradually. In some recipes, the liquid is added to the yolks and beaten until the mixture is very light.

whites, breaking up any blobs of white with the spatula. Turn into the 2 cake pans.

Bake for 20 to 25 minutes, or until the top springs back to the touch. Let cool in the pans on racks for 10 minutes, then turn out onto the racks and let cool completely.

FRUITCAKES

Dark Fruitcake

Serves: 20

> $3^{1}/_{2}$ cups ($1^{1}/_{2}$ pounds) mixed candied
>   diced fruits and peels for fruitcake
> $1^{1}/_{4}$ cups (8 ounces) dark raisins
> $1^{1}/_{4}$ cups (8 ounces) golden raisins
> 1 cup (4 ounces) walnuts, chopped
> 1 cup (4 ounces) pecans, chopped
> 3 cups sifted flour
> 1 teaspoon baking powder
> 1 teaspoon salt
> 1 teaspoon ground cinnamon
> 1 teaspoon ground allspice
> $^{1}/_{2}$ teaspoon ground nutmeg
> $^{1}/_{2}$ teaspoon ground cloves
> 1 cup vegetable shortening
> 2 cups packed brown sugar
> 4 eggs
> $^{3}/_{4}$ cup grape juice

Preheat an oven to 275°F. Line two $8^{1}/_{2}$-by-$4^{1}/_{2}$-by-$2^{1}/_{2}$-inch loaf pans with wax paper, allowing $^{1}/_{2}$ inch to extend above the sides.

In a large bowl, mix together the fruits and peels, raisins, and nuts. Sift together flour,

baking powder, salt, and spices into another bowl. Sprinkle $^1/_4$ cup of the flour mixture over the fruit mixture, mixing well. In yet another bowl, cream together the shortening and sugar until light and fluffy. Beat in the eggs one at a time, beating well after each addition. Add the flour mixture to the creamed mixture alternately with the grape juice, beating until smooth after each addition. Pour over the fruits and mix well. Pour the batter into the pans, filling each one three-fourths full. Do not flatten.

Place a pan of water on the bottom shelf of the oven. Place the loaf pans on the center shelf and bake for 3 to $3^1/_2$ hours, or until lightly browned. Cool on racks.

If desired, wrap the cakes in cheesecloth and moisten on all sides with brandy or wine. Wrap in aluminum foil and store in the refrigerator or a cool place for 3 to 4 weeks, moistening again once a week.

White Wedding Fruitcake

Serves: 20

> 4 cups ($1^3/_4$ pounds) mixed candied diced
>   fruits and peels for fruitcake
> $^1/_2$ cup pitted dates, cut up
> $^1/_2$ cup dried apricots, cut up
> $^1/_2$ cup dried figs, cut up
> $1^1/_4$ cups (8 ounces) golden raisins
> 2 cups (8 ounces) slivered, blanched
>   almonds
> 2 cups flaked dried coconut

> 2 cups sifted flour
> $1^1/_2$ teaspoons baking powder
> 1 teaspoon salt
> 1 cup vegetable shortening
> 1 cup sugar
> 1 teaspoon rum flavoring
> 5 eggs
> $^1/_2$ cup unsweetened pineapple juice

Preheat an oven to 275°F. Line two $8^1/_2$-by-$4^1/_2$-by-$2^1/_2$-inch pans with wax paper, allowing $^1/_2$ inch to extend above the sides.

In a large bowl, mix together the candied fruits and peels, dates, apricots, figs, raisins, almonds, and coconut. Sift together the flour, baking powder, and salt into another bowl. Sprinkle $^1/_2$ cup of the flour mixture over the fruit mixture, mixing well. In a large bowl, cream together the shortening, sugar, and rum flavoring. Add the eggs, one at a time, beating well after each addition. Add the flour mixture to the creamed mixture alternately with the pineapple juice, beating until smooth after each addition. Add the fruit mixture, stirring until well mixed. Pour the batter into the pans, filling each one three-fourths full.

Place a pan of water on the bottom shelf of the oven while baking. Place the loaf pans on the center shelf and bake for $2^1/_2$ hours, or until lightly browned. Cool on a rack.

Fruitcakes that People Will Eat

You know all the jokes about holiday fruitcakes: better used for doorstops, and so on. Have you ever actually seen someone eat a piece of fruitcake except on December 25? If you are a stickler for the quality of the ingredients that go into your fruitcake, you shouldn't have a problem. Here's a hint: don't tell your guests it's a fruitcake, and then watch their faces as you inform them of the truth after they've polished off seconds.

Pineapple Fruitcake Glaze

Makes: Enough glaze to give double coat to 6 pounds fruitcake

$^3/_4$ cup unsweetened pineapple juice
$^1/_2$ cup light corn syrup

Combine the pineapple juice and corn syrup in a saucepan and bring quickly to a rolling boil. Remove from the heat. Immediately brush over cooled fruitcakes. Decorate the tops of the cakes with blanched almonds, candied cherries, or candies. When set, brush on a second coat of glaze. (Reheat glaze to boiling each time you use it.) Allow glaze to dry thoroughly before wrapping or storing cakes.

Belgian Loaf

Serves: 12

2 cups sugar
2 cups raisins
2 cups milk
1 cup butter or margarine
4 cups flour
1 teaspoon baking soda
1 teaspoon cream of tartar
8 ounces glacéed cherries

Preheat an oven to 350°F. Have ready a 9-inch tube pan.

Stir together the sugar, raisins, milk, and butter in a saucepan and bring to a boil. Remove from the heat, pour into a bowl, and let cool. In another bowl, combine the flour,

baking soda, cream of tartar, and cherries and stir to mix. Add the flour mixture to the sugar mixture and mix well. Pour into the tube pan.

Bake for 1 hour, or until a knife comes out clean. Cool on a rack.

TRIFLES

A trifle is a unique kind of dessert that is simple to assemble, but rarely considered anymore in the traditional vernacular of dessert-making in America today. Considered to be too British? Perhaps, but the basic ingredients and the briefest of times involved to put one together—along with the fact that most people have never been exposed to this sweet treat, make this an ideal dessert for busy people who want to have something just a bit different for dessert. A variation on the theme of a trifle is the jelly roll, so I've included some of these recipes in this section as well.

For the best results, make sure that the cake you use for a trifle is dry; even slightly stale cake would work.

Leftover Trifle

Serves: 8

    1 package (4 ounces) vanilla pudding
    2 cups milk
    $1/2$ teaspoon vanilla or almond extract or
        rum flavoring
    3 or more slices leftover cake, each
        $1/2$-inch thick
    jam or preserves of choice

    $1 1/2$ cups fresh or canned cut-up fruit such
        as peaches, pears, bananas, kiwifruits,
        or berries
    $3/4$ cup almonds, chopped
    $1/2$ cup whipping cream, whipped stiff
    $1/4$ cup almonds, chopped and toasted

Following the package directions, prepare the pudding, using the milk and flavoring with vanilla. Remove from the heat and let cool. Line a standard loaf pan with wax paper. Spread one side of each cake slice with jam and place coated side up, in the bottom of the loaf pan, covering the bottom completely. Place half of the fruit and half of the untoasted almonds evenly over the cake. Cover with half of the pudding. Repeat the layers, then top with a third cake layer. Spread the whipped cream on top and sprinkle with the toasted nuts. Cover and chill for at least 3 hours before serving.

Celebration Trifle

Serves: 12

    $1/4$ cup sugar
    2 tablespoons cornstarch
    4 egg yolks
    1 cup milk
    3 cups whipping cream
    1 teaspoon vanilla extract
    2 packages (8 ounces each) ladyfingers
    1 cup raspberry preserves combined with
        $1/4$ cup framboise liqueur
    $1/2$ cup sweet or medium-dry sherry

(continued)

In the top pan of a double boiler placed over (not touching) gently simmering water, mix together the sugar, cornstarch, and egg yolks. Heat, stirring constantly, until warm. In a saucepan, combine the milk and 1 cup of the cream and heat until warm. Add to the mixture in the double boiler. Stir constantly for about 10 minutes, or until the mixture thickens and coats the back of a spoon. Never allow it to come to a boil. Remove from the heat and stir in the vanilla. Allow the mixture to cool. Whip the remaining 2 cups cream until stiff and fold half of it into the cooled custard. Cover and refrigerate the remaining whipped cream.

Split the ladyfingers. Spread one cut side with the preserves-framboise mixture, and then reassemble the ladyfingers and cut in half crosswise. Line the bottom and sides of a 4-quart glass bowl with half of the ladyfingers. Sprinkle with ¼ cup of sherry. Pour in half of the custard. Cover with plastic wrap and chill until partially set. Layer with the remaining ladyfingers, sprinkle with the remaining sherry, and spread the remaining custard on top. Cover and chill until set. Garnish with the reserved whipped cream.

Trifle in the Grand Manner

Serves: 8

1 pound cake
¼ cup dry sherry
¼ cup cognac or other brandy
½ cup strawberry or raspberry jam

Crème Anglaise:
½ cup sugar
4 egg yolks
1 teaspoon cornstarch
1¾ cups milk
½ teaspoon almond extract

1 cup whipping cream
¼ cup slivered almonds, toasted

Cut the pound cake into 2-inch square chunks and place in a single layer in a shallow dish. Combine the sherry and cognac and pour evenly over the cake. Let soak for 10 minutes. Spread each piece of cake with some of the jam. Place in a large glass bowl or trifle bowl and let stand for a couple of hours.

To make the crème anglaise, in a bowl combine the sugar and egg yolks and beat until the mixture is very thick and creamy, pale yellow, and forms ribbons that fall back on themselves when the beaters are lifted. This will take about 5 minutes. Beat in the cornstarch. In a saucepan, heat the milk until a film shines on top. Do not allow to boil. While beating constantly, add the hot milk to the yolk mixture in a thin, steady stream. Place over very low heat and cook, stirring constantly, with a wooden spoon, until sauce thickens enough to coat the back of a spoon, about 10 minutes. (The sauce should never come to a simmer.) Remove from the heat. Beat for a minute or two to cool. Then beat in the almond extract. Pour the hot crème anglaise over the soaked cake, let cool, cover,

and chill. Just before serving, whip the cream until stiff peaks form and spread over the trifle. Stick the almonds upright over the surface.

Bee Sting Cake

Serves: 8

Filling:

1 cup milk
¼ cup sugar
pinch of salt
2 tablespoons cornstarch
3 egg yolks
1 tablespoon Amaretto liqueur
1 teaspoon vanilla extract
⅛ teaspoon almond extract
⅓ cup whipping cream

Cake:

1¾ cups flour
2 teaspoons baking powder
¼ teaspoon salt
*½ cup unsalted butter, at room
    temperature*
⅔ cup sugar
2 eggs
1 teaspoon vanilla extract
¼ teaspoon almond extract
½ cup milk

(continued)

A Trifle Trifle

Although Americans customarily think of trifle as a peculiarly British dessert, we should learn to appreciate it not only because of its simple assembly, but also because it gives us the excuse to resurrect cake that has turned just a bit dry. Trifle's Italian cousin is _tiramisù_, so if you add a touch of Amaretto to the custard or cream, it's entirely possible to pass the dessert off as the equivalent of spending a night in Italy.

Topping:

³/₄ cup blanched sliced or slivered almonds
¹/₂ cup granulated sugar
¹/₄ cup unsalted butter
2 tablespoons whipping cream
confectioners' sugar

To make the filling, in a small, heavy saucepan over medium heat, combine ²/₃ cup of the milk, the sugar, and salt. Bring to a boil, stirring to dissolve the sugar. Pour the rest of the milk into a small bowl; beat in the cornstarch, then the egg yolks.

Whisking constantly, add a little of the hot milk to the egg yolk mixture. Bring the remaining milk mixture in the saucepan back to a boil over medium heat. Whisking constantly, pour the eggs into the saucepan.

Cook, stirring constantly, until the mixture comes to a boil. Reduce the heat to low and simmer for 1 minute longer. Immediately remove the saucepan from the heat, add the Amaretto and vanilla and almond extracts, and pour the custard into a small bowl. Cover with plastic wrap, pressing it directly on the surface, and chill well or for up to 24 hours. Reserve the cream for mixing with the custard just before filling cake.

Preheat an oven to 350°F. Butter and flour a 9-inch springform pan.

To make the cake, in a bowl, sift together the flour, baking powder, and salt. In a larger bowl, using an electric mixer set on high speed, cream the butter until light. Gradually add the sugar and continue beating until the mixture is very light and fluffy. Reduce the speed to medium and add the eggs, one at a time, beating well after each addition. Add the vanilla and almond extracts and beat well.

Reduce the speed to low. Alternately mix in the flour mixture and the milk, one-third at a time, beginning and ending with the flour mixture and beating only until combined. Pour the batter into the prepared pan.

To make the topping, in a small saucepan, combine the almonds, sugar, butter, and cream. Place over medium heat until the butter melts. Pour the topping over the cake batter, spreading lightly.

Bake for almost 40 minutes, or until the top is golden and a toothpick inserted in the center comes out clean. Let cool in the pan on a wire rack for 20 minutes. Using a sharp knife, loosen the cake from the pan sides, then carefully remove from the pan. Let cool completely.

In a bowl, beat the cream for the custard filling until it forms soft peaks. Stir about 2 tablespoons of the whipped cream into the chilled custard to lighten it, then fold in the remainder. Slice the cake in half horizontally and place the bottom half, cut side up, on a serving platter. Spread the custard filling on the cake, then top with the remaining half, cut side down. Cover and refrigerate until ready to serve. Dust lightly with confectioners' sugar, just before serving.

Tiramisù

Serves: 12

Sponge Cake:
4 eggs, separated
1 teaspoon vanilla extract
³/₄ cup sugar
½ cup flour
½ cup cornstarch
Pinch of salt

Espresso Syrup:
⅓ cup sugar
¼ cup water
½ cup very strong brewed espresso
¼ cup brandy

Zabaglione Filling:
3 egg yolks
⅓ cup sugar
⅓ cup Marsala wine
½ pound mascarpone cheese, at room temperature
⅔ cup whipping cream

Preheat an oven to 350°F. Butter a 9-inch round cake pan and line with wax paper.

To make the sponge cake, in a bowl, using an electric mixer set on medium speed, beat together the egg yolks and vanilla until well mixed. Add half of the sugar and beat until very light and frothy, about 5 minutes. Set aside. In a separate bowl, sift together the flour and cornstarch. Set aside.

In yet another bowl, using clean beaters, beat together the egg whites and salt at medium speed until soft peaks form. Increase the speed to high and add the rest of the sugar in a slow, continuous steam, until the egg whites hold a firm peak.

Using a rubber spatula fold the whites into the yolk mixture. Sift the flour and cornstarch over the eggs in three additions, folding in after each addition. Pour the batter into the prepared pan.

Bake for 30 to 40 minutes, or until well risen and feels slightly firm when pressed gently with the palm of your hand. Remove from the oven and immediately loosen the cake from the pan sides with a small knife. Invert onto a rack, lift off the pan, and peel away the paper. Turn the cake right side up and let cool.

To make the syrup, in a saucepan, combine the sugar and water and bring to a boil, stirring to dissolve the sugar. Remove from the heat, let cool, and stir in the espresso and brandy.

To make the filling, in a heatproof bowl, using an electric mixer set at medium speed, beat the egg yolks until thick. Add the sugar and Marsala and beat well until combined. Place over a pan of simmering water and continue to beat at medium speed until thickened. Remove from over the water and continue to beat at medium speed until cool.

In a bowl, stir the mascarpone with a rubber spatula until it is smooth. Fold in the

(continued)

The Frosting Formula

I'm a frosting fan. My biggest problem is making sure I have enough frosting left over to cover the sides of the cake. A simple formula has helped me to gauge more accurately any recipe: Allocate about one-third of the frosting in the bowl for the filling between the layers, and use the rest for the top and sides. This only works, however, if you don't snitch too much for yourself during the process.

cooled egg mixture. In another bowl, whip the cream until soft peaks form. Fold into the egg-cheese mixture.

To assemble, cut the cake vertically into slices about $\frac{1}{4}$ inch thick. Place a layer of the slices in the bottom of a shallow 2-quart dish. Pour one-third of the espresso syrup over the cake. Spread with half of the filling.

Add another layer of cake, and then half of the remaining syrup. Top with the rest of the filling. Place the remaining cake on top and soak with the rest of the syrup.

In a separate bowl, whip 1 cup whipping cream with 2 tablespoons of the sugar until it holds its shape and spread it on the surface of the dessert. Sprinkle the top of the cake with cinnamon and ground coffee, or cocoa powder. Refrigerate for several hours before serving.

FROSTINGS

Sour Cream Frosting

Makes: 3 cups frosting, enough to frost 2 2-layer cakes

> 2 cups sour cream
> 2 cups sugar
> 1 teaspoon vanilla extract
> $1\frac{1}{2}$ cups walnuts, chopped

In a heavy saucepan, combine the sour cream and sugar. Cook over medium heat, stirring occasionally, for about 10 minutes, or until the mixture registers 234°F on a candy

thermometer. Alternatively, test by dropping a nugget of the mixture into cold water; it should form a soft ball. Remove from the heat and let cool to lukewarm. Stir in the vanilla and nuts.

Cream Cheese Frosting

Makes: About 1¹⁄₂ cups, enough for a 2-layer cake

> 1¹⁄₂ cups (12 ounces) cream cheese, softened
> ¹⁄₂ teaspoon vanilla extract
> 6 tablespoons maple syrup or ¹⁄₄ cup honey

In a bowl, combine all the ingredients and mix until smooth. This frosting tastes best on carrot cake.

Mocha Frosting

Makes: 1¹⁄₂ cups, enough for a 2-layer cake

> 1¹⁄₂ cups (12 ounces) cream cheese, softened
> 1 square (1 ounce) unsweetened chocolate, melted and cooled
> ¹⁄₄ cup honey
> 2 teaspoons instant coffee crystals, dissolved in 1 tablespoon of hot water

In a bowl, combine all the ingredients and mix until smooth.

Lemon Frosting

Makes: About 1 cup, enough to frost a 9-by-13 sheet cake

> 1 cup confectioners' sugar
> 1¹⁄₂ tablespoons water
> 2 tablespoons lemon juice
> 1 tablespoon grated lemon rind

In a bowl, combine the water, lemon juice, and lemon rind. Beat in the confectioners' sugar, ¹⁄₂ cup at a time, until smooth.

North Country Frosting

Makes: About 2 cups, enough to frost a 2-layer cake

> ¹⁄₂ cup butter or margarine, softened
> 2 cups confectioners' sugar
> 1 tablespoon whipping cream
> ¹⁄₂ teaspoon vanilla extract

In a bowl, cream together the butter and confectioners' sugar until light. Add the cream and vanilla and mix well.

Essential Chocolate Frosting

Makes: About 2 cups frosting, enough for a 2-layer cake

> ¹⁄₄ cup butter or margarine, softened
> 2 cups confectioners' sugar
> 2 squares (2 ounces) semisweet chocolate, melted and cooled

(continued)

Fancy Frosting

I used to live upstairs from a woman who ran a cake-designing business from her home kitchen. I would watch while she gracefully handled the pastry bag and effortlessly created rosebuds and letters from sugar, butter, and food coloring. Using a pastry bag is easy, especially with the wide variety of tips now available. Practice with your grip and the pressure you exert on the bag, and in no time you could become a professional cake designer, too.

$^1/_2$ teaspoon vanilla extract
pinch of salt
2 or 3 tablespoons light cream

In a bowl, cream the butter until light. Gradually stir in 1 cup of the confectioners' sugar, then the melted chocolate, and then the rest of the sugar as needed. Stir in the vanilla, salt, and enough cream to create a good frosting consistency. Blend well.

Pillow-Top Chocolate Frosting

Makes: About 2 cups, enough for a 2-layer cake

$^1/_4$ cup butter or margarine, softened
$1^1/_2$ cups confectioners' sugar
1 teaspoon vanilla extract
3 squares (3 ounces) semisweet chocolate, melted and cooled
$^1/_4$ teaspoon salt
2 egg whites

In a bowl, cream together the butter and $^3/_4$ cup of the sugar until light. Add the vanilla, melted chocolate, and salt. Mix well. In another bowl, beat the egg whites until stiff peaks form. Fold the remaining $^3/_4$ cup sugar, 2 tablespoons at a time, into the egg whites. Fold in the chocolate mixture gently, just enough to blend.

The Everything
Dessert Cookbook

Chapter 6: Squares and Bars

S quare and bar cookies are among the most perfect desserts for the hectic lives that most of us lead these days: they're portable, they're compact, and they don't tend to crumb all that much. Another added benefit is that you can cram a good number of nutritious ingredients into them—like dried fruit and nuts—so in a pinch, they could serve as a meal on the go, with a glass of milk.

Square and bar cookies also mean a minimum of cleanup time, since you usually only need a couple of bowls and utensils for the recipes. And they work as well being served as an elegant dessert with a dollop of cream on top as handed out to kids at the playground.

Frosted Snow Squares

Makes: 12 squares

1 envelope unflavored gelatin
1 tablespoon cold water
1 cup boiling water
²/₃ cup sugar
3 egg whites
¹/₄ teaspoon salt
1 teaspoon vanilla extract

Sauce:
3 egg yolks
¹/₃ cup butter, melted
1 tablespoon lemon juice
¹/₃ cup sugar

¹/₄ cup graham cracker crumbs

In a large bowl, soften the gelatin in the cold water. Add the boiling water and sugar and stir until the sugar dissolves. Let cool. Add the egg whites, salt, and vanilla and beat until very light (like angel food cake). Pour into an 8-inch square pan and place in the refrigerator for an hour, or until set.

To make the sauce, in the top pan of a double boiler over low-medium heat, whisk together the egg yolks, butter, lemon juice, and sugar. Cook, stirring constantly, for 7 to 10 minutes, or until thick enough to coat the back of a spoon. Remove from the heat and cool slightly. Sprinkle with graham cracker crumbs.

Apricot Squares

Makes: 12 squares

²/₃ cup dried apricots, chopped
²/₃ cup water
¹/₂ cup butter, softened
¹/₄ cup granulated sugar
1¹/₂ cups sifted flour
¹/₂ teaspoon baking powder
¹/₄ teaspoon salt
2 eggs
³/₄ cup packed brown sugar
¹/₂ teaspoon vanilla extract
¹/₂ cup flaked dried coconut

Icing:
¹/₃ cup butter, softened
2 tablespoons lemon juice
about 1¹/₂ cups confectioners' sugar

Preheat an oven to 350°F. Have ready an 8-inch square pan.

Combine the apricots and water in a small saucepan, bring to a simmer, and cook for 15 minutes, or until soft. Remove from the heat and let cool. Meanwhile, in a bowl, mix together the butter, granulated sugar, and 1 cup of the sifted flour until well blended.

Press into the pan. Bake for 20 minutes. Remove from the oven and let cool in pan. Sift together the remaining ¹/₂ cup sifted flour, baking powder, and salt into a bowl. In another bowl, beat together the eggs and brown sugar until blended. Add the flour mixture and mix well. Stir in the vanilla,

coconut, and apricots. Spread over the baked base and return to the oven.

Bake for 30 minutes.

Remove from the oven and cool.

To make the icing, in a bowl beat together the butter, lemon juice, and enough sugar to make a spreadable mixture. Spread the icing over the baked sheet. Cut into squares.

Coconut Honey Bars

Makes: 12 squares

¹/₄ cup butter or margarine, melted
¹/₄ cup packed brown sugar
1¹/₂ cup flaked dried coconut
¹/₂ teaspoon vanilla extract
2 cups quick-cooking rolled oats
¹/₄ cup honey

Preheat an oven to 400°F. Grease an 8-inch square pan.

In a bowl, combine the butter, sugar, coconut, vanilla, oats, and honey and stir until blended. Spread or press into the prepared pan.

Bake for 15 minutes, or just until golden. Let cool on a wire rack and cut into squares.

Nanaimo Bars

Makes: 12 squares

²/₃ cup plus 3 tablespoons butter
3 tablespoons unsweetened cocoa powder
¹/₄ cup granulated sugar
1 egg

(continued)

1 ¹/₂ cups graham cracker crumbs
1 cup flaked dried coconut
¹/₄ chopped walnuts
1 cup confectioners' sugar
3 tablespoons custard powder such as
   Bird's Custard Powder
milk or whipping cream
1 teaspoon vanilla extract
2 squares (2 ounces) semisweet
   chocolate

Have ready a 9-inch square pan.

Melt together $^1/_3$ cup butter and the cocoa in a saucepan. Remove from the heat and stir in the granulated sugar and egg. Add the graham cracker crumbs, coconut, and chopped nuts and mix well. Pat into the pan and place in the refrigerator for 20 minutes. In a bowl, cream together $^1/_3$ cup butter, the confectioners' sugar, custard powder, and milk or cream.

Add the vanilla. Spread over the base. In a small saucepan, melt together the chocolate and the 3 tablespoons butter. Spread evenly over the top. Let cool. Cut into 2-inch squares before the chocolate hardens. In Canada, these bars are is known as Nanaimo bars, named for a town on Vancouver Island, British Columbia. In the United States, they are commonly called New York specials.

Marshmallow Squares

Makes: 15 squares

$^1/_2$ cup butter, softened
$^1/_4$ cup packed brown sugar
1 cup flour
2 tablespoons unflavored gelatin
$^1/_2$ cup cold water
2 cups granulated sugar
$^3/_4$ cup boiling water
$^1/_2$ teaspoon distilled white vinegar
1 teaspoon vanilla extract
few drops of green food coloring (optional)
6 to 8 maraschino cherries, sliced (optional)
$^1/_4$ cup flaked dried coconut (optional)
$^1/_4$ cup slivered almonds (optional)

Preheat an oven to 350°F. Have ready a 12-inch square pan.

In a bowl, mix together the butter, brown sugar, and flour until well mixed. Press into the pan. Bake for 10 minutes, or until lightly browned.

Dissolve the gelatin in the cold water and let stand for 5 minutes. In a saucepan, combine the granulated sugar and boiling water. Stir to dissolve the sugar and bring to a boil. Boil to 234°F on a candy thermometer. Stir in the gelatin and set aside to cool.

Add the vinegar and vanilla and, if you wish the topping tinted, the food coloring. Beat until very stiff. Pour over the base. If desired, decorate with the cherries, coconut, and almonds. Cut into 3-inch squares.

Oatmeal Squares

Makes: 16 squares

1 egg, beaten
$\frac{1}{2}$ cup granulated sugar
$\frac{1}{2}$ cup packed brown sugar
1 teaspoon vanilla extract or $\frac{1}{2}$ teaspoon lemon flavoring
$\frac{1}{2}$ cup sifted flour
$\frac{1}{2}$ teaspoon salt
$\frac{1}{2}$ teaspoon baking soda
$\frac{1}{2}$ teaspoon ground nutmeg
$\frac{1}{3}$ cup vegetable shortening, melted and cooled
1 cup quick-cooking rolled oats
$\frac{1}{2}$ cup walnuts, chopped

In a large bowl, combine the egg, sugars, and flavoring and beat well. Sift together the sifted flour, salt, baking soda, and nutmeg into another bowl. Gradually add the flour mixture to the egg mixture, beating well. Stir in the shortening, oats, and nuts. Cover and chill the dough for about 1 hour.

Preheat an oven to 350°F. Grease a baking sheet.

Spread the dough $\frac{1}{4}$ inch thick on the prepared baking sheet, leaving a 1-inch border around the edges of the sheet. Bake for about 15 minutes, or until golden brown and flat in the center. Remove from the oven and cut into squares at once. Remove from the pan and let cool on a rack.

It's Cool to Be Square

With the advent of prepackaged cookie bars, granola bars, and energy squares that promise to keep you going at full tilt from dawn to dusk, many kids feel that their lunchboxes are as good as empty without one of these bars tucked inside. Use one of the recipes in this section to create a personalized energy bar that's full of your kids' favorite things. Although they taste just as good as the squares that come wrapped in foil, the ones you bake will be a lot healthier for them.

Date-Nut Bars

Makes: About 24 squares

> ¹/₂ cup vegetable shortening
> 1 cup sugar
> 1 teaspoon vanilla extract
> 2 eggs
> 2 cups sifted flour
> 2 teaspoons baking powder
> ¹/₂ teaspoon salt
> 1 teaspoon ground cinnamon
> ¹/₂ teaspoon ground cloves
> ¹/₂ teaspoon ground nutmeg
> 1 cup pitted dates, cut up, or raisins
> ¹/₂ cup walnuts, chopped

Preheat an oven to 375°F. Grease 2 baking sheets.

In a bowl, cream together the shortening, sugar, and vanilla until light. Add the eggs and beat well. Sift together the sifted flour, baking powder, salt, and all the spices into a bowl. Stir the flour mixture into the shortening mixture. Add the dates and nuts and mix well. Divide into 4 equal portions. Using 1 prepared sheet for 2 portions, spread each portion into a strip 12 inches long by 2¹/₂ inches wide by ¹/₂ inch thick. Space the strips 3 inches apart to allow for spreading during baking.

Bake for about 15 minutes, or until lightly browned. Remove from the oven and cut into 2-inch-wide bars while still warm. Remove to a rack to cool.

Orange Bars

Makes: About 24 bars

> ¹/₂ cup vegetable shortening
> ¹/₂ cup packed brown sugar
> 2 eggs
> 2 tablespoons grated orange rind
> 3 tablespoons orange juice
> 2 cups sifted flour
> 1 teaspoon baking soda
> ¹/₂ teaspoon salt
> 1 teaspoon ground cinnamon
> ¹/₂ teaspoon ground nutmeg
> ¹/₄ teaspoon ground cloves
> 1 cup raisins
> 1 cup walnuts, chopped
> confectioners' sugar for dusting (optional)

Preheat an oven to 350°F. Grease a 15¹/₂-by-10¹/₂-by-1-inch jelly-roll pan.

In a large bowl, cream together the shortening, brown sugar, and eggs until light. Stir in the orange rind and juice. Sift together the sifted flour, baking soda, salt, and all the spices into a bowl. Add to the creamed mixture and mix well. Stir in the raisins and nuts. Spread in the prepared jelly-roll pan.

Bake for about 30 minutes, or until lightly browned. Let cool, then cut into 2-inch bars or diamonds. If you like, sift confectioners' sugar over the tops.

Apple-Nut Squares

Makes: About 20 squares

3 eggs
³⁄₄ cup sugar
1 cup vegetable oil
2 teaspoons vanilla extract
2 cups flour
1 teaspoon baking soda
1 teaspoon salt
1 ¹⁄₂ teaspoons ground cinnamon
2 cups peeled and diced apples
¹⁄₂ cup nuts, chopped
whipped cream

Preheat an oven to 325°F. Lightly grease a 9-by-13-by-2-inch baking pan.

In a large bowl, combine the eggs, sugar, oil, and vanilla and mix well. In another bowl, sift together the flour, baking soda, salt, and cinnamon. Add the flour mixture to the egg mixture and mix well. Fold in the apples and nuts. Spread the batter in the prepared pan.

Bake for 1 hour, or until lightly brown. Let cool in pan. Cut into 1 ¹⁄₂-inch squares and serve with whipped cream.

Orange-Coconut Bars

Makes: About 12 squares

Base:
¹⁄₃ cup butter or margarine, softened
¹⁄₄ cup granulated sugar
grated rind of ¹⁄₂ fresh orange
1 cup flour

Filling:
¹⁄₂ cup packed light brown sugar, packed
¹⁄₂ cup nuts, chopped
¹⁄₂ cup flaked dried coconut
1 egg
2 tablespoons flour
¹⁄₄ teaspoon baking powder
grated rind of ¹⁄₂ orange

confectioners' sugar for dusting (optional)

Preheat an oven to 350°F. Have ready an 8-inch square baking pan.

To make the base, cream together the butter, sugar, and orange rind. Gradually stir in the flour. (The mixture will be crumbly.) Press evenly onto the bottom of the baking pan. Bake for 15 minutes, or until lightly browned.

Meanwhile, make the filling: In a bowl, combine all the ingredients, mixing well. Spread over the baked base and return to the oven. Bake for 20 minutes, or until the top is lightly browned. Remove from the oven and sprinkle with confectioners' sugar, if desired. Let cool, then cut into 2-inch bars.

Fruit Jelly Squares

Makes: 24 squares

1 ¹⁄₂ cups flour
1 ¹⁄₂ teaspoons baking powder
¹⁄₄ teaspoon salt
1 teaspoon ground cinnamon
¹⁄₂ teaspoon ground ginger

(continued)

1 cup sugar-coated fruit jellies (about 10 ounces), cut in half
½ cup pitted dates, cut into 2-inch pieces
1 cup walnuts, coarsely chopped
½ cup golden raisins
½ cup unsalted butter, softened
1½ cups packed light brown sugar
2 eggs
2 teaspoons vanilla extract
confectioners' sugar for dusting (optional)

Preheat an oven to 300°F. Butter a 9-inch square pan.

In a large bowl, sift together the flour, baking powder, salt, cinnamon, and ginger. Add the fruit jellies, dates, walnuts, and raisins, and stir just to combine the fruit and nuts with the flour mixture.

In a large bowl, using an electric mixer set on medium speed, beat together the butter and brown sugar until smooth. Add the eggs and vanilla and beat for 1 minute, stopping the mixer once at the midway point to scrape down the bowl sides with a rubber spatula. Reduce the speed to low and add the flour mixture, mixing just until incorporated. Spread the batter evenly in the prepared pan.

Bake for 1 hour, or until a toothpick inserted in the center comes out clean. Let cool in the pan on a rack for about 2 hours.

If desired, dust the top with confectioners' sugar. Cut into 24 squares and remove them from the pan. To store, wrap individually in plastic wrap and store in an airtight container.

Chocolate Date-Nut Bars

Makes: 20 bars

2 eggs
½ cup sugar
½ cup sifted flour
1 teaspoon baking powder
1 teaspoon vanilla extract
6 tablespoons chocolate syrup
½ cup walnuts, chopped
½ cup pitted dates, chopped
confectioners' sugar for dusting

Preheat an oven to 350°F. Grease a 9-by-13-by-2-inch baking pan.

In a large bowl, beat the eggs until well blended. Gradually beat in the sugar. In another bowl, sift together the flour and baking powder. Add the flour mixture to the egg mixture and beat until blended. Add the vanilla, chocolate syrup, walnuts, and dates. Beat together well. Spread in the prepared baking pan.

Bake for 25 minutes, or until lightly browned. Let cool, then cut into 1-by-3-inch bars. Dust with confectioners' sugar.

Rocky Road Bars

Makes: 10 squares

¼ cup sifted flour
¼ teaspoon baking powder
⅛ teaspoon salt
¾ cup packed light brown sugar
1 egg

1 tablespoon butter, softened
$^1/_2$ teaspoon vanilla extract
$^1/_2$ cup walnuts, finely chopped
1 cup marshmallows, quartered, or
    miniature marshmallows
$^1/_2$ cup walnuts, coarsely chopped
1 package (6 ounces) semisweet chocolate
    morsels

Preheat an oven to 350°F. Grease a 9-inch square pan.

Sift together the sifted flour, baking powder, and salt into a large bowl. Add the brown sugar, egg, butter, and vanilla and beat until smooth. Stir in the finely chopped walnuts. Turn into the prepared pan.

Bake for 15 minutes, or until the top is lightly browned and springs back when lightly touched. Remove from the oven and cover the top with, in the order given, the marsh-mallows, coarsely chopped walnuts, and chocolate morsels. Return the pan to the oven and bake for 12 minutes, or until the choco-late is softened. Remove from the oven, and swirl the chocolate through the marshmallows and walnuts. Let cool until the chocolate is set, then cut into 2-inch bars.

Cranberry-Pecan Bars

Makes: 20 bars

1$^1/_2$ cups pecans
2 cups flour
$^3/_4$ cup packed brown sugar

Cutting Bar Cookies

Here is the best way to cut bar cookies so they don't tear apart: As soon as you take the pan out of the oven, score the bars with a sharp knife. The next part is the hardest, however, for you must wait until the bars cool, and then cut along the scored lines.

(continued)

1 cup unsalted butter, chilled and cut into
bits
1 jar (10 ounces) seedless raspberry
preserves
³/₄ cup dried cranberries
¹/₃ cup flaked dried coconut

Preheat an oven to 350°F. Grease a 9-by-13-by-2-inch pan.

In a food processor, coarsely chop ¹/₂ cup of the pecans and place in a bowl. Add the remaining 1 cup pecans to the processor along with the flour, brown sugar, and butter and process until the dough clumps together, occasionally scraping down the sides of the processor bowl with a rubber spatula. Remove the dough from the processor and measure out 1 cup. Add the reserved pecans to the 1 cup dough and set aside. Pat the remaining dough onto the bottom of the prepared pan.

In a bowl, mix together the preserves and cranberries, then spread over the dough in the pan. Mix the coconut with the reserved nut mixture, pressing some together to form clumps. Sprinkle over the preserves layer in the pan.

Bake for 40 minutes, or until the top browns. Let cool on a rack, then cut into 2-inch bars.

Raspberry Streusel Squares

Makes: 20 squares

1¹/₂ cups flour
1 teaspoon baking powder
¹/₄ teaspoon salt
¹/₂ cup granulated sugar
¹/₂ cup packed light brown sugar
³/₄ cup butter, chilled
¹/₂ cup quick-cooking rolled oats
1 jar (10 ounces) red raspberry preserves
(³/₄ cup)
1 cup almonds, chopped
confectioners' sugar for dusting

Preheat an oven to 375°F. Lightly grease a 9-by-13-by-2-inch baking pan.

In a bowl, combine the flour, baking powder, and salt. Stir in the sugars. Add the butter and cut in with a pastry blender until crumbly; stir in the oats. Press ²/₃ cup of the crumb mixture onto the bottom of the prepared pan. Spread the preserves evenly over the dough. Add the almonds to the remaining crumb mixture, toss to mix, and then sprinkle over the preserves. Pat down lightly.

Bake for 30 to 35 minutes, or until golden. Let cool on a wire rack. Sprinkle with confectioners' sugar and cut into squares.

Golden Nugget Fudge Squares

Makes: 16 squares

> 2 squares (2 ounces) unsweetened
>   chocolate
> $1/2$ cup vegetable shortening
> 1 cup sugar
> 2 eggs, lightly beaten
> 1 teaspoon vanilla extract
> $1/2$ cup flour
> $1/4$ teaspoon salt (optional)
> 1 cup golden raisins, chopped
> $1/2$ cups walnuts, chopped

Preheat an oven to 350°F. Grease the bottom only of a 9-inch square baking pan.

In a saucepan, melt together the chocolate and shortening. Remove from the heat. Stir in the sugar, eggs, and vanilla until well mixed. Stir in the flour and the salt, if using, and then add the raisins and nuts. Pour into the prepared pan.

Bake for 25 to 30 minutes, or until firm. Let cool on a wire rack, then cut into squares.

BROWNIES

Elegant Brownies

Makes: About 12 brownies

> 1 package (4 ounces) sweet cooking
>   chocolate, broken into pieces
> $1/3$ cup butter or margarine

(continued)

Easy Brownie Cleanup

For easy cleanup when making brownies, try this: Line an 8-inch square baking pan with a large sheet of wax paper, letting the paper overhang the edges of the pan by 1 inch, then pour in the brownie batter. Bake and cool the brownies as directed, then simply lift them out of the pan by grasping the edges of the wax paper.

Coffee Royale

Serves: 1

1 teaspoon sugar
½ cup hot freshly brewed coffee
2 tablespoons brandy
2 tablespoons whipping cream

In a mug or Irish coffee glass, dissolve the sugar in the coffee. Add the brandy and stir well. Add the cream by pouring it over the back of a spoon so that it floats on top.

⅔ cup sifted flour
½ teaspoon baking powder
¼ teaspoon salt
2 eggs
½ cup sugar
½ cup walnuts, chopped
1 teaspoon vanilla extract

Preheat an oven to 350°F. Grease an 8- or 9-inch square pan.

In a saucepan, melt together the chocolate and butter over low heat, stirring constantly; let cool slightly. Meanwhile, sift together the flour, baking powder, and salt into a bowl. In a large bowl, beat the eggs until thick and light in color. Gradually beat in sugar, and then blend in the chocolate mixture. Add the flour mixture and mix well. Stir in the nuts and vanilla. Spread in the prepared pan.

Bake for 20 to 25 minutes for moist, chewy brownies, or 25 to 30 minutes for cakelike brownies. Let cool in the pan on a wire rack. Cut into squares or rectangles.

Espresso Brownies

Makes: About 24 brownies

1 tablespoon butter, melted
⅔ cup flour
⅓ cup unsweetened cocoa powder
5 teaspoons instant espresso coffee powder
¼ teaspoon salt
4 eggs
2 cups sugar

1 square (1 ounce) unsweetened
  chocolate, chopped
³/₄ cup butter
¹/₃ cup sour cream
1 teaspoon vanilla extract
2¹/₂ cups walnuts, chopped

Preheat an oven to 400°F. Line a 15¹/₂-by-10-by-1-inch jelly-roll pan with aluminum foil and brush with the melted butter. Sift together the flour, cocoa, espresso powder, and salt into a bowl; set aside. In a large bowl, cream the butter and sugar and beat on high speed for about 2 minutes, or until thickened. Beat in the eggs, sour cream, and vanilla. Add the warm chocolate mixture and the flour mixture all at once and beat on low speed until just blended. Fold in the nuts. Spread in the prepared pan.

Bake for 20 to 25 minutes, or until a knife comes out clean. Let cool on a wire rack, then cut into 2-inch squares.

Yummy Chocolate Marshmallow Squares

Makes: 36 squares

³/₄ cup unsalted butter, softened
1¹/₂ cups sugar
3 eggs
1 teaspoon vanilla extract
1¹/₃ cups flour
¹/₂ teaspoon baking powder
¹/₂ teaspoon salt
3 tablespoons unsweetened cocoa powder

¹/₂ cup chopped pecans (optional)
4 cups miniature marshmallows

Topping:
1¹/₂ cups (8 ounces) semisweet chocolate
  chips
3 tablespoons unsalted butter
1 cup chunky peanut butter
2 cups crisped rice cereal

Preheat an oven to 350°F. Grease a 9-by-13-inch jelly-roll pan.

In a bowl, using an electric mixer set on medium speed, cream together the butter and sugar. Add the eggs and vanilla and beat on high speed until fluffy. In another bowl, stir together the flour, baking powder, salt, and cocoa. Add the flour mixture to the butter mixture and beat until well combined. Stir in the nuts, if desired. Spread in the prepared pan.

Bake for 15 to 18 minutes. Remove from the oven. Sprinkle the marshmallows evenly over the cake and return to the oven for 2 to 3 minutes, or until marshmallows are lightly brown. Remove from the oven and, using a knife dipped in water, spread the melted marshmallows evenly over the cake. Let cool completely on a rack.

To make the topping, in a small saucepan, combine the chocolate chips, butter, and peanut butter. Place over low heat and cook, stirring constantly, until melted and well blended. Remove from the heat and stir in

(continued)

the cereal. Spread over the bars. Chill well, then cut into squares to serve.

Coffee Chocolate Chip Squares

Makes: 12 squares

$1/2$ cup vegetable oil
2 cups packed brown sugar
2 eggs
3 cups flour
1 teaspoon baking powder
1 teaspoon baking soda
1 teaspoon ground cinnamon
$1/2$ teaspoon salt
1 teaspoon vanilla extract
1 cup brewed coffee (cold)
2 cups (12 ounces) semisweet chocolate chips

Preheat an oven to 350°F. Grease a large baking sheet.

In a bowl, stir together the oil, sugar, and eggs, mixing well. In another bowl, stir together the flour, baking powder, baking soda, cinnamon, and salt. Add the flour mixture to the oil, blending well. Add the vanilla and coffee, mixing well. Stir in the chocolate chips, mixing well. Spread on the prepared baking sheet.

Bake for 15 minutes, or until a cake tester comes out clean. Let cool on a rack, then cut into squares to serve.

Sourdough Gingerbread

Serves: 6

$1/2$ cup packed brown sugar
$1/2$ cup shortening
$1/2$ cup dark molasses
1 egg
$1 1/2$ cups unbleached flour
1 teaspoon ground ginger
1 teaspoon ground cinnamon
1 teaspoon baking soda
$1/2$ teaspoon salt
$1/2$ cup hot water
1 cup active sourdough starter

Preheat an oven to 375°F. Grease an 8-inch pan.

In a large bowl, using an electric mixer set on medium speed, beat together the brown sugar and shortening until creamy. Then add the molasses and egg, beating continuously. In another bowl, sift together the flour, ginger, cinnamon, baking soda, and salt. Add the hot water and mix well, then beat the flour mixture into the creamed mixture. Finally, slowly add the sourdough starter, mixing carefully to maintain a bubbly batter. Transfer to pan.

Bake for about 30 minutes, or until a knife comes out clean. Serve with ice cream or whipped cream while still warm.

Chapter 7: Dessert Muffins and Breads

Serving muffins or a thin slice of a dessert bread at the end of a meal is becoming more popular as a perfect ending to a light meal of salad or pasta. And these sweet breads are also great during other times of the day, lightly toasted with a smear of butter or cream cheese on top.

You can add a mix-in or two—like walnuts or raisins—but it's a good idea to not go overboard because too many chunky items can cause the muffin or bread to become too moist or too crumbly after baking.

Rhubarb Muffins

Makes: 12 muffins

>   2 cups finely chopped rhubarb
> $^3/_4$ cup sugar
>   1 teaspoon grated orange rind
>   2$^1/_2$ cups flour
> $^1/_2$ teaspoon baking powder
>   1 teaspoon baking soda
>   1 teaspoon salt
>   2 eggs, beaten
> $^3/_4$ cup buttermilk
>   3 tablespoons butter or margarine, melted
>   and cooled

Preheat an oven to 375°F. Grease 12 muffin-tin cups.

In a bowl, combine the rhubarb with $^1/_4$ cup of the sugar and orange rind. Let stand for 5 minutes. In another bowl, stir together the flour, the remaining $^1/_2$ cup sugar, baking powder, baking soda, and salt. Make a well in the center. Stir together the eggs, buttermilk, and butter and add all at once to the well.

Stir quickly just until moistened. The batter should be lumpy. Gently fold in the rhubarb mixture. Spoon into the prepared muffin cups, filling each two-thirds full.

Bake for 20 to 25 minutes, or until the top springs back when touched. Cool on a rack.

Cornmeal Apricot Muffins

Makes: 12 muffins

>   1 cup cornmeal
>   1 cup flour
>   1 teaspoon salt
>   2 teaspoons baking powder
> $^1/_2$ cup apricot jam
> $^1/_8$ teaspoon grated orange rind
> $^3/_4$ cup milk
>   2 eggs, beaten
> $^1/_4$ cup butter, melted

Preheat an oven to 425°F. Have ready a greased 12-cup muffin tin.

Sift together the cornmeal, flour, salt, and baking powder in a bowl. In a saucepan,

warm together the jam and orange rind until the jam liquefies. Remove from the heat and let cool. Mix the milk and beaten eggs into the jam. Add the egg mixture to the flour mixture along with the melted butter. Beat until smooth. Spoon into the muffin cups, filling them almost to the top.

Bake for 15 to 20 minutes, or until brown. If the muffins are browning too fast, turn the oven down to 400°F. Let cool on a rack.

Microwaved Cocoa Muffins

Makes: 8 muffins

1 cup flour
²/₃ cup sugar
¹/₄ cup unsweetened cocoa powder
2 teaspoons baking powder
¹/₂ teaspoon salt
¹/₂ cup milk
¹/₄ cup cooking oil
1 egg, lightly beaten
1 cup raisins
¹/₂ cup nuts, chopped
butter or cream cheese for serving
   (optional)

In a bowl, combine the flour, sugar, cocoa, baking powder, and salt. Mix together the milk, oil, and egg in another bowl, and then add all at once to the flour mixture. Stir until just moistened. Fold in the raisins and nuts. Use half of the batter to fill 7 paper muffin cups half-full. Place the cups in a

microwaveproof cupcake or muffin pan. Microwave on HIGH for 2 to 2¹/₂ minutes, or until the top springs back slightly when touched. Repeat with the remaining batter. Serve warm, spread with butter or cream cheese, if desired.

Note: The cooking time for this recipe is geared to 7 muffins. If you are cooking less at one time, shorten the cooking time.

Date-Orange Muffins

Makes: 8 muffins

1 orange
¹/₂ cup orange juice
¹/₂ cup pitted dates, chopped
1 egg
¹/₂ cup butter or margarine, softened
¹/₂ cup flour
1 teaspoon baking soda
1 teaspoon baking powder
³/₄ cup sugar
pinch of salt

Preheat an oven to 400°F. Have ready an 8-cup greased muffin tin.

Cut the orange into pieces. Remove and discard the seeds and place the pieces in a blender. Process until the rind is finely ground. Add the orange juice, dates, egg, and butter and whirl briefly. Sift together the flour, baking soda, baking powder, sugar, and salt into a large bowl. Pour the orange mixture

(continued)

113

over the flour mixture and stir lightly. Spoon into the muffin-tin cups, filling each $^2/_3$ full.

Bake for 15 minutes, or until a knife comes out clean. Cool on rack.

Banana Loaf

Makes: 1 loaf

$^1/_2$ cup butter or shortening, softened
$^1/_2$ cup sugar
2 eggs, well beaten
2 cups flour
1 teaspoon baking powder
1 teaspoon baking soda
$^1/_2$ teaspoon salt
$^1/_3$ cup buttermilk
1 cup mashed ripe bananas
1 teaspoon vanilla extract
1 cup chopped nuts (optional)

Preheat an oven to 350°F. Grease and flour a loaf pan.

In a bowl, cream the butter until smooth. Gradually add the sugar, beating well. Stir in the eggs. In another bowl, sift together the flour, baking powder, baking soda, and salt. In yet another bowl, combine the buttermilk and bananas. Add the flour mixture to the butter mixture alternately with the banana mixture. Stir in the vanilla and fold in the nuts. Spread the batter in the prepared pan.

Bake for 30 minutes, or until a knife comes out clean. Cool on a rack.

Applesauce Bread

Makes: 1 loaf

$^1/_2$ cup butter or margarine, softened
1 cup sugar
1 cup applesauce
2 cups flour
1 teaspoon baking soda
1 teaspoon ground cinnamon
$^1/_2$ teaspoon ground cloves
1 cup raisins
1 cup nuts, chopped

Preheat an oven to 350°F. Grease and flour a 9-by-5-by-3-inch loaf pan.

In a large bowl, cream the butter until smooth. Gradually add the sugar, beating well. Add the applesauce and mix thoroughly. In another bowl, sift together the flour, baking soda, and all the spices. Add the flour mixture to the applesauce mixture. Stir in the raisins and nuts. Spread in the prepared pan.

Bake for 50 to 60 minutes, or until a knife comes out clean. Let cool on a rack.

Glazed Applesauce Bread

Makes: 1 loaf

$^1/_2$ cup vegetable shortening
1 cup granulated sugar
2 eggs
$^3/_4$ cup sifted flour
1 teaspoon salt

1 teaspoon baking powder
$^1/_2$ teaspoon baking soda
$^1/_2$ teaspoon ground cinnamon
$^1/_2$ teaspoon ground nutmeg
1 cup sweetened applesauce
$^1/_2$ cup walnuts, chopped

Sugar Glaze:

$^1/_2$ cup sifted confectioners' sugar
1 tablespoon water

Preheat an oven to 350°F. Grease a 9-by-5-by-3-inch loaf pan.

In a large bowl, stir the shortening to soften. Gradually add the granulated sugar, creaming until light. Add the eggs and beat until light and fluffy. In another bowl, sift together the flour, salt, baking powder, baking soda, cinnamon, and nutmeg. Add the flour mixture to the shortening mixture alternately with the applesauce, beating well after each addition. Stir in the nuts. Pour into the prepared pan.

Bake about 1 hour, or until a knife comes out clean. Let cool in the pan on a rack for 10 minutes, then turn out onto the rack.

Meanwhile, make the glaze: In a bowl, stir together the confectioners' sugar and water until smooth. While the loaf is still warm, spread the top with the glaze.

Apple-Date Bread

Serves: 1 loaf

$1^1/_2$ cups all-purpose flour
$1^1/_2$ cups whole-wheat flour
1 cup sugar
1 tablespoon baking powder
$1^1/_2$ teaspoons salt
1 cup flaked dried coconut
$1^1/_2$ cups milk
1 egg, lightly beaten
1 cup pitted dates, diced
1 cup peeled, seeded, and finely chopped
   apples

Topping:

$^3/_4$ cup packed light brown sugar
$^3/_4$ cup nuts, chopped
2 tablespoons butter, softened
$^1/_4$ cup all-purpose flour
$^1/_4$ teaspoon ground cinnamon
$^1/_4$ teaspoon salt

Preheat an oven to 350°F. Grease and flour a 9-by-5-by-3-inch loaf pan.

In a large bowl, mix together the flours, sugar, baking powder, and salt; stir in the coconut. In a small bowl, whisk together the milk and egg. Add to the flour mixture, blending well. Add the apples and dates. Mix well. Pour into the prepared pan. To make the topping, combine all the ingredients in a bowl and rub together with your fingertips until crumbly. Sprinkle the topping over the batter.

Bake for $1^1/_4$ hours, or until a knife comes out clean. Let cool on rack.

Pear Tea Bread with Lemon Glaze

Makes: 1 loaf

> 1 can (16 ounces) pear halves
> 2 $\frac{1}{2}$ cups flour
> $\frac{1}{2}$ cup granulated sugar
> 1 tablespoon baking powder
> 1 teaspoon salt
> $\frac{1}{8}$ teaspoon ground cardamom
> $\frac{1}{4}$ cup corn oil
> 1 egg, lightly beaten
> 2 teaspoons grated lemon rind
> $\frac{1}{2}$ cup pecans, chopped

Lemon Glaze:
> 1 tablespoon lemon juice
> $\frac{1}{2}$ cup confectioners' sugar

Preheat an oven to 350°F. Grease a 9-by-5-by-3-inch loaf pan.

Drain the pears, reserving the syrup. Set aside 1 pear half for garnish. Purée the remaining pear halves in a blender or food processor. Add enough of the reserved pear syrup to puréed pears to measure 1 cup. In a large bowl, lightly stir together the flour, granulated sugar, baking powder, salt, and cardamom. In another bowl, combine the puréed pear mixture with the oil, egg, and lemon rind. Stir the pear mixture into the flour mixture. Fold in the nuts. Pour into the prepared pan. Slice the reserved pear half into sixths; arrange the slices over the top of the batter.

Bake for 50 to 55 minutes, or until a knife comes out clean. While the tea bread is baking, make the glaze: In a bowl, stir together the lemon juice and confectioners' sugar to make a thin glaze. When the tea bread is ready, let cool in the pan on a rack for 5 minutes, then turn out onto the rack and spoon the glaze over the top. Let cool completely; wrap in aluminum foil and let stand overnight before serving.

Chocolate Banana Bread

Makes: 1 loaf

> 1 $\frac{1}{2}$ cups flour
> $\frac{1}{2}$ cup unsweetened cocoa powder
> $\frac{2}{3}$ cup granulated sugar
> 1 teaspoon baking powder
> $\frac{1}{2}$ teaspoon baking soda
> $\frac{1}{2}$ teaspoon salt
> $\frac{1}{2}$ cup vegetable shortening
> 1 cup mashed ripe bananas
> 2 eggs, lightly beaten
> confectioners' sugar

Preheat an oven to 350°F. Grease and flour a 9-by-5-by-3-inch loaf pan.

In a large bowl, combine the flour, cocoa, granulated sugar, baking powder, baking soda, and salt. Cut in the shortening with a pastry blender until the mixture resembles coarse crumbs. Add the bananas and eggs and stir with a fork just until blended. Spread in the prepared pan.

Bake for 50 to 55 minutes, or until a knife comes out clean. Let cool in the pan on a rack for 10 minutes, then turn out onto the rack to cool completely. Sprinkle with confectioners' sugar before serving.

Double Chocolate Babka

Serves: 10

1 cup semisweet chocolate chips
1 cup finely chopped pecans
1 1/2 cups sugar
2 teaspoons ground cinnamon
2 cups flour
1/3 cup unsweetened cocoa powder
1 1/2 teaspoons baking powder
3/4 teaspoon baking soda
1/2 teaspoon salt
1 cup unsalted butter, softened
1 1/4 cups sugar
1 teaspoon vanilla extract
3 eggs
1 cup sour cream

Preheat an oven to 350°F. Lightly grease a 10-inch tube pan.

To prepare the crumbs, in a small bowl, combine the chocolate chips, pecans, 1/4 cup of the sugar, and 1 teaspoon of the cinnamon; set aside. Onto a sheet of wax paper, sift together the flour, cocoa powder, baking powder, baking soda, the remaining 1 teaspoon cinnamon, and the salt.

In a bowl, using an electric mixer on high speed, beat together the butter and sugar until light and fluffy. Reduce the speed to medium and beat in the vanilla, and then the eggs one at a time.

Reduce the mixer speed to low. Beat in the flour mixture in three batches alternating with the sour cream, beginning and ending with the flour mixture and beating only until blended.

Spread half of the batter in the bottom of the prepared pan. Sprinkle with half of the crumb mixture. Top with the remaining batter and then the remaining crumb mixture, pressing the crumbs in lightly so they adhere. Cut through the batter and crumbs with a knife to swirl. Tap the pan once against a hard surface to settle the ingredients.

Bake for 40 minutes, then cover with aluminum foil. Continue baking for about 20 minutes longer, or until a knife inserted into the cake comes out clean. Let cool in the pan on a rack for 30 minutes. Using a sharp knife, carefully loosen the edges of the cake from around the sides of the pan and of the tube. Invert onto the rack, turn right side up, and let cool completely.

Dessert Egg Rolls

Serves: 6

3 pounds tart green apples, peeled, cored, and thinly sliced
1/4 cup apple juice
1/2 cup sugar, plus extra for sprinkling
1/2 cup apricot jam
grated zest of 2 lemons

(continued)

ground nutmeg to taste
apple pie spice to taste
1 cup chopped walnuts
12 egg roll wrappers
$1/2$ cup unsalted butter, melted
1 cup caramel sauce

Preheat a broiler. Butter a baking sheet.

In a large, heavy skillet, combine the apples, apple juice, $1/2$ cup sugar, jam, zest, nutmeg, and apple pie spice. Place over medium heat, cover, and cook until the apples are tender, 10 to 15 minutes. Stir in the walnuts, then taste and adjust the seasonings to taste.

Place several tablespoons of the apples in the center of an egg roll wrapper. Roll up. Fold in sides. Lightly moisten edges with water to seal. Place seam side down on the prepared baking sheet. Repeat until all the apples are used. Brush the tops with the melted butter and sprinkle with sugar.

Slip under the broiler for 3 to 5 minutes, or until golden. To serve, spoon a pool of caramel sauce onto each of 6 individual dessert plates. Place 2 egg rolls on each plate. Serve at once.

Vermont Maple-Cinnamon Swirls

Makes: 25

2 cups flour
$1/4$ cup plus 2 tablespoons granulated sugar
1 cup unsalted butter, chilled and cut into pieces

$1/4$ cup pure maple syrup, chilled, plus $1/2$ cup
2 tablespoons ice water
2 tablespoons brown sugar
4 teaspoons ground cinnamon

To make the pastry, in a bowl, using an electric mixer set on medium speed, briefly mix together the flour and the $1/4$ cup sugar. Add the butter and mix until the mixture forms large crumbs. Add the $1/4$ cup chilled maple syrup and the ice water. Reduce the speed to low and beat until the dough comes together in a rough mass. Do not overmix. Divide the dough in half and form each half into a disk. Wrap in plastic wrap and chill for 2 hours.

Preheat an oven to 325°F. In a small bowl, mix together the 2 tablespoons granulated sugar, the brown sugar, and the cinnamon. On a floured surface, roll out a dough disk into a 10-by-15-inch rectangle about $1/8$ inch thick. Sprinkle the dough with half of the cinnamon-sugar filling. Starting from a narrow side, roll up the dough into a log. Dampen the seam with water and press to seal. Repeat with the other dough disk. Wrap each log in plastic wrap and chill for 1 hour.

Using a sharp knife, cut each log into slices $1/4$ inch thick and place cut side down on an ungreased baking sheet about 1 inch apart. Brush the tops with the remaining $1/2$ cup maple syrup. Bake for about 20 minutes, or until light golden brown. Transfer to cool surface.

Chocolate Swirl Brioche

(Courtesy of Godiva Chocolates)

Makes: 2 loaves

Brioche dough:

2 tablespoons lukewarm water (110 °F to 115 °F)

1 teaspoon plus 2 tablespoons granulated sugar

2 teaspoons active dry yeast

3 1/2 cups flour

1 1/2 teaspoons salt

8 eggs, at room temperature

1 cup unsalted butter, softened

Chocolate filling:

3 squares (3 ounces) semisweet chocolate, finely chopped

1/2 cup whipping cream

1 egg, lightly beaten

1 teaspoon vanilla extract

1 egg lightly beaten with 1 teaspoon water

To make the brioche dough, in a small bowl, combine the lukewarm water with 1 teaspoon of the sugar. Sprinkle the yeast over the water and set the mixture aside for 10 minutes, or until foamy. (If the mixture is not foamy, the yeast may be inactive and should not be used.)

In the 4 1/2-quart bowl of a heavy-duty electric mixer fitted with the paddle attachment, combine the flour, the 2 tablespoons sugar, the salt, and the yeast mixture. Beat briefly on low speed until mixed. Add the eggs, one at a time, and beat until combined after each addition. Increase the speed to medium and continue to beat the mixture until the dough is smooth and elastic, about 3 minutes. Reduce the speed to low, and add the butter, 1 tablespoon at a time, beating after each addition until fully incorporated. Transfer the dough to a large, buttered bowl and turn to coat with butter. Cover the bowl with a tea towel and allow the dough to rise in a warm, draft-free place until almost doubled in bulk, about 1 1/2 hours.

While the dough is rising, make the chocolate filling: Place the chocolate in a bowl. In a small saucepan, bring the cream to a gentle boil. Pour the hot cream over the chocolate. Let stand for 30 seconds to melt the chocolate. Gently whisk the chocolate mixture until smooth. Whisk in the beaten egg and vanilla. Transfer the filling to a small bowl, cover with plastic wrap, and refrigerate until the brioche dough is ready to fill.

To shape the brioche dough, punch down the dough in the bowl, cover with plastic wrap, and refrigerate for at least 8 hours or for up to 2 days.

Butter two 8 1/2-by-4 1/2-by-2 1/2-inch loaf pans. On a floured work surface, divide the brioche dough in two. Working with one half of the dough at a time, roll each piece into a 7-by-15-inch rectangle. Spread half of the chilled chocolate filling over each rectangle and, starting at a narrow side, roll up each into a tight roll. Gently place each roll, seam

(continued)

side down, into one of the prepared pans. Cover the pans with a tea towel and allow the brioche loaves to rise at room temperature for 1 hour.

Preheat an oven to 375°F. Using a pastry brush, brush the egg wash over the tops of the brioche loaves. Bake the loaves for 35 to 40 minutes, or until they are a deep golden brown. Let cool in the pans on a wire rack for 10 minutes, then unmold and let cool completely on the rack before slicing.

White Chocolate Cranberry Quick Bread
(Courtesy of Godiva Chocolates)

Makes: 1 loaf

> $2^1/_4$ cups flour
> $^1/_2$ teaspoon salt
> $^1/_4$ teaspoon baking soda
> 5 squares (5 ounces) white chocolate, coarsely chopped
> $^1/_2$ cup unsalted butter, softened
> 1 cup sugar
> 3 eggs, at room temperature
> $^1/_2$ cup buttermilk
> 3 tablespoons orange juice
> 1 teaspoon grated orange rind
> 1 teaspoon vanilla extract
> $^3/_4$ cup dried cranberries, chopped

Preheat an oven to 350°F. Lightly butter and flour a 9-by-5-inch loaf pan. Tap out the excess flour.

In a bowl, using a wire whisk, stir together the flour, salt, and baking soda. Set aside.

In the top of a double boiler or in a heat-proof bowl, melt the white chocolate over simmering water. Set aside to cool.

In the $4^1/_2$-quart bowl of a heavy-duty electric mixer fitted with the paddle attachment, beat the butter at medium speed for 2 minutes until creamy. While continuing to beat the butter, gradually add the sugar 1 teaspoon at a time until completely incorporated into the butter. Beat in the eggs, one at a time. Using a rubber spatula, scrape down the sides of the bowl and beat the mixture for 1 minute more. Reduce the speed to low and beat in the buttermilk. At this point the batter will look curdled. Add the melted white chocolate, orange juice, orange rind, and vanilla to the batter and mix just until blended.

At low speed, add the flour mixture to the batter one-third at a time and mix until blended. Stir in the cranberries. Scrape the batter into the prepared loaf pan.

Bake for 70 to 75 minutes, or until a toothpick inserted in the center of the bread comes out clean. Let cool on a rack for 15 minutes. Turn the bread out of the pan and let cool completely on the rack.

SCONES

Simple Scones

Makes: 8 scones

> 2 cups flour
> $^1/_3$ cup sugar
> 2 teaspoons baking powder
> $^1/_4$ teaspoon salt

$^1/_3$ cup unsalted butter, chilled and cut into
    $^1/_2$-inch pieces
$^1/_2$ cup whipping cream
1 egg, lightly beaten
1 teaspoon vanilla extract
1 egg beaten with whipping cream

Preheat an oven to 375°F. Lightly grease a baking sheet.

In a large bowl, stir together the flour, sugar, baking powder, and salt. Add the butter and, using a pastry blender, work in the butter until coarse crumbs form. In a small bowl, combine the cream, egg, and vanilla. Add to the flour mixture and stir until just combined.

Turn out the dough onto a lightly floured work surface. Knead the dough gently until well mixed. Roll out into a 7-inch round. Cut into 8 wedges. Place the wedges on the baking sheet 2 to 3 inches apart. Brush the scones with the egg-cream mixture.

Bake for about 15 minutes, or until lightly browned. Cool on a rack.

Chocolate Scones

Makes: 8 scones

$1^2/_3$ cups flour
$^1/_3$ cup unsweetened cocoa powder
$^1/_3$ cup plus 1 tablespoon sugar, plus extra
    for sprinkling
1 teaspoon baking powder
$^1/_4$ teaspoon salt

$^1/_2$ cup unsalted butter, chilled and cut into
    bits
$^3/_4$ cup whipping cream
1 large egg, lightly beaten

Preheat an oven to 425°F. Lightly grease a baking sheet.

In a bowl, stir together the flour, cocoa, $^1/_3$ cup plus 1 tablespoon sugar, baking powder, and salt. Add the butter and, using a pastry blender, cut in until the mixture forms coarse crumbs. Add the cream and stir and toss with a fork just until the mixture starts to hold together.

Transfer the dough to a lightly floured board and knead lightly for a minute until the dough forms a ball. Form the dough into a 7-inch round. Cut into 8 wedges. Place the scones on the baking sheet. Brush the tops with the egg and sprinkle with the sugar.

Bake for 15 minutes, or until the edges feel firm. Let cool on a rack for 10 minutes before serving.

Apple-Cinnamon Scones

Makes: 12 scones

$^1/_2$ cup flour
$^1/_2$ cup whole-wheat flour
$1^1/_2$ teaspoons baking powder
$^1/_2$ teaspoon ground cinnamon
$^1/_3$ cup unsalted chilled butter, cut into
    small pieces
1 small apple, peeled, cored, and finely
    chopped

(continued)

1 cup quick-cooking rolled oats
2 egg whites
2 tablespoons apple juice
2 tablespoons honey

Preheat an oven to 400°F. Lightly grease a baking sheet.

In a bowl, stir together the flours, baking powder, and cinnamon. Add the butter and, using a pastry cutter, cut in until the mixture resembles coarse meal. Add the apple and rolled oats and mix thoroughly. Mix in the egg whites, apple juice, and honey; mix well. The dough will be sticky.

Form the dough into a 7-inch round directly on the baking sheet. Using a sharp knife, cut the dough into 12 wedges.

Bake for 10 to 12 minutes, or until golden. Cool on a rack.

Oatmeal Raisin Scones

Makes: 12 scones

> 4 cups flour
> $3^3/_4$ teaspoons baking powder
> 1 teaspoon baking soda
> 1 teaspoon salt
> 1 tablespoon ground cinnamon
> $1^1/_4$ teaspoons ground nutmeg
> $^1/_2$ teaspoon ground allspice
> $^1/_4$ teaspoon ground cloves
> $^1/_2$ cup granulated sugar, plus $^1/_3$ cup for topping
> $^1/_4$ cup packed light brown sugar
> $1^1/_2$ cups quick-cooking rolled oats

10 tablespoons unsalted butter, cut into cubes
2 tablespoons vegetable shortening
1 cup whipping cream
4 eggs
1 tablespoon vanilla extract
$1^1/_2$ cups dark raisins

Preheat an oven to 400°F. Set out 2 cookie sheets or rimmed baking sheets.

In a large bowl, whisk together the flour, baking powder, baking soda, salt, cinnamon, nutmeg, allspice, cloves, and the $^1/_2$ cup granulated sugar. Crumble over the brown sugar and blend it into the dry ingredients with your fingertips to disperse the small pellet-sized lumps of sugar. Stir in the rolled oats.

Drop in the chunks of butter and shortening and, using a pastry blender, cut the chunks into the flour until they are reduced to nuggets the size of large pearls.

In a bowl, whisk together the cream, eggs, and vanilla extract. Add the raisins to the flour along with the liquid mixture and stir to form a dough; it will be moist and sticky.

Turn out the dough onto a lightly floured work surface and knead 8 to 10 times. As necessary, continue to sprinkle the dough and work surface with extra flour, but avoid adding too much flour. (The dough should be very soft to the touch, and it will stick to the knife when cutting into wedges.)

Divide the dough in half, and form each piece into a $7^1/_2$-inch round. Cut each round into 6 pie-shaped wedges. Using a small metal

spatula, transfer the scones to the baking sheet, spacing them $2\frac{1}{2}$ to 3 inches apart. Sprinkle the tops of the scones with the $\frac{1}{3}$ cup sugar.

Bake the scones for 16 to 18 minutes, or until set. Let cool on the baking sheet for 1 minute, then remove them to a rack. Serve warm, or let cool completely, store in an airtight container, and reheat at another time.

Cherry Almond Scones

Makes: 12 scones

4 cups flour
$\frac{1}{4}$ cup finely ground almonds
4 teaspoons baking powder
$\frac{1}{2}$ teaspoon baking soda
1 teaspoon salt
2 teaspoons ground nutmeg
$\frac{3}{4}$ cup unsalted butter, cubed
$\frac{1}{2}$ cup superfine sugar
4 eggs
1 cup whipping cream
$1\frac{1}{2}$ tablespoons almond extract
1 tablespoon vanilla extract
1 cup dried pitted cherries
1 cup packed light brown sugar

Preheat an oven to 400°F.
In a large bowl, whisk together the flour, almonds, baking powder, baking soda, salt, and nutmeg. Drop in the chunks of butter and, using a pastry blender, cut the chunks into the flour until they are reduced to nuggets the size of large pearls. Stir in the superfine sugar.

In a bowl, whisk together the eggs, cream, almond extract, and vanilla extract. Add the dried cherries and the egg mixture to the flour mixture and stir to form a dough; it will be moist. Turn out the dough onto a lightly floured work surface and knead lightly about 10 times. If the dough is too sticky to handle, sprinkle the dough and work surface with extra flour. The dough should be soft to the touch.

Divide the dough in half, and form each piece into a $6\frac{1}{2}$- to 7-inch round about 1 inch thick. Cut each round into 6 pie-shaped wedges. Using a small metal spatula, transfer the scones to the baking sheet, spacing them about 2 inches apart. Sprinkle the tops with the brown sugar.

Bake for 17 to 18 minutes, or until set and light golden on top. Let cool on the baking sheet for 1 minute, then remove them to a rack. Serve warm, or let cool completely, store in an airtight container, and reheat at another time.

123

The Everything Dessert Cookbook

Chapter 8: Cookies

Whenever I remember the drop cookies cooling on wire racks after school, and the way the aroma wafted its way up to my bedroom, my blood pressure immediately drops a couple of points. The way the oven warmed the kitchen, and the sweet, often spicy smell of the cookies combined with the knowledge that school was over for another day, well, that was one of the best memories of childhood.

Probably more so than any other dessert, home-baked cookies represent a security blanket to many people. Whenever someone brings something from home into the office, inevitably it's cookies. You don't need utensils or plates, and even people who are watching their weight will treat themselves to one, because the average cookie is pretty small.

These days, people need more security blankets. Cookies are an easy, delicious way to fit the bill.

Snow Drops

Makes: 24 cookies

$^{7}/_{8}$ cup butter or margarine, softened
$^{1}/_{2}$ cup confectioners' sugar
2 cups cake flour
1 cup walnuts, chopped
2 teaspoons vanilla extract
1 teaspoon water
sifted confectioners' sugar for coating

In a large bowl, cream together the butter and confectioners' sugar. Stir in the flour, walnuts, vanilla, and water. Mix well. Cover and chill until firm enough to shape with your fingers.

Preheat an oven to 400°F. Form the dough into small date-shaped pieces and place on a greased baking sheet.

Bake for 10 to 12 minutes, or until lightly browned. Remove from the oven and immediately roll in sifted confectioners' sugar to coat evenly. Let cool completely on a rack.

Almond and Citron Cookies

Makes: 24 cookies

4 eggs, well beaten
2 cups sugar
$^{1}/_{2}$ cup flour
2 teaspoons baking powder

grated rind of 1 lemon
2 teaspoons ground cinnamon
1 teaspoon ground cloves
1 cup almonds, ground
1 package (8 ounces) candied citron, cut
   into small pieces

Preheat an oven to 400°F. Coat a baking sheet with nonstick cooking spray.

In a large bowl, combine the eggs and sugar and beat well. Add the flour, baking powder, lemon rind, cinnamon, cloves, ground almonds, and citron; mix thoroughly. Drop by level tablespoonfuls onto the prepared baking sheet, spacing them 1 inch apart.

Bake for about 8 minutes or until lightly browned. Do not overbake or the cookies will harden. Let cool completely on a rack, then store in a tightly covered container or freeze.

Apricot Crescents

Makes: 30 crescents

1 cup butter or margarine
1 package (8 ounces) cream cheese
2 cups flour
1 can (12 ounces) apricot pastry filling
   or jam
3 egg whites, lightly beaten
1 cup confectioners' sugar

In a bowl, combine the butter, cream cheese, and flour, blending to form a dough. Shape into 1-inch balls and chill for an hour.

Desserts on the Go

If you're planning a picnic, a quick lunch for yourself while traveling, or a walking or hiking excursion, the best desserts to bring are those that stand up to the rigors of the road without crumbling or melting. Of course, cookies fill the bill nicely. Bar or drop cookies made with dried fruits and nuts provide an extra nutrition boost in case you have to miss a meal.

(continued)

Cookie Storage

After you've gone to all the trouble of making great cookies, you want them to stay that way for a few days. Cookies should be kept in tins that can be tightly covered. Bar cookies can be stored in the baking pan lightly covered with aluminum foil for a day or two. If there are still some left after that, store in a cookie tin.

Preheat an oven to 350°F. On a floured surface, roll out the balls into 2-inch diameter circles. Spoon $1/2$ teaspoon filling onto the center of each circle. Fold the circles in half and then shape into crescents. On a plate, combine the nuts and sugar. In a shallow bowl, lightly beat the egg whites. Dip one side of each crescent first into the egg white and then into the nut mixture. Place coated side up on an ungreased baking sheet.

Bake for 25 to 30 minutes, or until golden brown. Let cool on a rack.

Scottish Shortbread

Makes: 24 wedges

4 cups flour
2 cups butter or margarine, softened
$1/2$ cup confectioners' sugar
1 teaspoon baking powder
$1/2$ teaspoon salt

Preheat an oven to 325°F.

In a large bowl, combine all the ingredients, blending and kneading by hand until well mixed and a soft dough forms. Divide the dough in half. Lightly press each half into the bottom of two 9-inch round cake pans or deep-dish pie plates. Prick the dough with a fork.

Bake for 45 minutes, or until golden brown. Cut each shortbread into 12 wedges; let cool completely in the pan on a rack. Remove from the pans and store in a tightly covered container.

Pineapple Shortbread Cookies

Makes: 36 cookies

1 cup margarine or butter, softened
1 package (3 ounces) cream cheese, softened
1 cup sugar
1 egg, lightly beaten
2 tablespoons thawed frozen orange juice concentrate
2¹/₂ cups flour
1 teaspoon baking powder
1 can (8¹/₂ ounces) crushed pineapple, drained

In a large bowl, cream together the margarine and cream cheese. Slowly beat in the sugar until light. Add the egg and juice concentrate and mix well. In another bowl, sift together the flour and baking powder. Mix into the cream cheese mixture. Fold in the pineapple and cover and chill for 30 minutes.

Preheat an oven to 375°F. Grease a baking sheet. Drop the dough by tablespoonfuls onto the prepared baking sheet. Bake for 10 to 12 minutes, or until lightly browned. Let cool completely on the baking sheet on a rack.

Hazelnut Espresso Shortbread Cookies

Makes: 48 cookies

2 cups flour
1 cup packed brown sugar
3 tablespoons cornstarch
4 teaspoons instant espresso powder
1 teaspoon salt
1 cup unsalted butter, chilled and cubed
1 teaspoon vanilla extract
²/₃ cup hazelnuts, coarsely chopped
2 tablespoons hot water
2 squares (2 ounces) semisweet chocolate, coarsely chopped

Preheat an oven to 350°F. Lightly grease two 9-inch round cake pans.

In a food processor, combine the flour, brown sugar, cornstarch, 3 teaspoons of the espresso powder, and the salt. Process until well blended. Add the butter and vanilla. Process until the mixture resembles coarse meal. Add the nuts and blend until finely chopped.

Transfer the dough to a floured work surface. Knead briefly until the dough forms a ball. Divide the dough in half and press into the bottoms of the prepared pans.

Bake for about 25 minutes, or until a deep golden brown. Let cool on a rack for 2 minutes. Place on a cutting board and cut each shortbread round into 24 wedges. Let cool completely.

In a small saucepan, stir together the hot water and the remaining 1 teaspoon espresso powder. Add the chocolate and stir over low heat until the chocolate is smooth. Remove from the heat and let cool for 10 minutes. Place the chocolate mixture in a pastry bag fitted with a ¹/₂-inch round tip and pipe the chocolate over the shortbread. Let stand until the chocolate hardens.

Mint Meringue Cookies

Makes: 16 cookies

2 egg whites
¹/₂ teaspoon cream of tartar
³/₄ cup sugar
¹/₄ teaspoon peppermint flavoring
few drops of green food coloring
1 cup semisweet chocolate morsels

Preheat an oven to 350°F.

In a bowl, beat together the egg whites and cream of tartar until fluffy. Add the sugar and beat until very stiff. Add the flavoring and the food coloring. Fold in the chocolate morsels. Drop by teaspoonfuls onto an ungreased baking sheet. The cookies will not spread during cooking, so they can be placed close together.

Place in the preheated oven and turn off the oven. Leave the cookies in the oven overnight, or until the oven cools.

Cake Mix Cookies

Makes: 36 to 40 cookies

1 package yellow cake mix
¹/₄ cup vegetable oil
2 teaspoons water
2 eggs
1 cup semisweet chocolate morsels
1 cup nuts

Preheat an oven to 375°F.

In a large bowl, mix together all the ingredients to form a soft dough. Using your hands, form the dough into small balls the size of walnuts. Place on ungreased baking sheets, spacing the balls about 2 inches apart.

Bake for 10 to 12 minutes, or until delicately browned. Let cool on the baking sheets for a few minutes before removing to racks to cool completely.

Almond Cookies

Makes: 20 cookies

¹/₂ cup butter or margarine
¹/₂ cup superfine sugar
¹/₂ teaspoon salt
¹/₄ teaspoon almond extract
1 egg yolk
1 cup unsifted flour
blanched almonds or walnut pieces

Preheat an oven to 350°F.

In a large bowl, cream together the butter, sugar, salt, and almond flavoring until light. Thoroughly beat in the egg yolk. Stir in the flour. Cover and chill for an hour before shaping. Using a level tablespoon for each, shape the dough into small balls and place them 1 inch apart on an ungreased baking sheet. Press an almond or piece of walnut onto the center of each cookie. The sides will crack slightly.

Bake for 15 to 18 minutes, or until the bottoms of the cookies are browned but the tops are still light. The edges will turn tan. Carefully remove to a rack to cool.

Pinwheel Cookies

Makes: About 36 cookies

¹/₂ cup butter or margarine, softened
1 package (3 ounces) cream cheese,
  softened
1 cup sugar
1 egg
1 teaspoon vanilla extract
2¹/₄ cups flour
¹/₂ teaspoon baking powder
¹/₂ teaspoon salt
¹/₈ teaspoon baking soda
¹/₂ cup unsweetened cocoa powder

In a large bowl, cream together the butter, cream cheese, sugar, egg, and vanilla until light. In another bowl, combine 1¹/₂ cups of the flour, the baking powder, salt, and baking soda. Mix the flour mixture into the butter mixture. Divide the dough in half. Add the cocoa to half of the dough and add the remaining ³/₄ cup flour to the remaining half. Roll each half into a 9-inch square. (If the dough is too soft to roll, chill it for 15 minutes.) Place the chocolate square on top of the vanilla square. Roll up jelly-roll style. Wrap tightly in wax paper or plastic wrap and chill for at least 1 hour or as long as overnight.

Preheat an oven to 350°F. Slice the dough into rounds ¹/₄ inch thick. Place the rounds on an ungreased baking sheet. Bake for 12 to 15 minutes, or until lightly browned. Remove to a rack to cool completely.

Sesame Cookies

Makes: 60 cookies

³/₄ cup butter or margarine, softened
1¹/₄ cups packed light brown sugar
1¹/₂ teaspoons vanilla extract
3 cups sifted flour
¹/₂ teaspoon salt
2¹/₄ teaspoons baking powder
1 egg
¹/₄ cup sesame seeds

Preheat an oven to 400°F.

In a large bowl, cream together the butter, sugar, and vanilla until light. Beat in the egg. In another bowl, sift together the sifted flour, salt, and baking soda. Stir the flour mixture into the butter mixture. (At this point the dough can be covered and refrigerated for up to an hour.) Shape into 1-inch balls. Dip the tops in the sesame seeds and place on ungreased baking sheets, spacing them about 1 inch apart. Using a fork, flatten each ball, forming a crisscross pattern on top.

Bake for 5 to 6 minutes, or until lightly browned. Let cool on the baking sheet on a rack.

Cocoa Indians

Makes: 40 cookies

²/₃ cup raisins, plumped in hot water to
  cover, drained
1 cup flour
¹/₄ teaspoon baking powder
¹/₄ teaspoon salt

(continued)

$^{1}/_{4}$ cup unsweetened cocoa powder
$^{1}/_{2}$ cup plus 2 tablespoons vegetable
    shortening
1 cup sugar
2 eggs
$^{1}/_{2}$ teaspoon vanilla extract
$^{1}/_{4}$ cup milk

Preheat an oven to 350°F.

In a bowl, combine the raisins, flour, baking powder, salt, and cocoa. In a large bowl, cream together the shortening and sugar until light. Beat in the eggs and vanilla. Add the flour mixture and the milk to the shortening mixture, combining thoroughly. Drop by teaspoonfuls onto a greased baking sheet.

Bake for 25 minutes, or until lightly browned. Let cool on a rack.

Peanut Butter Crackles

Makes: About 24 cookies

$^{1}/_{2}$ cup flour
1 teaspoon baking soda
$^{1}/_{2}$ teaspoon salt
$^{1}/_{2}$ cup margarine, softened
$^{1}/_{2}$ cup creamy or chunk-style peanut butter
$^{1}/_{2}$ cup granulated sugar
$^{1}/_{2}$ cup packed light brown sugar
1 egg
1 teaspoon vanilla extract
granulated sugar for coating (optional)
chocolate candy kisses or stars

Preheat an oven to 375°F.

In a bowl, stir together the flour, baking soda, and salt; set aside. In a large bowl, using an electric mixer set on medium speed, beat together the margarine and peanut butter until smooth. Beat in the sugars until blended, then beat in the egg and vanilla. Reduce the speed to low. Add the flour mixture, beating well. Shape the dough into $^{3}/_{4}$-inch balls. Roll in the granulated sugar to coat, if desired, and place on a baking sheet.

Bake for 10 minutes, or until lightly browned. Remove from the oven and quickly press a piece of chocolate candy firmly into the top of each cookie. (The cookies will crack around the edges.) Remove from the baking sheet and let cool on paper towels on a counter top.

Microwaved Chocolate Crackles

Makes: 30 cookies

$^{1}/_{4}$ cup butter or margarine
2 squares (2 ounces) unsweetened
    chocolate, premelted or solid
1 cup granulated sugar
2 eggs
2 teaspoons baking powder
1 teaspoon vanilla extract
$^{1}/_{2}$ teaspoon salt
$^{1}/_{2}$ cup nuts, chopped
2 cups flour
confectioners' sugar for coating

In a bowl, combine the butter and chocolate and microwave on MEDIUM for 1 to 4 minutes, or until melted. Stir well. Beat in the granulated sugar, eggs, baking powder, vanilla, and salt until well mixed. Stir in the flour and nuts. Cover and refrigerate overnight.

The next day, shape the dough into 1-inch balls and roll in confectioners' sugar. Put 6 to 8 balls in a large ring on a wax paper–lined microwaveproof baking sheet, dinner plate, pie plate, or paper plate. Put a single ball in the center. Microwave on MEDIUM for 1¼ to 3 minutes, or just until surface is dry, rotating the baking sheet or plate one-quarter turn every 30 seconds. Remove the wax paper with cookies to a countertop. Let cool. Repeat with the remaining dough.

Cherry Winks

Makes: 48 cookies

> 2⅔ cups cornflakes
> 2¼ cups sifted flour
> 1 teaspoon baking powder
> ½ teaspoon baking soda
> ½ teaspoon salt
> ¾ cup butter, softened
> 1 cup sugar
> 2 eggs
> 2 tablespoons milk
> 1 teaspoon vanilla extract
> 1 cup nuts, chopped
> 1 cup pitted dates, finely chopped
> ⅓ cup maraschino cherries, finely chopped
> 18 maraschino cherries, cut into quarters

Preheat an oven to 375°F. Grease a baking sheet.

Crush the cornflakes into fine crumbs; set aside. In a bowl, sift together the sifted flour, baking powder, baking soda, and salt; set aside. In a large bowl, beat together the butter and sugar until light and fluffy. Add the eggs and beat well. Stir in the milk and vanilla. Add the flour mixture to the butter mixture and mix well. Add the nuts, dates, and finely chopped cherries. Using a level tablespoon as a measure, shape the dough into balls. Roll the balls in the cornflake crumbs to coat. Top each ball with a cherry quarter and place on the prepared baking sheet.

Bake for 12 minutes, or until lightly browned. Cool on a rack.

Lace Cookies

Makes: 30 cookies

> ⅓ cup butter or margarine, softened
> ⅔ cup packed light brown sugar
> ¼ teaspoon salt
> ½ teaspoon baking powder
> 1 cup old-fashioned rolled oats
> ½ cup pecans, chopped
> 1 tablespoon milk
> ¼ teaspoon lemon flavoring

Preheat an oven to 350°F.

In a large bowl, cream together the butter and sugar until light and fluffy. Add the salt, baking powder, oats, pecans, milk, and lemon flavoring and mix well. Drop by teaspoonfuls about 2 inches apart onto an ungreased baking sheet.

(continued)

Bake for about 8 minutes, or until lightly browned. Let cool for 2 to 3 minutes, then remove from the baking sheet. (If the cookies harden before removal from the sheet, reheat them in the oven for a few minutes to soften.) The cookies will be very thin and lacy and must be very warm to roll into cornucopias. Roll cookies, one by one, to form a cornucopia, pinching the points slightly. Let cool completely on a rack.

Hermits

Makes: 30 cookies

1 cup packed light brown sugar
$1/4$ cup margarine, softened
$1/4$ cup vegetable shortening
$1/4$ cup cold strong brewed coffee
1 egg
$1/2$ teaspoon ground cinnamon
$1/2$ teaspoon ground nutmeg
$1^3/4$ cups flour
$1/2$ teaspoon baking soda
$1/2$ teaspoon salt
$1^1/4$ cups raisins
$3/4$ cup nuts, chopped

Preheat an oven to 375°F.

In a large bowl, mix together the brown sugar, margarine, shortening, coffee, egg, cinnamon, and nutmeg. Stir in the flour, baking soda, salt, raisins, and nuts. Mix well. Drop the dough by rounded teaspoonfuls 2 inches apart onto an ungreased baking sheet.

Bake for 8 to 10 minutes, or until almost no indentation remains when touched. Immediately remove to racks to cool.

Peanut Butter Sandwich Cookies

Makes: 20 cookies

$1^1/2$ cups flour
$1/2$ teaspoon baking soda
$1/4$ teaspoon salt
$1/2$ cup margarine, softened
$3/4$ cup creamy or chunk-style peanut butter
$1/2$ cup sugar
$1/4$ cup light corn syrup
1 tablespoon milk
$1/4$ cup strawberry preserves

In a bowl, stir together the flour, baking soda, and salt; set aside. In a large bowl, beat together the margarine and $1/2$ cup of the peanut butter until smooth. Beat in the sugar until blended, then beat in the corn syrup and milk. Add the flour mixture, beating only until smooth. Shape the dough into 2 logs, each 2 inches in diameter. Wrap in wax paper and refrigerate for 2 hours.

Preheat an oven to 350°F.

Slice the logs into $1/8$ inch-thick rounds. Place half of the cookies on ungreased baking sheets 2 inches apart. Spread $1/2$ teaspoon of the remaining peanut butter on each cookie. Top each cookie with $1/2$ teaspoon strawberry preserves.

Seal the edges by pressing lightly with a fork. Bake for 12 to 15 minutes, or until lightly browned. Remove to racks to cool.

Old-Fashioned Sugar Cookies

Makes: 48 cookies

> $3^1/_2$ cups sifted flour
> $^1/_2$ teaspoon salt
> 1 tablespoon baking powder
> 1 teaspoon ground nutmeg
> $^1/_2$ teaspoon ground cloves
> 1 cup lard, softened
> $^2/_3$ cup sugar
> 3 eggs
> 3 tablespoons milk
> sugar for sprinkling

Preheat an oven to 400°F. Grease 2 baking sheets.

In a bowl, sift together the flour, salt, baking powder, nutmeg, and cloves; set aside. In a large bowl, cream together the lard and sugar until light. Add the eggs one at a time, beating well after each addition. Add 1 cup of the flour mixture to the lard mixture and mix well. Stir in the milk. Add the remaining flour mixture. On a lightly floured work surface, roll out the dough $^1/_4$ inch thick. Using a round cookie cutter 3 inches in diameter, cut out cookies. Sprinkle with additional sugar. Place on the prepared baking sheets.

Bake for 8 to 10 minutes, or until lightly browned. Cool on a rack.

Cookie Baking Hints

For the best cookies ever, follow these tips: Always put your cookie batter on a cold baking sheet, to help the cookies retain their shape. If possible, and if your patience allows, try to bake only 1 sheetful of cookies at a time. This will help them to cook and brown more evenly. And finally, to add a bit of crispiness and a glow to sugar cookies, brush the cookies with a little beaten egg yolk before baking.

Chocolate Chip Cookies

Makes: 30 cookies

$^1/_2$ pound butter, softened
$^3/_4$ cup packed brown sugar
$^3/_4$ cup granulated sugar
2 eggs, beaten
1 teaspoon baking soda
1 teaspoon hot water
$1^1/_4$ cups sifted flour
1 teaspoon salt
1 teaspoon crème de cacao, or to taste
1 package (6 ounces) semisweet chocolate
   morsels
1 cup macadamia nuts, chopped

Preheat an oven to 375°F.

In a large bowl, cream together the butter
and sugars. Add the eggs and beat well. Add,
in the order given, the baking soda, hot
water, sifted flour, salt, and crème de cacao
and mix well. Fold in the chocolate chips and
the nuts. Drop by rounded teaspoonfuls onto
ungreased baking sheets.

Bake for 10 to 12 minutes, or until lightly
browned. Let cool on a rack.

Chocolate Chippers

Makes: 20 cookies

$^1/_2$ cup vegetable shortening
$^1/_2$ cup granulated sugar
$^1/_2$ cup packed brown sugar
1 egg
2 teaspoons vanilla extract

1 cup sifted flour
$^3/_4$ teaspoon salt
$^1/_2$ teaspoon baking soda
1 package (6 ounces) semisweet chocolate
   morsels
2 large candy canes, crushed
$^1/_2$ cup walnuts, chopped

Preheat an oven to 375°F. Grease a baking
sheet.

In a large bowl, cream together the shortening, sugars, egg, and vanilla until light and
fluffy. In another bowl, sift together the sifted
flour, salt, and baking soda. Stir the flour
mixture into the shortening mixture, mixing
well. Fold in the chocolate morsels, candy
canes, and walnut pieces. Drop by teaspoonfuls onto the prepared baking sheet, spacing
them about 2 inches apart.

Bake for 10 to 12 minutes, or until firm.
Remove immediately to racks to cool.

Chocolate Crinkles

Makes: 24 cookies

$^1/_2$ cup vegetable shortening
$^2/_3$ cup granulated sugar
2 teaspoons vanilla extract
2 eggs
2 squares (2 ounces) unsweetened
   chocolate, melted and cooled
2 cups sifted flour
2 teaspoons baking powder
$^1/_2$ teaspoon salt
$^1/_3$ cup milk

1/2 cup walnuts, chopped
sifted confectioners' sugar for coating

Preheat an oven to 350°F. Grease a baking sheet.

In a large bowl, cream together the shortening, sugar, and vanilla until light. Beat in the eggs, and then the chocolate. In another bowl, sift together the sifted flour, baking powder, and salt. Add the flour mixture to the shortening mixture alternately with the milk. Fold in the nuts. Cover and chill for 3 hours. Form into 1-inch balls. Roll in the confectioners' sugar to coat and place on the prepared baking sheet, spacing 2 to 3 inches apart.

Bake for about 15 minutes, or until firm on top. Let cool slightly on the pan, then remove to racks to cool completely.

Oatmeal Cookies

Makes: 30 cookies

1 cup vegetable shortening
1 1/2 cups packed brown sugar
2 eggs
1/2 cup buttermilk
1 3/4 cups sifted flour
1 teaspoon baking soda
1 teaspoon baking powder
1 teaspoon salt
1 teaspoon ground cinnamon
1 teaspoon ground nutmeg
3 cups quick-cooking rolled oats
3/4 cup raisins

1/2 cup walnuts, chopped
30 walnut halves (optional)

Preheat an oven to 400°F. Grease a baking sheet.

In a large bowl, cream together the shortening, brown sugar, and eggs until light and fluffy. Stir in the buttermilk. In another bowl, sift together the sifted flour, baking soda, baking powder, salt, cinnamon, and nutmeg. Stir the flour mixture into the shortening mixture. Stir in the rolled oats, raisins, and chopped nuts. Drop by tablespoonfuls onto the prepared baking sheet, spacing them 2 inches apart. Top each with a walnut half, if desired.

Bake for about 8 minutes, or until lightly browned. Let cool slightly, then remove to racks to cool completely.

Oatmeal Drop Cookies

Makes: About 6 dozen

1 cup vegetable shortening
1 cup granulated sugar
1 cup packed brown sugar
2 eggs
1/4 cup milk
1 tablespoon vanilla extract
1 1/2 cups flour
1 teaspoon baking soda
1 teaspoon cream of tartar
2 1/2 cups quick-cooking rolled oats
1 cup raisins
1 cup peanuts
1 package (6 ounces) chocolate morsels

(continued)

Preheat an oven to 350°F.

In a large bowl, cream together the shortening and sugars until light. Beat in the eggs, milk, and vanilla until well mixed. Stir in the flour, soda, cream of tartar, and oats. Stir in the raisins, nuts, and chocolate. Drop by teaspoonfuls onto ungreased baking sheets.

Bake for 10 to 12 minutes, or until light brown on the bottoms. Do not overbake. Let cool completely on racks.

Oatmeal Crispies

Makes: 60 cookies

1 cup vegetable shortening
1 cup packed brown sugar
1 cup granulated sugar
2 eggs, well beaten
1 teaspoon vanilla extract
$1/2$ cup sifted flour
1 teaspoon salt
1 teaspoon baking soda
2 cups quick-cooking rolled oats
$1/2$ cup walnuts, chopped
1 package (6 ounces) semisweet chocolate morsels

Preheat an oven to 350°F. Grease a baking sheet.

In a large bowl, cream together the shortening and sugars. Add the eggs and vanilla, mixing well. In another bowl, sift together the sifted flour, salt, and baking soda. Add the flour mixture to the shortening mixture. Add the oats, nuts, and chocolate morsels and

mix well. Drop by teaspoonfuls on the prepared baking sheet.

Bake for 10 minutes, or until lightly browned. Let cool on a rack.

Oatmeal Caramelinos

Makes: 16 squares

$1/2$ cups plus $4/2$ tablespoons flour
$1/2$ cups quick-cooking rolled oats
1 cup plus 2 tablespoons brown sugar
$3/4$ teaspoon baking soda
$1/2$ teaspoon salt
1 cup plus 2 tablespoons margarine, melted and cooled
$3/4$ cup chopped nuts
$1/2$ cups semisweet chocolate morsels
1 jar (12 ounces) caramel topping

Preheat an oven to 350°F.

In a bowl, combine the $1/2$ cups flour, the oats, brown sugar, baking soda, salt, and margarine. Mix well until crumbly. Divide the mixture in half and press half into an 8-by-10-inch pan.

Bake for 10 minutes, or until lightly brown on top. Remove from the oven. Sprinkle the chocolate morsels and nuts over the baked base. In a bowl, mix together the caramel topping and the $4/2$ tablespoons flour. Pour over the chocolate and nuts to cover. Sprinkle with the remaining oat crumb mixture.

Bake for 10 to 15 minutes, or until golden brown. Refrigerate or let cool at room temperature for 1 to 2 hours. Cut into squares.

Easter Cookies

Makes: 60 cookies

½ pound butter, softened
1½ cups sugar
3 eggs
½ cup orange juice
6 cups flour
2 teaspoons baking powder
½ teaspoon baking soda
1½ teaspoons vanilla extract
1½ teaspoons anise flavoring
1 egg beaten with 5 tablespoons milk, for glaze
sesame seeds
60 whole cloves

Preheat an oven to 375°F for aluminum pans or 350°F for dark nonstick pans. Grease 2 baking sheets.

In a large bowl, cream together the butter until soft. Add the sugar and mix thoroughly. Add the eggs one at a time, mixing well after each addition. Add the orange juice and mix well. Add the flour, baking powder, and baking soda and beat to combine. Add the vanilla and anise flavorings. Mix thoroughly. The mixture will be stiff and you may have to knead by hand in order to mix thoroughly. Shape into desired forms—usually a small figure 8—and place on the prepared baking sheets. Brush each cookie with the egg-milk mixture. Sprinkle with sesame seeds and place a whole clove in the center of each cookie.

Bake for 15 to 20 minutes, or until lightly brown. Let cool on a rack.

Coconut Kisses

Makes: About 18

2 egg whites
pinch of salt
1 cup sugar
½ teaspoon vanilla extract
2 cups cornflakes
1¼ cups flaked dried coconut
½ cup walnuts, chopped.

Preheat an oven to 350°F. Liberally grease a baking sheet.

In a bowl, beat the egg whites with the salt until soft peaks form. Gradually add the sugar, beating until stiff peaks form. Fold in the vanilla, cornflakes, coconut, and walnuts. Drop by teaspoonfuls onto the prepared baking sheet.

Bake for 20 minutes, or until done. Remove the cookies immediately to a rack. (If the cookies stick, return them to the oven to soften.) You can make them special with a spiral of melted chocolate, if you like.

Easy Coconut Macaroons

Makes: 24 macaroons

1 package (8 ounces) flaked dried coconut
⅔ cup sweetened condensed milk
1 teaspoon vanilla extract

(continued)

Preheat an oven to 350°F. Liberally grease a baking sheet.

In a bowl, mix together the coconut and condensed milk. Add the vanilla and mix well. Drop by teaspoonfuls onto the prepared baking sheet, spacing about 1 inch apart.

Bake for 8 to 10 minutes, or until firm. Let cool slightly on the baking sheet, then remove to a rack to cool.

Chewy Ginger Cookies

Makes: 30 cookies

$1/4$ cup vegetable shortening
$1/2$ cup sugar
1 egg
$1/3$ cup dark molasses
2 cups sifted flour
$1/2$ teaspoon baking soda
$1/2$ teaspoon salt
1 teaspoon ground ginger
$1/2$ teaspoon ground cinnamon
$1/2$ teaspoon ground cloves
$1/2$ cup water

Confectioners' Sugar Icing:

1 cup confectioners' sugar
$1/3$ cup butter
milk or whipping cream to moisten

30 pecan halves

Preheat an oven to 400°F. Grease a baking sheet.

In a large bowl, cream together the shortening and sugar until light. Beat in the egg,

then stir in the molasses. In another bowl, sift together the sifted flour, baking soda, salt, ginger, cinnamon, and cloves. Add the flour mixture to the shortening mixture alternately with the water. Drop by teaspoonfuls onto the prepared baking sheet, spacing them about 2 inches apart.

Bake for about 8 minutes, or until lightly browned. Meanwhile, make the icing: In a bowl, cream together the sugar and butter until light. Add the milk or cream as needed to form a smooth consistency. Stir until smooth.

When the cookies are ready, cool on a rack. While still warm, frost the tops with the icing. Top each cookie with a pecan half.

Gingersnaps

Makes: 40 cookies

$3/4$ cup vegetable shortening
1 cup packed brown sugar
$1/4$ cup dark molasses
1 egg
$2 1/4$ cups sifted flour
2 teaspoons baking soda
$1/2$ teaspoon salt
1 teaspoon ground ginger
1 teaspoon ground cinnamon
$1/2$ teaspoon ground cloves
granulated sugar for coating

Preheat an oven to 375°F. Grease a baking sheet.

In a bowl, cream together the shortening, brown sugar, molasses, and egg until fluffy. In

another bowl, sift together the sifted flour, baking soda, and all the spices. Stir the flour mixture into the molasses mixture until well mixed. Form into 1-inch balls. Roll in granulated sugar to coat and place on the prepared baking sheet, spacing them 2 inches apart.

Bake for about 10 minutes, or until lightly browned. Let cool slightly on the baking sheet on a rack, then remove to the rack to cool.

Peanut Butter Cookies

Makes: 48 cookies

> 1 cup vegetable shortening
> 1 cup granulated sugar
> 1 cup packed brown sugar
> 2 eggs
> 1 teaspoon vanilla extract
> 1 cup creamy peanut butter
> 3 cups sifted flour
> 2 teaspoons baking soda
> $1/2$ teaspoon salt

Preheat an oven to 350°F.

In a bowl, cream together the shortening, sugars, eggs, and vanilla until light and fluffy. Stir in the peanut butter. In another bowl, sift together the sifted flour, baking soda, and salt. Stir the flour mixture into the creamed mixture. Drop by rounded teaspoonfuls onto an ungreased baking sheet. Using the back of a floured fork, press each cookie to form a crisscross pattern.

Bake for about 10 minutes, or until light brown. Let cool on a rack.

Richer Peanut Butter Cookies

If you want a peanut butter cookie that is richer in taste and texture than the traditional variety made in the previous recipe, reduce the amount of flour that you use from 3 cups down to 2 cups. The ratio of flour to butter—whether butter or peanut butter—is what determines how rich a cookie will be.

Pecan Sandies

Makes: 48 cookies

1 cup butter or margarine, softened
1 cup granulated sugar
2 teaspoons vanilla extract
2 teaspoons water
2 cups flour
1 cup pecans, chopped
confectioners' sugar for coating

Thin Chocolate Icing (optional):

¹/₃ cup butter or margarine, softened
about 1 cup confectioners' sugar
¹/₄ cup chocolate syrup

Preheat an oven to 325°F.

In a large bowl, cream together the butter and granulated sugar until light. Add the vanilla and water, mixing well. Add the flour and again mix well. Stir in the pecans. Shape into small balls or sticks. Place on an ungreased baking sheet. Bake for about 20 minutes, or until lightly browned. Remove to a rack and let cool slightly. Meanwhile, if desired, make the icing: In a bowl, cream together the butter and half of the confectioners' sugar. Gradually add as much of the remaining sugar as needed to form a smooth consistency. Stir in the chocolate syrup. Roll the warm cookies in confectioners' sugar. If desired, dip one end of each stick in thin chocolate icing.

Black-Eyed Susans

Makes: About 30 cookies

³/₄ cup butter, softened
¹/₂ cup sugar
1 egg
1 teaspoon vanilla extract
¹/₄ teaspoon salt
1³/₄ cups sifted flour
1 package (7 ounces) chocolate-mint candy wafers (not cream filled)

In a large bowl, cream together the butter, sugar, and egg until light. Add the vanilla and salt and mix well. Stir in the flour. Cover and chill for 1 hour. Preheat an oven to 400°F. Shape the dough into 1-inch balls and place on an ungreased baking sheet. Top each cookie with a chocolate-mint candy wafer.

Bake for 8 to 10 minutes, or until lightly browned. Let cool on a rack.

Chocolate Lime Swirl

Serves: 8

1 package (20 ounces) chocolate wafers
3 tablespoons butter, melted and cooled
1 package (3.4 ounces) lemon Jell-O
¹/₂ cup hot water
¹/₄ cup lemon juice
¹/₄ cup granulated sugar
1 can (8 ounces) evaporated milk
1 teaspoon grated lemon rind
few drops of green food coloring

Butter a deep 9-inch glass pie plate. Line the edges with whole wafers. Crush the remaining wafers. Mix three-fourths of the crumbs with the melted butter. Spread on the bottom of the pie plate. In a bowl, dissolve the Jell-O in the hot water. Add the lemon juice and sugar. Whip the evaporated milk until soft peaks form. Add the Jell-O mixture, rind, and coloring and stir well. Turn into the pie plate. Sprinkle with the remaining one-fourth of wafer crumbs. Freeze.

Marshmallow Refrigerator Squares

Makes: 30 squares

> 30 marshmallows, quartered
> 8 maraschino cherries, cut up
> $1/2$ cup walnuts, chopped
> 2 cups graham cracker crumbs
> 1 can (14 ounces) condensed milk
> $1/2$ cup flaked dried coconut

In a bowl, mix together the marshmallows, cherries, walnuts, and cracker crumbs. Add the milk and mix well. Butter a 9-by-13-by-2-inch pan. Sprinkle the bottom of the prepared pan with $1/4$ cup of the coconut. Add the mixture and press down. Sprinkle with the remaining $1/4$ cup coconut. Cover and chill. Cut into squares.

Crispy Oatmeal Cookies

Makes: 48 cookies

> 1 cup vegetable shortening
> 1 cup packed brown sugar
> 1 cup granulated sugar
> 2 eggs
> 1 teaspoon vanilla extract
> $1 1/2$ cups sifted flour
> 1 teaspoon salt
> 1 teaspoon baking soda
> 3 cups quick-cooking rolled oats
> $1/2$ cup walnuts, chopped

In a large bowl, cream together the shortening and sugars. Add the eggs and vanilla and mix well. In another bowl, sift together the flour, salt, and baking soda. Add the flour mixture to the shortening mixture. Stir in the rolled oats and nuts. Mix well. Form the dough into logs, 1 to $1 1/2$ inches in diameter. Wrap in wax paper, aluminum foil, or plastic wrap. Chill well.

Preheat an oven to 350°F. Slice the logs about $1/4$ inch thick. Arrange the cookies on an ungreased baking sheet.

Bake for 10 minutes, or until lightly browned. Let cool on a rack.

Spicy Slices

Makes: 36 cookies

> 1 cup vegetable shortening
> $1/2$ cup granulated sugar
> $1/2$ cup packed brown sugar

(continued)

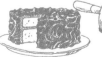

143

1 egg
2 1/4 cups sifted flour
1/2 teaspoon baking soda
1/2 teaspoon salt
2 teaspoons ground cinnamon
1/4 teaspoon ground nutmeg
1/4 teaspoon ground cloves
1/2 cup walnuts, finely chopped

In a bowl, cream together the shortening and sugars until light. Add the egg and beat well. In another bowl, sift together the sifted flour, baking soda, salt, and all the spices. Stir the flour mixture into the shortening mixture. Fold in the nuts. Shape into logs about 2 1/2 inches in diameter. Wrap in wax paper, aluminum foil, or plastic wrap. Chill well.

Preheat an oven to 375°F. Lightly grease a baking sheet. Slice the logs 1/8-inch-thick or less. Arrange the cookies on the prepared baking sheet. Bake for 5 to 7 minutes, or until delicately browned. Remove at once to a rack to cool.

Candy Bar Cookies

Makes: 24 cookies

1 1/4 cups flour
3/4 teaspoon baking powder
1/4 teaspoon salt
1/2 cup unsalted butter, softened
1/2 cup sugar
1 egg
1 teaspoon vanilla extract

1 cup chopped chocolate-covered candy bars (about 5 to 6 ounces, 1/2-inch pieces)

Preheat an oven to 325°F.

In a bowl, sift together the flour, baking powder, and salt. In a large bowl, using an electric mixer set on medium speed, beat together the butter and sugar until fluffy and smooth, about 30 seconds. Mix in the egg and vanilla and beat for 1 minute, stopping the mixer once at the midway point to scrape down the sides with a rubber spatula. Reduce the speed to low and add the flour mixture, mixing just until incorporated. Gently mix in the candy bar pieces.

Drop the batter by large tablespoons onto ungreased baking sheets.

Bake for 15 minutes, or until lightly browned. Remove while warm to prevent sticking. Cool on wire racks.

Amaretto Cookies

Makes: 48 cookies

8 ounces marzipan or almond paste
1 cup sugar, plus extra for sprinkling on cookies
2 egg whites

Preheat an oven to 375°F. Lightly grease 2 baking sheets with shortening.

In a large mixing bowl, combine the marzipan with the 1 cup sugar. Using an electric mixer set on low speed, beat until the

mixture resembles sugar granules. Add the egg whites in two stages, mixing well after each stage. Increase the speed to medium and beat until smooth, about 5 minutes.

Fill a pastry bag with the mixture, and fit the bag with a 1/2-inch round tip. Pipe the mixture onto the prepared pans in 2-inch rounds spaced about 1 inch apart. Using a damp teaspoon, lightly press down on the surface of each cookie to smooth the surface. Sprinkle sugar on each cookie.

Bake for 15 minutes, or until cookies are lightly browned. Cool on a rack.

Chocolate Chip Madeleines

Makes: 24 cookies

> $^1/_2$ cup unsalted butter
> 1 cup flour
> $^1/_2$ teaspoon baking powder
> pinch of salt
> 3 eggs
> $^2/_3$ cup granulated sugar
> 1 teaspoon vanilla extract
> $^1/_2$ cup semisweet chocolate chips
> confectioners' sugar for dusting

In a small saucepan, melt the butter over low heat just until it starts to turn a light golden brown color, about 5 minutes. Remove from the heat and let cool until almost at room temperature.

In a small bowl, whisk together the flour, baking powder, and salt until well blended. In a large bowl, using an electric mixer set

on medium speed, beat together the eggs and granulated sugar until the mixture forms a thick ribbon when the beaters are lifted, about 8 to 10 minutes. Beat in the vanilla.

Gently fold the flour mixture into the egg mixture in two stages. Follow by folding in the melted butter in two stages, and then fold in the chocolate chips. Cover with plastic wrap and refrigerate for 30 minutes, until it becomes slightly firm.

Preheat an oven to 375°F. Grease and flour two 12-mold madeleine pans.

Drop a heaping tablespoonful of the batter into each prepared mold; do not flatten or smooth the centers.

Bake for 15 minutes, or until the edges have browned slightly and the centers spring back when touched with a finger. Remove from the oven and tap each mold with a knife to free the madeleines. Place on a rack to cool completely.

To serve, dust with confectioners' sugar.

Brandy Snaps Filled with Whipped Cream

Makes: 30 cookies

> $^1/_2$ cup plus 2 tablespoons unsalted butter
> $^2/_3$ cup light corn syrup
> $^1/_4$ cup packed light brown sugar
> $1^1/_4$ teaspoons ground ginger
> pinch of salt
> 1 cup flour
> 1 tablespoon brandy

(continued)

Whipped Cream Filling:

2 cups whipping cream
1 tablespoon sugar
2 teaspoons brandy
1 teaspoon vanilla extract

Preheat an oven to 350°F. Generously butter a baking sheet.

In a large saucepan over high heat, combine the butter, corn syrup, brown sugar, ginger, and salt. Bring to a boil, stirring often. Remove from the heat and stir in the flour and brandy.

Drop the batter by tablespoonfuls onto the prepared baking sheet. Since the snaps will spread out to 4 inches in diameter, bake only 4 cookies at a time on each sheet.

Bake for 7 minutes, or until the cookies turn golden brown. Remove from the oven and let the cookies cool on the sheet for 30 to 60 seconds, or until they can be lifted with a spatula without creasing. Taking 1 snap at a time, roll it tightly around the handle of a wooden spoon. After it is rolled, place each cookie, seam side down, on a rack to cool completely.

While the cookies are cooling, make the filling: In a large bowl, combine the cream, sugar, brandy, and vanilla. Cover and refrigerate for at least 30 minutes. Remove from the refrigerator and, using an electric mixer, beat until stiff peaks form.

Spoon the whipped cream into a pastry bag fitted with a large pastry tip and fill the brandy snaps with whipped cream.

Spice Cookies

Makes: About 40 cookies

^{2}/$_3$ cup dark corn syrup
^{1}/$_2$ cup packed light brown sugar
^{1}/$_2$ cup unsalted butter
scant 1 ^{1}/$_4$ cups slivered blanched almonds (about 6 ounces)
2 cups sifted flour
^{1}/$_4$ teaspoon baking soda
^{1}/$_2$ teaspoon ground allspice
2 teaspoons ground ginger
1 teaspoon ground cinnamon
1 teaspoon salt
^{1}/$_2$ teaspoon white pepper
4 teaspoons dark rum
^{1}/$_2$ teaspoon almond extract
finely grated rind of 2 large lemons

Preheat an oven to 350°F.

In a saucepan over medium heat, combine the corn syrup, sugar, and butter. Stir occasionally until the mixture comes to a boil. Boil for 2 minutes, then set aside to cool for 15 minutes.

Spread the almonds on a baking sheet and toast in the oven, stirring a few times, until lightly browned, about 12 minutes. Let cool.

In a bowl, sift together the flour, baking soda, allspice, ginger, cinnamon, salt, and pepper. Set aside.

Measure out about ^{1}/$_4$ cup of the toasted almonds and chop into small pieces. Set aside. Put the remaining almonds in a food

processor. Add $^1/_4$ cup of the flour mixture and process until the nuts are finely ground, about 30 seconds. Set aside.

Stir the rum, almond extract, and the grated rind into the corn syrup mixture. Add the processed nut mixture to the flour mixture and stir to mix. Add the corn syrup mixture and again stir to mix.

Measure out three 12-inch squares of plastic wrap. Place one-third of the mixture on each square. Flatten slightly, wrap, and chill for 1 hour or more.

Preheat an oven to 375°F. Lightly grease 2 baking sheets.

On a lightly floured work surface, roll out the dough $^1/_8$ inch thick. Using a 3-inch round cookie cutter, cut out rounds and transfer them to the prepared sheet, spacing 2 inches apart. Sprinkle with the $^1/_4$ cup chopped nuts.

Bake for 8 to 10 minutes, or until lightly browned. Let cool completely on racks. Store in an airtight container.

Chocolate Chocolate Cookies

Makes: 24 cookies

> 1 pound bittersweet or semisweet
>   chocolate, finely chopped
> 1$^1/_2$ cups sugar
> 4 eggs
> $^1/_4$ cup unsalted butter, melted
> 1 tablespoon vanilla extract
> 1 teaspoon instant coffee powder

> $^1/_2$ cup cake flour
> 1 teaspoon baking powder
> $^1/_2$ teaspoon salt
> 2$^1/_2$ cups semisweet chocolate chips
> 1 cup chopped walnuts

In the top of a double boiler, melt the chocolate over simmering water, stirring occasionally. Remove from the heat and let cool.

In a bowl, using an electric mixer set on medium speed, beat together the sugar and eggs until pale yellow, about 5 minutes. Stir in the melted chocolate, melted butter, vanilla, and coffee powder. Set aside. In a small bowl, sift together the flour, baking powder, and salt. Add the flour mixture to the chocolate mixture and stir until combined. Then stir in the chocolate chips and nuts. Cover and refrigerate until firm, about 30 minutes.

Preheat an oven to 350°F. Lightly grease 2 large baking sheets.

Drop the batter by $^1/_4$ cupfuls onto the prepared sheets. Press with moist fingertips to form 4-inch rounds.

Bake about 15 minutes, or until the tops crack. Let cool completely on a rack. Store in an airtight container.

Chocolate-Walnut Truffle Cookies

Makes: 48 cookies

Cookie Dough:
1$^3/_4$ cups flour
$^3/_4$ cup unsweetened cocoa powder

(continued)

$^1/_2$ teaspoon salt
$^3/_4$ cup packed light brown sugar
$^1/_4$ cup granulated sugar
$^1/_3$ cup chopped walnuts
1 cup unsalted butter, chilled and cubed
1 teaspoon vanilla extract

Truffle Filling:

8 squares (8 ounces) semisweet or
    bittersweet chocolate, chopped
$^1/_2$ cup whipping cream
2 tablespoons unsalted butter, softened,
    cubed
2 tablespoons brandy

Preheat an oven to 300°F. Lightly grease 2 baking sheets.

To make the cookie dough, stir together the flour, cocoa powder, and salt. Set aside.

Place the sugars and walnuts in a food processor. Process until the nuts are finely ground, about 30 seconds. With the motor running, add the butter and the vanilla and process for a few seconds more, until the mixture is smooth and creamy. Add the flour mixture and process for about 15 seconds until a ball of dough forms.

Transfer the dough to a lightly floured work surface and divide it in half. Roll out each half $^1/_8$ inch thick. Using a 2-inch round cookie cutter, cut out cookies and transfer to the baking sheet. Repeat with the rest of the dough.

Bake for about 10 minutes, or until the cookies crack on top. Let them cool on the sheets for 5 minutes and then transfer to racks to cool completely.

While the cookies are cooling, prepare the truffle mixture: Place the chocolate into a heatproof bowl. In a small saucepan over medium heat, bring the cream to a boil and pour over the chocolate. Stir until the chocolate is fully melted and smooth. Mix in the butter and the brandy. Cover and chill for 15 minutes.

Arrange the cookies on lightly greased baking sheets. Put the truffle mixture into a pastry bag fitted with a large star tip and pipe a large star onto each cookie. Place 1 teaspoonful of the truffle mixture in the center of each cookie. Chill for at least 2 hours before serving.

Ladyfingers

Makes: 30 cookies

1 $^1/_4$ cups cake flour
$^1/_2$ cup granulated sugar
4 egg whites, at room temperature
6 egg yolks, at room temperature
1 teaspoon vanilla extract
1 cup confectioners' sugar

Preheat an oven to 350°F. Line 2 baking sheets with wax paper.

In a large bowl, sift together the flour and the $^1/_4$ cup granulated sugar; set aside. In another bowl, using an electric mixer set on high speed, beat the egg yolks until the mixture thickens and is pale yellow, 3 to 5

minutes. Add the vanilla and beat briefly.
Set aside.

In a large bowl, using clean beaters, beat
the egg whites with an electric mixer set on
low speed until small bubbles appear, about
30 seconds. Increase the speed to medium
and add 1 teaspoon of the granulated sugar.
Continue whipping until soft, white peaks
form, about 1 minute. Add the rest of the
granulated sugar in a steady stream. Continue
whipping until thicker, stiffer, glossy peaks
form, about 2 minutes.

Using a rubber spatula, gently fold the
yolks into the egg white mixture with a few
strokes. Take about one-third of the flour
mixture, sprinkle it over the surface of the
eggs, and gently fold in with the spatula.
Repeat until the ingredients are blended.

Place the batter into a pastry bag fitted
with a 2-inch round tip. Pipe the batter into
5-inch-long ladyfingers, spacing them $1/2$ inch
apart. You'll have about 15 ladyfingers on
each sheet. With a sifter, gently dust the
confectioners' sugar over the ladyfingers.

Bake for about 10 minutes, or until the
ladyfingers spring back when lightly touched.
When done, remove the baking sheets from
the oven and remove the wax paper with the
ladyfingers on it to a wire rack. After 5
minutes, gently remove the ladyfingers to the
rack to cool thoroughly. To store, place in a
plastic container with wax paper between the
layers.

Balancing Your Menu

If you're leafing through *The Everything Dessert Book* in order to find the perfect dessert to balance a particular menu, try to keep in mind that opposites attract. In other words, if your entrée is rich, go for a light fruit-based dessert. Or if you are serving a light salad or sandwiches, choose a calories-be-damned chocolate dessert.

Peanut Butter Krisps

Makes: 60 krisps

4 cups chunky peanut butter
1 cup unsalted butter, softened
7 cups confectioners' sugar
5 cups crisped rice cereal
4 ounces paraffin, finely chopped
6 cups (2 1/4 pounds) milk chocolate chips

Lightly grease 4 baking sheets.

In a large bowl, using a large spoon, blend together the peanut butter and butter until smooth. Add the confectioners' sugar and the cereal and stir until thoroughly mixed. Form the mixture into 1-inch balls and place on the baking sheets. Chill well.

In the top of a double boiler over simmering water, melt the paraffin and the chocolate chips. Using a ladle, dip each ball in the chocolate mixture, coating thoroughly. Remove and set on wax paper to dry. Store in an airtight container.

Double-Chocolate Coconut Macaroons
(Courtesy of Godiva Chocolates)

Makes: About 4 dozen cookies

2 squares (2 ounces) bittersweet
chocolate, coarsely chopped
2 squares (2 ounces) semisweet chocolate,
coarsely chopped
2 egg whites, at room temperature
pinch of salt

2/3 cup sugar
1 teaspoon vanilla extract
2 2/3 cups (one 7-ounce bag) sweetened
shredded coconut
3/4 cup mini semisweet chocolate chips

Position a rack in the bottom third of an oven and another in the top third. Preheat to 325°F. Line 2 baking sheets with aluminum foil.

In the top of a double boiler or in a heat-proof bowl, combine the bittersweet and semi-sweet chocolates over simmering water and heat until melted. Stir until smooth and remove from over the water.

In a bowl, using an electric mixer set on low speed, beat together the egg whites and salt until frothy. Increase the speed to medium-high and beat until the whites start to form soft peaks. One tablespoon at a time, add the sugar, and continue beating until the whites form stiff, glossy peaks. Using a rubber spatula, fold in the melted chocolate and the vanilla. Fold in the coconut, and then the chocolate chips.

Drop the batter by rounded teaspoonfuls onto the prepared baking sheets, forming neat mounds and leaving about 1 1/2 inches between the cookies. Bake for 12 to 14 minutes, or until the cookies are just set and their surfaces look dull, switching the positions of the baking sheets halfway through baking for even baking. Do not overbake, or the macaroons will be dry.

Let the cookies cool on the baking sheets on racks for 2 to 3 minutes. Then, using a metal spatula, transfer the cookies to racks to cool completely. Repeat with the remaining batter. The cookies can be stored in an airtight container at room temperature for up to 5 days.

BISCOTTI

Orange Biscotti

Makes: 30 cookies

$1^2/_3$ cups flour
$^1/_2$ teaspoon baking soda
$^1/_4$ teaspoon salt
2 eggs
2 teaspoons Grand Marnier liqueur
1 teaspoon vanilla extract
grated zest of 2 oranges
$^3/_4$ cup sugar
$^2/_3$ cup whole blanched almonds, coarsely
    chopped

Preheat an oven to 300°F. Lightly grease a baking sheet.

In a bowl, stir together the flour, baking soda, and salt. Set aside. In another bowl, combine the eggs, liqueur, vanilla, orange zest, and sugar. Add the flour mixture to the egg mixture, stirring just to mix. Add the nuts and mix just until incorporated. You may want to mix it with your hands.

Divide the dough in half. On a floured surface, form each half into a 12-inch-long log

and place on the prepared sheet. Allow 3 inches between the logs.

Bake for 35 minutes, or until lightly browned. Transfer the pan to a cooling rack and let cool for 10 minutes.

Using a sharp knife, cut the logs on the diagonal into $^3/_4$-inch-thick slices. Place the biscotti on their cut sides on the baking sheet.

Bake for 8 minutes. Turn and bake on the seamed side for 8 minutes more, until lightly browned and dry. Cool on a rack.

Lemon Poppy Biscotti

Makes: About 36 cookies

$^1/_3$ cup butter, unsalted
$^2/_3$ cup sugar
4 teaspoons finely shredded lemon rind
1 tablespoon poppy seeds
1 teaspoon baking powder
$^1/_2$ teaspoon baking soda
2 eggs
$2^1/_2$ cups flour

Preheat an oven to 375°F.

In a large bowl, using an electric mixer set on medium speed, beat the butter until softened, about 30 seconds. Add the sugar, lemon rind, poppy seeds, baking powder, and baking soda, and beat until combined. Add the eggs and beat until combined. Add the flour and beat until thoroughly combined.

Divide the dough in half. Using floured hands, shape each dough half into a log 8 inches long and 2 inches in diameter. Place

(continued)

the logs on an ungreased baking sheet a few inches apart from each other.

Bake for about 20 minutes, or until a knife inserted in the center comes out clean. Let cool on the baking sheet or a wire rack for 1 hour. Turn off the oven while the cookies cool.

Preheat an oven to 325°F. Cut each roll crosswise into slices about $1/2$ inch thick. Arrange the slices about 4 inches apart on the baking sheet.

Bake for 8 minutes, then flip the slices over and bake for 8 more minutes, or until the cookies are crisp and lightly browned. Let cool on a wire rack.

CREAM PUFFS

Blackberry Cream Puffs

Makes: 8 cream puffs

Cream Puffs:
1 cup water
$1/2$ cup butter
1 cup sifted flour
4 eggs

Blackberry Filling:
1 package (3 ounces) blackberry Jell-O
1 cup boiling water
1 cup cold water
1 cup whipping cream, whipped stiff

confectioners' sugar for dusting

Preheat an oven to 400°F.

In a saucepan, combine the water and butter and bring to a boil. Stir in the flour, blending until the mixture forms a ball, leaving sides of pan, about 1 minute. Beat in the eggs one at a time, beating well after each addition. Beat until smooth. Drop by spoonfuls onto an ungreased baking sheet.

Bake for 45 to 50 minutes, or until puffed and dry. Let cool. When completely cool, cut off the tops and scoop out any soft dough. Set the tops aside until ready to fill.

Meanwhile, make the filling. Dissolve the Jell-O in the boiling water. Stir in the cold water. Chill for one hour, or until slightly thickened. Fold in the whipped cream and chill until firm.

To fill the cream puffs, stir the chilled filling until smooth. Spoon into the cream puff bases, using about $1/3$ cup filling for each puff. Replace the tops. Sprinkle the tops with confectioners' sugar.

The Everything Dessert Cookbook

Chapter 9: Classic French Desserts

Mousses and soufflés are the kind of dessert that always make me think of quiet times. Everyone tends to tiptoe around the house, but in the end, the reward for this good behavior is an exquisite, light dessert that you might as well eat before you eat dinner, since everyone is just going through the motions to get to dessert anyway.

Mousses require a light but firm folding technique that is equally persnickety. But the oohs and aahs you'll get as a result are worth all the whispers in the world.

Chocolate Fondue

Serves: 8

12 ounces milk chocolate
$^1/_2$ cup whipping cream
3 tablespoons orange-flavored liqueur
$^1/_2$ cup almonds, toasted and chopped
1 tablespoon honey
angel food cake squares
canned pineapple chunks, drained and chilled
canned mandarin oranges, drained and chilled
sliced bananas, chilled
strawberries, chilled

Combine the chocolate, cream, liqueur, almonds, and honey in a saucepan. Heat slowly until the chocolate is melted, stirring well. Pour the chocolate into a fondue pot placed over a low flame.

Arrange the cake squares, pineapple, oranges, bananas (dip in sugar water to prevent browning), and strawberries on a platter or in small bowls. Spear pieces of fruit and cake onto fondue forks and dip into the warm mixture.

Easy Chocolate Mousse

Serves: 6

1 package (6 ounces) chocolate pudding mix
$^3/_4$ cup milk
1 teaspoon instant coffee powder
1 package (8 ounces) cream cheese, cubed

In a saucepan, combine the pudding mix, milk, and instant coffee and stir well. Place over medium heat and cook, stirring constantly, until the mixture comes to a boil.

Add the cream cheese and beat until blended. Pour into a 1-quart mold. Place wax paper directly on the surface. Chill before serving.

Café Au Lait Mousse

Serves: 6

$^1/_2$ cup cornstarch
$1^1/_2$ cups sugar
2 cups double-strength brewed coffee
4 ounces cream cheese, cubed
$^1/_3$ cup Kahlúa liqueur
$1^1/_4$ cups whipping cream, whipped stiff
rind of 2 lemons, slivered
$^1/_2$ cup water

In a saucepan, combine the cornstarch and $1^1/_4$ cups of the sugar. Stir in the coffee and place over low heat. Cook, stirring, until the mixture bubbles and thickens. Remove from the heat and stir in the cream cheese and liqueur until smooth and well thickened. Cover and let cool at room temperature for 2 hours. Fold in 1 cup of the whipped cream, cover, and chill overnight.

The next day, spoon into serving dishes and garnish with the remaining whipped cream. Mix together the lemon rind, the remaining $^1/_4$ cup sugar, and the water in a saucepan. Bring to a boil and boil hard for about 10 to 15 minutes, or until almost all the syrup is absorbed. Spread the rind on a piece of greased aluminum foil and let cool. Sprinkle the lemon rind on top of the whipped cream and chill until serving.

Mousse

Some people feel that mousse is just another name for pudding. Not true. Mousse is a lighter form of pudding that is usually whipped at some point in the recipe. To ensure a light, fluffy mousse, be extra gentle when folding the whipped cream into the cooked mousse base.

Dark Chocolate Mousse

Serves: 6

> 4 squares (4 ounces) unsweetened
>   chocolate
> $^3/_4$ cup superfine sugar
> $^1/_4$ cup water or strong brewed coffee
> 5 eggs, separated
> $^1/_2$ teaspoon vanilla extract or 1 to 2
>   tablespoons brandy, rum, kirsch, or
>   Kahlúa

In the top pan of a double boiler, combine the chocolate, sugar, and water. Place over (not touching) boiling water and cook, stirring constantly, until the chocolate is melted and smooth. Remove the double boiler from the heat but leave the top in place. Beat in the yolks one at a time, beating well after each addition. Remove the top pan and let cool. When cool, stir in the vanilla.

Beat the egg whites until stiff peaks form. Fold the whites into the cooled chocolate mixture. Pour into custard cups. Cover with plastic wrap. Chill for 30 minutes before serving.

Honey Mousse

Serves: 4

> 6 egg yolks
> $^3/_4$ cup honey
> 2 teaspoons vanilla extract

> 3 egg whites
> $^1/_2$ cup whipping cream

In a large bowl, combine the egg yolks, honey, and vanilla and beat for about 5 minutes. The mixture should more than double in volume and be thick, foamy, and pale. In a clean bowl with clean beaters, beat the egg whites until they start to form stiff peaks. In a separate bowl, beat the cream until it forms stiff peaks. Scoop the cream and the egg whites onto the honey mixture and fold together until well blended. Scoop the mousse into individual cups or a large bowl. Cover with plastic wrap and freeze for several hours before serving.

Maple Charlotte

Serves: 6

> 1 envelope unflavored gelatin
> $^1/_4$ cup cold water
> $^1/_2$ cup milk, scalded
> 1 cup maple syrup
> 1 cup whipping cream

In a large bowl, soften the gelatin in the cold water. Add the hot milk and stir until the gelatin is dissolved. Stir in the maple syrup. Chill for about 20 minutes, or until partially set. Beat the syrup mixture until foamy. Whip the cream. Fold into the syrup mixture. Pour into 1-quart or individual molds. Chill until firm, about 2 hours.

Banana Soufflé

Serves: 6

3 ripe bananas
$1/2$ tablespoon lemon juice
$1/3$ cup sugar
1 tablespoon cornstarch
$1/8$ teaspoon salt
$1/2$ teaspoon ground nutmeg
$1/4$ teaspoon grated lemon rind
$3/4$ cup milk
3 eggs, separated
2 tablespoons butter
$1 1/2$ teaspoons vanilla extract
whipped cream

Preheat an oven to 350°F.

Peel and slice the bananas. Toss the slices with the lemon juice and set aside. In a saucepan, combine the sugar, cornstarch, salt, nutmeg, and lemon rind; add the milk and mix well. Cook over medium heat, stirring constantly, for 10 to 15 minutes, or until thickened. In a bowl, beat the egg yolks until blended. Add a little of the hot mixture to the beaten yolks, then mix with the remaining hot mixture. Stir in the butter and the bananas. Beat the egg whites until they stand in soft peaks. Fold into the banana mixture along with vanilla. Turn into an ungreased $1 1/2$-quart soufflé dish.

Place the soufflé dish in a baking pan and add hot water to the pan to reach three-fourths of the way up the sides of the dish.

Bake for 1 hour, or until firm. Serve at once with whipped cream.

Chocolate Soufflé

Serves: 8

5 egg yolks
$3/4$ cup granulated sugar
4 drops vanilla extract
1 cup flour
2 cups milk
2 squares (2 ounces) unsweetened
*   chocolate, melted and cooled*
8 egg whites, divided
confectioners' sugar
sweetened whipped cream

In a bowl, beat the egg yolks with $1/2$ cup of the granulated sugar and the vanilla until light and fluffy. Gradually beat in the flour until a paste forms. Meanwhile, scald the milk in a saucepan. Add the egg mixture to the milk mixture all at once and bring to a boil. With a wire whisk, quickly and vigorously beat until the paste is well incorporated into the milk and the mixture is smooth. Continue to stir with a wooden spoon until the mixture is thick. Add the melted chocolate, stirring to blend. Let cool.

Preheat an oven to 350°F. Grease 12 individual soufflé dishes or custard cups each 2 inches in diameter or 2 soufflé dishes each 5 inches in diameter.

Gradually add the remaining $1/4$ cup granulated sugar to the egg whites beaten in three stages as follows: Beat 3 egg whites, then add another 3 egg whites and beat them. Finally add 2 egg whites and beat until stiff and

(continued)

shiny but not dry. (The egg whites should not slide when the bowl is tipped.) Fold the egg whites into the soufflé batter just until no white streaks remain. Spoon the batter almost to the rim of the prepared dishes.

Bake for 30 minutes for individual soufflés or 1½ hours for larger soufflés, or until the top is firm. Dust with confectioners' sugar and serve topped with whipped cream.

Banana Mousse with Raspberries

Serves: 6

4 egg whites
1¼ cups sugar
1½ cups whipping cream
3 ripe bananas, puréed
¼ cup water
1 envelope unflavored gelatin
2 teaspoons natural banana extract

Raspberry sauce:
1 bag (12 ounces) frozen unsweetened
  raspberries
½ cup sugar
1 pint fresh raspberries

In the large bowl of a heavy-duty electric mixer fitted with the wire whip attachment, whip the egg whites and sugar at low speed until blended. Remove the bowl from the mixer stand and place over a saucepan half filled with simmering water. Cook, whisking constantly, for 10 to 15 minutes, or until the

mixture is hot to the touch and registers 140°F on an instant-read thermometer.

Return the bowl to the mixer stand and beat at medium-high speed until stiff, shiny peaks form and the mixture is cool.

In a chilled bowl, using a handheld electric mixer set at medium speed, beat the cream until soft peaks start to form. Do not overwhip the cream. Cover and refrigerate until ready to use.

Place the banana purée in a bowl. Place the water in a small saucepan. Sprinkle the gelatin over the water and let stand for 5 minutes to soften. Place the saucepan over low heat and cook, stirring constantly with a wooden spoon for 2 to 3 minutes, or until the gelatin granules dissolve completely and the mixture is clear. Stir the dissolved gelatin mixture and the banana extract into the banana purée.

Using a large rubber spatula, fold the banana-gelatin mixture into the egg white mixture. Gently fold one-third of the whipped cream into the banana mixture to lighten it. Fold in the remaining whipped cream just until white streaks remain. Cover with plastic wrap, pressing it directly onto the surface of the mousse, and refrigerate for at least 2 hours, or until almost set.

To make the raspberry sauce, in a saucepan, combine the frozen raspberries and the sugar. Cook over medium-low heat, stirring constantly with a wooden spoon, until the sugar dissolves completely and the berries

soften. Remove from the heat. Strain the mixture through a fine-meshed sieve into a bowl. Cover the bowl with plastic wrap and refrigerate until serving.

To assemble the dessert, fill a pastry bag fitted with a 2-inch round tip with the banana mousse. For each serving, pipe a generous amount of the banana mousse into an ice cream dish and top with 6 fresh raspberries. Pipe another layer of mousse onto the berries and top with more berries. Top with a few spoonfuls of raspberry sauce and serve.

Eggnog Mold

Serve: 6

> 2 envelopes unflavored gelatin
> $1/2$ cup water
> 1 quart eggnog
> 1 cup blanched almonds, ground
> 1 can (12 ounces) mandarin oranges, drained

> Oil a 5-cup mold.

In a saucepan, sprinkle the gelatin over the water and let stand for 5 minutes to soften. Place over low heat and cook, stirring constantly, for 2 to 3 minutes, or until the gelatin granules dissolve completely and the mixture is clear. Add the eggnog, stirring until blended. Add the almonds. Pour into the prepared mold.

Cover and refrigerate until set, about 3 hours. To serve, unmold and garnish with the mandarin oranges.

Café Brûlot

Serves: 6

> 6 strips orange rind
> 2 cinnamon sticks
> 12 whole cloves
> 1 cup brandy
> 8 sugar cubes
> 6 cups hot freshly brewed coffee

Put the orange peel, cinnamon sticks, cloves, brandy, and sugar cubes in a heatproof bowl. Using a long match, ignite the brandy and stir until the sugar has melted and is bubbling. Pour in the hot coffee, stir well, and ladle into cups to serve.

The Everything
Dessert Cookbook

Chapter 10: Comfort Desserts

Many people feel that puddings and custards are too childish for them to eat. Ice cream and cookies are okay as adult dessert choices, but they feel puddings and custards somehow convey the feeling that you're two years old again and all you can manage is baby food because it's going to end up on the floor anyway.

That's okay. To please these people, you just have to put a spin of maturity on a pudding or custard: add a splash of flavored liqueur, broil it so the edges get nice and sugary, or just call it flan. Or just wrap it up in one of the pudding cake recipes that follow. But keep in mind that there are those of us who absolutely revel in this "baby food" and wouldn't think of leaving a diner without ordering a dish of "fish-eye pudding," or what my sister used to call tapioca pudding to gross me out.

No matter what side of the road you're on, try some of these recipes next time for a sweet, light ending to any kind of meal.

Baked Maple Pudding

Serves: 6

3 slices toast
1/2 cup milk
3/4 cup maple syrup
1 tablespoon butter
1/4 teaspoon salt
1 egg, lightly beaten
4 apples
whipping cream, whipped stiff, if desired

Preheat an oven to 350°F.

Cut the toast into quarters and arrange in layers in an 8-inch square pan. Heat the milk until scalded. Add the syrup and stir to blend.

Mix in the butter, salt, and egg. Pour over the toast. Peel, quarter, core, and slice the apples thinly. Place over the toast to form a top crust.

Bake for 40 to 45 minutes, or until a knife comes out clean. Serve hot with cream or whipped cream.

Sherried Egg White Custard

Serves: 6

2 tablespoons sugar
1/8 teaspoon salt
1 1/3 cups milk
1/4 teaspoon vanilla extract
2 to 3 teaspoons sherry or rum flavoring
3 egg whites, lightly beaten

Spiced Cherry Sauce:

1 can (8 ounces) pitted cherries, drained
few drops of red food coloring
1 teaspoon cornstarch mixed into 2
*   teaspoons water or lemon juice*
pinch of ground cloves
pinch of ground cinnamon
pinch of ground ginger

Preheat an oven to 325°F.

In a saucepan, heat together the sugar, salt, and milk until the sugar dissolves. Remove from the heat and let cool. Add the vanilla, sherry, and egg whites. Stir well and pour through a strainer into a 2-cup baking dish.

Place in a baking pan and add hot water to the pan to reach three-fourths up the sides of the dish. Bake for about 1 hour, until a knife comes out clean. Meanwhile, make the sauce: Pour the cherries into a saucepan and add the food coloring. Place over low heat and stir in the cornstarch mixture. Cook, stirring, for 3 minutes, or until clear. Mix in the cloves, cinnamon, and ginger. Remove the custard from the oven and cool. Drizzle with the cherry sauce.

Easy Rice Pudding

Serves: 6

1 cup cooked white rice
4 cups milk
¼ cup sugar

(continued)

Coconut Custard Topping

¼ cup flaked dried coconut
2 tablespoons brown sugar
1 tablespoon butter or
**   margarine, softened**

Preheat a broiler.
Combine coconut, sugar, and butter in a bowl and mix well. Sprinkle the mixture on warm or chilled custard. Place the cups on a baking sheet. Slip under the broiler 3 to 4 inches from the heat and broil for about 5 minutes, until the tops are brown.

Preheat an oven to 350°F.

In a bowl, combine the rice, milk, and sugar. Mix well. Pour into a 2-quart casserole dish.

Bake for about 1 1/2 hours, or until creamy. Do not overcook. Occasionally break the skin with a spoon while baking. Let cool. Serve warm or cold.

Classic Rice Pudding

Serves: 6

4 cups milk
1 orange
1/2 cup long-grain white rice
1/2 cup sugar
3/4 teaspoon salt
1 cup light cream
2 egg yolks
1/2 teaspoon vanilla extract
equal parts cinnamon and sugar
whipped cream (optional)

Pour the milk into the top pan of a double boiler and scald over (not touching) simmering water. Peel the orange as if it were an apple, going round and round so the rind is in one long spiral. Add the orange peel, rice, sugar, and salt to the milk and stir to dissolve the sugar. Cover and cook over boiling water for about 45 minutes, or until the rice is tender. Stir occasionally during the first part of cooking. Remove and discard the orange rind.

In a bowl, whisk together the cream and egg yolks. Stir a small amount of the hot rice mixture into the cream mixture, then stir the cream mixture into the rice mixture. Continue cooking, covered, for about 20 minutes, or until the mixture thickens. Stir now and then. Add the vanilla and mix well. Pour into dessert dishes and let cool. Sprinkle the tops with the cinnamon-sugar mixture. Garnish with whipped cream, if you like.

Party Rice Pudding

Serves: 6

1 can (9 ounces) crushed pineapple
2/3 cup packaged quick cooking rice
2/3 cup water
1/2 teaspoon salt
1 1/2 cups miniature marshmallows
1 ripe banana, peeled and diced
2 teaspoons lemon juice
1 cup whipping cream, whipped stiff

Drain the pineapple, reserving the syrup. In a saucepan, combine the rice, water, pineapple syrup, and salt; mix just to moisten the rice. Bring quickly to a boil. Reduce the heat, cover, and simmer for 5 minutes. Remove from the heat and let stand for 5 minutes. Stir in the marshmallows, pineapple, banana, and lemon juice. Turn into a bowl and let cool.

Fold in the cream and chill well before serving.

Rice Pudding for a Crowd

Serves: 24

3 quarts milk
4 cups water
3 cups long-grain white rice
1 teaspoon salt
3 eggs, beaten
3 cups sugar
2 teaspoons vanilla extract
ground cinnamon

In a large pot, combine the milk and water, and heat until warm. Add the rice and salt and bring to a boil. Lower heat. In a bowl, combine the eggs, sugar, and vanilla and mix well. When the rice is cooked, pour in the egg mixture. Stir a few times. Turn off the heat and let stand for 5 minutes. Pour into a large dish. Let cool. Add cinnamon to taste. Serve warm or cold.

Chocolate Sundae Rice Pudding

Serves: 8

2 cups cooked white rice
2 cups milk
$^1/_2$ teaspoon salt
1 teaspoon vanilla extract
1 cup marshmallow creme
$^1/_2$ cup chocolate syrup

(continued)

Rice Pudding Memories

For me and for many other people, a cold dish of rice pudding conjures up all kinds of good feelings about childhood: it's sweet, it's not much work to eat it, and if your grandmother prepared it in a slightly different way than your mother, you probably liked your grandmother's better. Today, you can create new memories for you and your family by giving rice pudding your own personal touch. Grated chocolate on top is always nice, but a nip of Amaretto stirred into the pudding after cooking, or using candied citron instead of raisins are new ways to add spice.

Perfect Custard, Part 1

Custard is an easy dish to prepare, but because it's so delicate, many cooks are nervous about doing it right. The best way to ensure a perfect custard is to make sure that it's fully cooked before you take it out of the oven. To test the custard, simply insert a clean knife into the middle of the custard. If it comes out clean, it is done.

In a saucepan, combine the rice, milk, and salt and bring to a simmer. Simmer for about 15 minutes, or until thick and creamy. Remove from the heat, add the vanilla, and let cool.

Fold $^3/_4$ cup of the marshmallow creme into the rice mixture. Spoon into dessert dishes. Top with the remaining $^1/_4$ cup marshmallow creme and the chocolate syrup.

Classic Baked Custard

Serves: 6

3 eggs, lightly beaten
$^1/_4$ cup sugar
$^1/_4$ teaspoon salt
2 cups milk, scalded and cooled slightly
$^1/_2$ to 1 teaspoon vanilla extract

Preheat an oven to 325°F.

In a bowl, combine the eggs, sugar, and salt and beat until well mixed. Slowly stir in the milk and the vanilla to taste. Set six 5-ounce custard cups in a baking pan. Pour hot water into the baking pan to a depth of 1 inch. Pour the custard into the cups.

Bake for 40 to 45 minutes, or until a knife inserted halfway between the outside edge and the center comes out clean. Serve warm or chilled.

Note: for 1 large custard, bake in a 1-quart baking dish for about 60 minutes, or until it tests done.

Custard

Serves: 10 to 12

>   5 eggs
>   1 cup sugar
>   4 cups milk
>   1 teaspoon vanilla extract
>   ground nutmeg (optional)

Preheat an oven to 375°F to 390°F.

In a bowl, beat the eggs until blended. Gradually add the sugar, beating constantly. Pour in the milk, stir well, and add the vanilla. Pour into a deep 2-quart baking dish and place in a baking pan. Sprinkle nutmeg on top. Pour hot water into the baking pan to a depth of 3 inches.

Bake for 55 minutes, or until a knife comes out clean.

Stove-Top Custard

Serves: 10 to 12

In the top pan of a double boiler, combine the same ingredients as for the previous custard recipe, except the vanilla. Cook over (not touching) hot—not boiling—water, stirring constantly. As soon as the custard coats a metal spoon, after about 10 minutes, remove from the heat. Place the pan in a sink or bowl of cold water and stir a minute or two to cool immediately. Add the vanilla and chill well before serving.

Perfect Custard, Part 2

You can do away with knife slits in the top of baked custards by getting to know what a fully bake custard looks like when its mold is shaken. Jiggle the custard very gently. If the top quivers like a bowl of Jell-O, the custard is done. If, however, the surface shakes like a bowl of milk, the custard needs to bake a little longer.

Perfect Custard, Part 3

To make sure that your custard comes out of its mold in one fell swoop, first wait until the custard has cooled completely. Loosen the custard from the sides of the mold with a blunt knife. Then slip the point of the knife down the side to let in air. Invert onto dessert plates.

Crème Caramel

Serves: 10 to 12

> $1\frac{1}{2}$ cups sugar
> $\frac{1}{4}$ cup water
> pinch of cream of tartar
> 4 cups light cream
> $\frac{1}{2}$ cup milk
> 5 whole eggs
> 5 egg yolks
> 3 tablespoons Cointreau or other orange-
>   flavored liqueur

Preheat an oven to 325°F.

In a heavy skillet, combine $\frac{3}{4}$ cup of the sugar and the water with the cream of tartar. Place over low heat and cook for 10 minutes, or until caramel colored. Pour the caramel into a heated 6-cup mold and swirl around the sides until it stops running. In the top pan of a double boiler, combine the cream and milk and heat over (not touching) simmering water to just below a boil. Meanwhile, in a bowl, beat together the whole eggs and egg yolks slightly with the remaining $\frac{3}{4}$ cup sugar. Continue to beat until thick and lemon colored. Slowly pour the hot milk mixture into the egg mixture, beating constantly. Add the Cointreau and mix well. Pour into the prepared mold. Cover the mold with aluminum foil. Place in a baking pan and add hot water to the pan to a depth of 2 inches.

Bake for about 1 hour and 40 minutes if the mold is deep like a soufflé dish, or until a knife comes out clean. It may take as long as

2 hours, depending on the mold used. Let cool. Cover and refrigerate for at least 8 hours. To serve, dip the base of the mold in a pan of hot water, then invert onto a serving plate, allowing all the caramel to drizzle out of the mold.

Crème Brûlée

Serves: 8

> 3 eggs, lightly beaten
> 1 cup granulated sugar
> $1/4$ teaspoon salt
> 2 cups light cream, scalded
> 1 teaspoon vanilla extract
> $1/2$ cup packed brown sugar
> peach slices or other prepared fruit
>   (optional)

In the top pan of a double boiler, combine the eggs, granulated sugar, and salt. Slowly stir in the hot cream and vanilla. Cook over (not touching) hot (not boiling) water for about 8 minutes, or until the custard coats a metal spoon. Continue cooking for about 2 minutes longer, or until the custard thickens slightly. Pour into an 8-inch round baking dish with 3-inch sides. Cover and chill well.

Preheat a broiler.

Sift the brown sugar evenly over the surface of the custard. Set in a shallow pan, surround the dish with ice cubes and a little cold water. Slip under the broiler about 8 inches from the heat and broil for about 5 minutes, or until the custard has a bubbly brown crust. Serve immediately, or chill, being careful not to break the crust. Serve as is, or spoon over peaches.

Chocolate Pudding

Serves: 5 to 6

> $1/2$ cup sugar
> $1/3$ cup unsweetened cocoa powder
> 3 tablespoons cornstarch
> $1/4$ teaspoon salt
> $1/2$ cup milk
> $1/2$ teaspoon vanilla extract

In a saucepan, stir together the sugar, cocoa, cornstarch, and salt. Gradually blend in the milk. Cook over medium heat, stirring constantly, for about 10 minutes, until the mixture thickens. Cook for 2 to 3 minutes longer until set. Add the vanilla. Pour into 5 or 6 custard cups. Chill before serving.

Vanilla Pudding Variation: Follow directions for Chocolate Pudding but omit the cocoa and decrease the sugar to $1/3$ cup.

Caramel Pudding

Serves: 6

> $1/2$ cup sugar
> $1/2$ cup boiling water
> 3 tablespoons cornstarch
> $1/4$ teaspoon salt
> 2 cups milk
> $1 1/2$ teaspoon vanilla extract

(continued)

In a small, heavy skillet, melt $^1/_4$ cup of the sugar over low heat, stirring constantly, until it is a rich medium brown. Remove from the heat. Slowly add the boiling water. Return to the heat and stir until the lumps dissolve. Remove from the heat. This is the caramel syrup.

In a saucepan, combine the remaining $^1/_4$ cup sugar, the cornstarch, and salt. Stir in the milk and then the caramel syrup. Place over medium heat and cook, stirring constantly, for about 10 minutes, or until thick. Cook for 2 minutes longer, or until it coats the back of a spoon. Add the vanilla. Pour into custard cups. Chill before serving.

Sweet Potato Pudding

Serves: 6

    $1^2/_3$ cups flour
    $1^1/_3$ cups sugar
    1 teaspoon baking soda
    $^1/_4$ teaspoon baking powder
    $^1/_2$ teaspoon salt
    $^1/_2$ teaspoon ground cinnamon
    $^1/_2$ teaspoon ground allspice
    $^1/_4$ teaspoon ground cloves
    1 cup cooked sweet potato, mashed
    $^1/_2$ cup butter, softened
    $^1/_3$ cup water
    1 egg

Preheat an oven to 350°F. Grease an 8-inch square cake pan.

In a bowl, sift together the flour, sugar, baking soda, baking powder, salt, and all the spices. Add the sweet potato, butter, and water and, using an electric mixer set on medium speed, beat for 2 minutes. Add the egg and beat for 2 minutes longer. Pour into the prepared pan.

Bake for 40 minutes, or until set.

Tapioca Pudding

Serves: 6

    4 cups milk
    $^1/_4$ cup quick-cooking tapioca
    $^1/_2$ cup sugar
    $^1/_4$ teaspoon salt
    3 egg yolks, lightly beaten
    $^1/_2$ teaspoon vanilla extract
    3 egg whites
    whipped cream or fresh or canned sliced
        fruit (optional)

In a saucepan, combine the milk, tapioca, sugar, and salt. Mix well and let stand for 5 minutes. Add the egg yolks and mix well. Bring quickly to a boil, stirring constantly. Remove from the heat (the mixture will be thin). Add the vanilla. Beat the egg whites until soft peaks form. Put about one-third of the egg whites in a large bowl. Slowly stir in the hot tapioca mixture. Fold in the remaining egg whites, leaving little blobs of white visible. Cover and chill well.

Pile the pudding into dessert dishes. Top with whipped cream or fresh or canned fruit, if you like.

Classic Bread Pudding

Serves: 8

2 cups day-old bread cubes (1-inch cubes)
$1^1/_4$ cups milk
2 eggs, lightly beaten
$1/_2$ cup packed brown sugar
1 teaspoon ground cinnamon
1 teaspoon vanilla extract
$1/_4$ teaspoon salt
$1/_2$ cup raisins

Preheat an oven to 350°F. Grease an 8-inch square baking dish with 2-inch sides.

Place the bread cubes in a large bowl. In a bowl or pitcher, stir together the milk and eggs. Pour the milk mixture over the bread cubes and add the brown sugar, cinnamon, vanilla, salt, and raisins. Toss lightly to blend. Spread in the prepared baking dish. Place the dish in a baking pan and pour hot water into the pan to a depth of 1 inch.

Bake for about 35 to 40 minutes, or until a knife inserted halfway between the center and the outside edge comes out clean. Serve warm or cold.

Old-Fashioned Lemon Bread Pudding

Serves: 8

1 cup soft white bread cubes (1-inch cubes)
2 tablespoons grated lemon rind
$1/_2$ teaspoon salt

2 cups milk
$2/_3$ cup granulated sugar
3 tablespoons butter
4 eggs, separated
5 tablespoons lemon juice
confectioners' sugar

Place the bread cubes in a large bowl. Sprinkle with the lemon rind and salt. In a saucepan, combine the milk and granulated sugar and bring just to a boil. Add the butter and stir to melt. Pour the milk mixture over the bread; let cool.

Preheat an oven to 350°F. Grease a $1^1/_2$-quart baking dish. In a bowl, beat the egg yolks until blended. Add to the cooled bread mixture along with the lemon juice. Mix well. Beat the egg whites until stiff but not dry. Fold the egg whites into the bread mixture. Pour into the prepared baking dish. Sprinkle with confectioners' sugar. Place the dish in a baking pan. Pour hot water into the pan to a depth of 3 inches.

Bake for 1 hour, or until firm. Serve warm or cold.

Microwaved Raisin Bread Pudding with Whiskey Sauce

Serves: 8

7 slices raisin bread, cut into 1-inch cubes (about 2 cups)
$1/_4$ cup packed light brown sugar
$1/_4$ teaspoon salt

(continued)

2 cups milk
$1/4$ cup butter, cut into pieces
2 eggs, beaten

Whiskey Sauce:
1 cup sugar
2 tablespoons bourbon
$1/4$ cup butter, cut into pieces
1 egg, beaten

Spread the bread cubes in a 10-by-6-inch glass baking dish. Sprinkle with the brown sugar and salt. Place the milk and butter in a 4-cup glass measure and microwave for about 4 minutes, or until hot. Whisk in the eggs and pour evenly over the bread cubes. Microwave on HIGH for 9 minutes, or until a knife inserted into the center comes out clean. Turn the dish once 180 degrees at the midway point.

To make the sauce, mix the sugar and bourbon in a 2-cup glass measure; stir in the butter. Microwave for 2 minutes, or until the mixture is bubbly. Stir some of the sauce mixture into the egg, then pour the egg back into the bourbon mixture and whisk until smooth. Serve the sauce warm over the warm bread pudding.

Apple-Buttered Rum Pudding with Apple Topping

Serves: 6 to 8

2 cups light cream
1 cup cooked white rice

$1/3$ cup sugar
$1/2$ teaspoon salt
1 envelope unflavored gelatin
$1/4$ cup water
2 tablespoons rum or 1 teaspoon rum flavoring
1 cup sour cream

Apple Topping:
$1/2$ to $3/4$ cup packed light brown sugar
2 tablespoons cornstarch
$1/4$ teaspoon salt
$1/2$ teaspoon ground cinnamon
$1/2$ cup water
1 can (20 ounces) pie-sliced apples
1 tablespoon butter or margarine
2 tablespoons rum or 1 teaspoon rum flavoring

In a saucepan, combine the cream, rice, sugar, and salt and bring to a boil. Reduce the heat to low and simmer for 20 minutes, stirring occasionally. Meanwhile, in a bowl, soften the gelatin in the water for 5 minutes. Remove the rice mixture from the heat and stir in the gelatin mixture until the gelatin dissolves. Let cool until thickened but not set. Fold in the rum and sour cream. Spoon into individual molds and chill until firm.

To make the topping, combine the brown sugar, cornstarch, salt, cinnamon, and water in a saucepan and stir well. Add the apples and bring to a boil. Reduce the heat to low and simmer for 15 to 20 minutes, or until the apples are tender, stirring occasionally.

Remove from the heat and add the butter and rum.

To serve, unmold the puddings onto individual plates. Reheat the topping until hot, if necessary, and spoon over the puddings.

Banana-Coconut Pudding

Serves: 6

$^2/_3$ cup milk
$^2/_3$ cup flaked dried coconut
2 eggs
3 tablespoons sugar
1 cup mashed ripe bananas
$^1/_4$ teaspoon ground nutmeg

Preheat an oven to 350°F. Grease a 1-quart baking dish.

Combine the milk and coconut in a small saucepan. Simmer, stirring occasionally, for 2 minutes. Remove from the heat. Beat the eggs in a large bowl. Gradually stir in the coconut-milk mixture, sugar, bananas, and nutmeg. Turn into the prepared baking dish. Place in a baking pan and add hot water to reach halfway up the sides of the dish.

Bake for about 30 minutes, or until set and the top is slightly brown. Serve warm.

Indian Pudding

Serves: 8

4 cups milk
$^1/_2$ cup light molasses
$^1/_2$ cup yellow cornmeal
$^1/_4$ cup sugar
1 teaspoon ground cinnamon

(continued)

Skinless Pudding

To prevent skin from forming on a pudding after cooking, immediately transfer the hot pudding to a bowl or individual serving dishes. Lay a sheet of wax paper or plastic wrap directly on the pudding surface. Let cool as directed.

¹/₂ *teaspoon ground nutmeg*
¹/₂ *teaspoon salt*
2 eggs, beaten
2 tablespoons grated orange rind
ice cream (optional)

In a 2-quart saucepan, combine the milk and molasses and bring to just below a boil. Meanwhile, in a small bowl, combine the cornmeal, sugar, cinnamon, nutmeg, and salt and mix well. Gradually add the cornmeal mixture to the milk-molasses mixture, stirring constantly. Cook over low heat, stirring constantly, for 5 to 10 minutes, or until the mixture thickens and comes to a boil. Add a little of the hot mixture to the beaten eggs, stirring constantly. Add the eggs to the saucepan and cook for 1 minute longer. Stir in the orange rind. Pour into a bowl, cover, and chill. Serve with ice cream, if desired.

French Fruit Pudding

Serves: 8

3 cups seedless grapes
2 large apples, peeled, cored, and diced
¹/₂ *cup walnuts, chopped*
¹/₂ *cup milk*
4 eggs
2 teaspoons vanilla extract
¹/₂ *cup flour*
¹/₂ *cup granulated sugar*
confectioners' sugar for dusting
ground cinnamon for dusting
sweetened whipped cream

Preheat an oven to 350°F. Grease a 2-quart baking dish.

Scatter the fruit and nuts over the bottom of the prepared baking dish. In a blender, combine the milk, eggs, and vanilla and blend until well mixed. Add the flour and sugar and blend thoroughly. Pour over the fruit and nuts.

Bake for 1 ¹/₂ hours, or until firm. Let cool slightly, then dust with confectioners' sugar and cinnamon. Serve warm with whipped cream.

Old-Fashioned Apple Dumplings with Rum Hard Sauce

Serves: 6

¹/₂ *cup packed light brown sugar*
¹/₄ *cup plus* ²/₃ *cup margarine, softened*
¹/₂ *teaspoon ground cinnamon*
¹/₄ *teaspoon ground allspice*
¹/₄ *teaspoon ground nutmeg*
2 cups flour
1 teaspoon salt
6 to 7 tablespoons ice water
6 large baking apples, peeled and cored
6 tablespoons orange marmalade

Rum Hard Sauce:

¹/₂ *cup butter or margarine, softened*
1 cup confectioners' sugar
1 tablespoon light rum

Preheat an oven to 350°F.

In a bowl, combine the brown sugar, $^1/_4$ cup margarine, cinnamon, allspice, and nutmeg. Cream together thoroughly and set aside.

Measure the flour and salt into a separate bowl. Using a pastry blender, cut in the $^2/_3$ cup margarine until the mixture resembles coarse meal. Using a fork, stir in enough of the ice water to form a dough. Gather into a ball. On a lightly floured board, roll out the dough into a 14-by-21-inch rectangle. Cut into six 7-inch squares. Place an apple in the center of each square. Spoon 1 tablespoon orange marmalade into the center of each apple and spread the brown sugar mixture on the sides of the apples. Bring up the corners of dough to meet in the center of the apple. Press together to seal well. Place in a large, shallow baking dish.

Bake for 1 hour. Meanwhile, make the hard sauce: In a bowl, cream the butter for about 5 minutes, or until very light and fluffy. Gradually beat in the confectioners' sugar. Mix in the rum. Cover and chill for at least 1 hour.

Serve the dumplings hot with Rum Hard Sauce.

PUDDINGS
Neapolitan Banana Delight

Serves: 4

$^3/_4$ cup ricotta cheese
1 large ripe banana, peeled and mashed
1 teaspoon lemon juice
$^1/_3$ cup confectioners' sugar

2 tablespoons grated unsweetened
   chocolate
$^1/_2$ teaspoon almond extract
2 ladyfingers or almond macaroons, crumbled
whipped cream (optional)
1 banana, sliced (optional)
additional grated sweetened chocolate
   (optional)

In a bowl, beat the ricotta cheese until smooth. Add the mashed banana, lemon juice, confectioners' sugar, the grated unsweetened chocolate, and the almond extract and beat until the mixture is light and fluffy. Sprinkle the cookie crumbs into dessert dishes. Spoon the pudding over the crumbs. Cover and chill.

Serve the pudding topped with whipped cream, banana slices, and grated sweetened chocolate, if desired.

Plum Kuchen

Serves: 8 to 10

$1^1/_2$ cups flour
$^1/_4$ teaspoon baking powder
$^3/_4$ cup sugar
pinch of salt
$^1/_2$ cup butter or margarine
1 egg, lightly beaten
3 cups pitted and sliced purple prune plums
$1^1/_2$ teaspoons grated orange rind
1 teaspoon ground cinnamon
$^1/_2$ cup whipping cream
1 egg yolk

(continued)

Preheat an oven to 375°F.

In a bowl, combine the flour, baking powder, $1/2$ cup of the sugar, and the salt. Using a pastry blender, cut in the butter until the mixture is crumbly. Stir in the beaten whole egg. Spread the dough onto the bottom and sides of an 8-inch square baking pan. Arrange the plum slices over the dough. Combine the remaining $1/4$ cup sugar, the orange rind, and the cinnamon in a small bowl and sprinkle evenly over the plum slices.

Bake for 20 minutes. Meanwhile, in a bowl, whisk together the cream and the egg yolk. Remove the kuchen from the oven, pour the cream mixture evenly over the top, and return to the oven to bake 30 minutes longer.

Serve warm.

Lemon Pudding Cake

Serves: 8

1 cup sugar
$1/4$ cup sifted flour
2 tablespoons vegetable oil
pinch of salt
2 teaspoons grated lemon rind
$1/3$ cup lemon juice
3 eggs, separated
$1^1/2$ cups milk, scalded

In a bowl, combine the sugar, flour, oil, and salt. Mix well. Add the lemon rind and juice and mix again. In another bowl, beat the egg yolks until blended. Gradually stir the

hot milk into the egg yolks, then add the yolk mixture to the lemon mixture. Beat the egg whites until stiff peaks form. Fold into the lemon mixture just until no white streaks remain. Pour into eight 5-ounce custard cups. Set the custard cups in a shallow baking pan and pour hot water into the pan to a depth of 1 inch.

Bake for 40 minutes, or until the cake part is done. Serve warm or cold.

Brownie Pudding Cake

Serves: 8

1 cup sifted flour
$3/4$ cup granulated sugar
6 tablespoons unsweetened cocoa powder
2 teaspoons baking powder
$1/2$ teaspoon salt
$1/2$ cup milk
1 tablespoon vegetable oil
1 teaspoon vanilla extract
$3/4$ to 1 cup walnuts, chopped
$3/4$ cup packed brown sugar
$1^3/4$ cups hot water

Preheat an oven to 350°F. Grease an 8-inch square cake pan.

In a bowl, sift together the sifted flour, granulated sugar, 2 tablespoons of the cocoa powder, the baking powder, and the salt. Add the milk, oil, and vanilla and blend together. Add the nuts. Pour into the prepared pan. In a small bowl, stir together the brown sugar

and the remaining 4 tablespoons cocoa. Sprinkle evenly over the batter. Pour the hot water over the entire batter.

Bake for about 45 minutes, or until a knife comes out clean. Cool on a rack.

Pumpkin Flan

Serves: 6

1 cup canned pumpkin purée
¼ cup honey
¾ teaspoon ground cinnamon
5 eggs
1 can (13 ounces) evaporated milk
1 teaspoon vanilla extract
1 tablespoon brandy
¼ cup packed brown sugar

Preheat an oven to 350°F.

In a bowl, stir together the pumpkin, honey, and cinnamon until well mixed. In another bowl, beat the eggs until blended. Add the evaporated milk, vanilla, and the pumpkin mixture, mixing well. Stir in the brandy, and again mix well.

Sprinkle the brown sugar over the bottom of a greased 10-inch baking dish. Slowly pour in the custard mixture, and place the baking dish in a baking pan. Add hot water to the baking pan to reach halfway up the sides of the dish.

Bake for 1 hour, or until a knife inserted into the center of the custard comes out clean. Let cool, cover, and chill for 2 to 4 hours before serving.

Minty Chocolate Baked Custard

Serves: 6

1½ cups regular whole milk
1 cup mint chocolate chips
1 cup sweetened condensed milk
2 eggs

Preheat an oven to 350°F. In a small saucepan over low heat, combine ½ cup of the whole milk and the mint chocolate chips. Cook, stirring constantly, until the chips are melted and the mixture is smooth. Set aside.

In a large bowl, combine the remaining 1 cup whole milk, the condensed milk, and the eggs. Beat until well blended. Add the chocolate mixture and beat well. Pour into a 4-cup baking dish. Place the baking dish in a baking pan. Add hot water to the baking pan to reach halfway up the sides of the dish.

Bake for 50 to 55 minutes, or until a knife inserted into the center comes out clean. Serve warm or let cool completely before serving.

Chocolate Custard

Serves: 8

1 cup semisweet chocolate chips
3 tablespoons half-and-half
3 cups milk
3 eggs
1 teaspoon vanilla extract
⅓ cup sugar

(continued)

Saving Your Custard

If, despite your best intentions, your custard ends up overcooking and curdling because you had to answer the phone, beat it on low speed with a handheld mixer for a few minutes to remove the lumps and make it presentable again. This technique also works if the custard becomes lumpy after it cools, or after it's been in the refrigerator for more than 5 days.

¹/₄ teaspoon salt
whipped cream (optional)

In the top of a double boiler or in a heatproof bowl, combine ²/₃ cup of the chocolate chips and the half-and-half and melt over gently simmering water. Stir until smooth.

Spoon about 1 tablespoon of the chocolate mixture into each of 8 custard cups or 10 individual soufflé dishes. Place in a baking pan and set aside.

Preheat an oven to 325°F.

Pour the milk into a saucepan and heat over medium heat until scalded. Melt the remaining ¹/₃ cup chocolate pieces in a heatproof bowl over simmering water. Remove from over the water, stir until smooth, and then gradually add the scalded milk, stirring until blended.

In a bowl, beat together the eggs, vanilla extract, sugar, and salt until blended. Gradually add the milk mixture, stirring constantly. Pour into the chocolate-lined cups or dishes. Add hot water to the baking pan to reach halfway up the sides of the cups or dishes.

Bake for 25 minutes, or until a knife inserted halfway between the center and the edge of a custard comes out clean. Remove the cups to a rack and let cool slightly. Refrigerate and serve when thoroughly cooled. Unmold and, if desired, garnish with whipped cream rosettes.

Walnut Pudding

Serves: 8

1 cup whipping cream
¼ cup freshly roasted coffee beans
4 teaspoons plus 2 tablespoons granulated sugar
1 vanilla bean, split in half lengthwise
4 squares (4 ounces) semisweet chocolate, coarsely chopped
2 tablespoons dark rum
1 tablespoon water
2 teaspoons instant coffee granules
1 cup dried bread crumbs
½ cup walnuts
pinch of salt
5 tablespoons unsalted butter, softened
⅓ cup confectioners' sugar
1 teaspoon vanilla extract
3 large egg yolks, at room temperature
4 large egg whites, at room temperature
2 tablespoons granulated sugar

Chocolate Glaze:

8 squares (8 ounces) semisweet chocolate, finely chopped
¾ cup plus 3 tablespoons whipping cream
3 tablespoons light corn syrup
1 teaspoon vanilla extract
8 walnut halves

In a saucepan, combine the cream, coffee beans, the 4 teaspoons sugar, and the vanilla bean. Cook over medium heat, stirring constantly with a wooden spoon, until the sugar is completely dissolved. Stop stirring and bring the mixture to a gentle boil. Pour the hot cream mixture into a small bowl. Let the mixture cool for 15 minutes. Cover with plastic wrap, pressing it directly onto the surface, and refrigerate for at least 6 hours or as long as overnight.

Preheat an oven to 350°F. Lightly butter six ¾-cup custard cups, then dust with sugar. Put the cups in a baking pan large enough to hold them easily.

In the top of a double boiler or in a heat-proof bowl over simmering water, melt together the chocolate, rum, water, and coffee. Whisk gently until smooth and let the melted chocolate mixture cool for 5 to 10 minutes, or until tepid.

In a food processor, combine the bread crumbs, walnuts, and salt. Process until the nuts are finely ground, 10 to 20 seconds. Scrape the mixture into a small bowl.

In a large bowl, using an electric mixer set on medium speed, beat together the butter and confectioners' sugar until creamy, 1 to 2 minutes. Beat in the vanilla. One at a time, beat in the egg yolks, beating well after each addition. Add the melted chocolate mixture and beat until smooth.

In a large bowl, using clean beaters, beat the egg whites at low speed until frothy. Gradually increase the speed to high and beat the whites until soft peaks start to form. One teaspoon at a time, gradually add the 2 tablespoons granulated sugar and continue beating the whites until stiff, shiny peaks form.

(continued)

Using a rubber spatula, fold one-third of the whites into the chocolate mixture to lighten it. Fold the remaining whites and the bread crumb–walnut mixture into the chocolate mixture.

Divide the pudding evenly among the prepared cups. Remove one of the corner cups from the baking pan. Hold a metal pancake spatula vertically inside that corner of the pan and slowly pour water against the spatula into the roasting pan. (The spatula will prevent the water from splashing the other cups.) Pour in enough water to reach halfway up the sides of the cups. Replace the cup in the pan.

Bake for 25 to 35 minutes, or until a wooden toothpick inserted into the center of each pudding comes out clean. Remove the pan from the oven and leave the puddings in the water bath to keep warm while preparing the chocolate glaze.

To make the glaze, put the chocolate in a 1-quart measuring cup with a pouring spout. In a small saucepan over medium heat, combine the cream and corn syrup and heat, stirring constantly with a wooden spoon, until the mixture comes to a boil. Pour the hot cream over the chocolate. Let the mixture stand for 30 seconds to melt the chocolate. Gently whisk until smooth. Stir in the vanilla.

One at a time, dip half of each walnut half in the warm chocolate glaze and set them on a plate. Unmold the puddings and place them on a wire rack set over a baking sheet. Pour the warm glaze over the tops of the puddings, letting it spill over the sides. Lift the puddings with a metal spatula and set them on individual dessert plates.

Strain the chilled coffee-vanilla cream into a large bowl. Discard the coffee beans and the vanilla bean pods. Using an electric mixer set on high speed, beat the cream for 1 to 3 minutes, or until it starts to form stiff peaks.

Fill a pastry bag fitted with a closed star tip with the whipped coffee-vanilla cream. Pipe a shell border around the base of each pudding. Pipe a swirled rosette on top of each pudding. Garnish each rosette with a half-dipped walnut. These puddings are best when served while still warm.

Chapter 11: Cheesecakes

M any people consider cheesecake to be among the most decadent dessert around, and with good reason. It's rich, dense and creamy, with probably more calories packed into each cubic inch than any other dessert.

But it's another case when a little goes a long way. When I order cheesecake in a restaurant, I've never received anything larger than a sliver. Cheesecake is meant to be savored slowly. Is it possible to eat a piece of cheesecake quickly? Maybe, but I, for one, can't do it. Anyway, who would want to?

Plain Vanilla Cheesecake

Serves: 12

> 1 package (8 ounces) cream cheese,
>   softened
> 2 cups (1 pint) sour cream
> 4 eggs
> 1 tablespoon vanilla extract
> 1½ cups sugar
> 3½ tablespoons cornstarch
> 2 tablespoons milk

Preheat an oven to 350°F. Grease a 10-inch springform pan.

In a large bowl, combine all the ingredients. Beat with an electric mixer on high speed for 20 minutes, or until smooth.

Bake for 50 to 60 minutes, or until the top of the cake cracks in the middle. Turn off the oven and let the cake sit in the oven for 1 hour. Cover and refrigerate overnight before serving.

Chilled Banana Cheesecake

Serves: 12

Crust:
2 cups graham cracker crumbs
⅓ cup sugar
1 teaspoon ground cinnamon
⅓ cup butter, melted

Filling:
1 cup sugar
2 envelopes unflavored gelatin
¼ teaspoon salt
2 eggs, separated
⅔ cup evaporated milk
1 teaspoon grated lemon rind
3 cups cream-style cottage cheese,
* sieved*
1 tablespoon lemon juice
½ teaspoon vanilla extract

1 cup whipping cream, whipped stiff
3 large ripe bananas, peeled and thinly
   sliced

To make the crust, combine the graham cracker crumbs, sugar, and cinnamon, mixing well. Stir in the melted butter. Press three-fourths of the mixture into the bottom and sides of an 8-inch springform pan. Reserve the rest for topping.

To make the filling, in the top of a double boiler, combine $^3/_4$ cup of the sugar, the gelatin, and salt. In a small bowl, whisk the egg yolks until blended. Stir the beaten yolks and the evaporated milk into the sugar mixture. Place over (not touching) simmering water and cook, stirring, for about 10 minutes, or until the gelatin is dissolved and the mixture thickens slightly. Remove from the heat and add the lemon rind. Let cool. Stir in the cottage cheese, lemon juice, and vanilla. Chill, stirring occasionally, until partially set.

Beat the egg whites until they form soft peaks. Slowly add the remaining $^1/_4$ cup sugar, beating until stiff peaks form. Fold the egg whites into the gelatin mixture. Fold in the whipped cream. Pour one-third of the filling into the crumb-lined pan. Cover with half of the banana slices. Add another one-third of the filling and top with the remaining banana slices. Top with the remaining filling. Sprinkle with the reserved crumbs. Cover and chill for 4 to 6 hours (or up to overnight), or until firm.

Blue Ribbon Cheesecake

Serves: 12

1 package (3 ounces) lemon Jell-O
1 cup boiling water
1 package (3 ounces) cream cheese,
   softened
1 cup sugar
2 teaspoons vanilla extract
2 cups whipping cream, beaten stiff
1 graham cracker crust recipe
   (see page 186)

In a small bowl, dissolve the Jell-O in the boiling water. Let cool until partially thickened. In a large bowl, combine the cream cheese, sugar, and vanilla and beat until smooth. Add the cooled Jell-O to the cream cheese mixture, mixing well. Fold the whipped cream into the cream cheese mixture.

Line the bottom and sides of a 9-by-13-by-2-inch baking pan with the graham cracker crust. Pour the creamed mixture into the lined pan. Cover and chill overnight before serving.

Rum Ricotta Cheesecake

Serves: 12

3 pounds ricotta cheese, made from whole
   or skim milk
1 $^1/_2$ cups sugar
8 eggs
1 teaspoon vanilla extract

(continued)

Cheesecake Success

It's always best to make a baked cheesecake the day before you need it so that it can cool thoroughly. Never try to slice a cheesecake within 2 or even 3 hours of baking. It also tastes better after spending the night in the refrigerator. Some people leave leftover cheesecake out on the counter, but since it contains cheese and eggs, it is always best and safest to keep it refrigerated, before, during, and after serving.

4 tablespoons dark rum
ground cinnamon
freshly grated nutmeg
1 package (10 ounces) frozen raspberries, thawed and drained (optional)

Preheat an oven to 300°F. Butter a 9-by-13-by-2-inch baking pan.

In a large bowl, combine the ricotta cheese, sugar, eggs, vanilla, and rum and beat until smooth. Pour into the prepared pan. Sprinkle with cinnamon and nutmeg.

Bake for 1 hour, or until the top cracks slightly and the cake is firm. Let cool in the pan on a rack. To serve, spoon the raspberries onto individual servings.

Hazelnut Cheesecake

Serves: 12

1 1/2 cups graham cracker crumbs
2 pounds cream cheese (four 8-ounce packages), softened
1/2 cup honey
1 3/4 cups sugar
4 eggs
1 teaspoon vanilla extract
1 cup hazelnuts, toasted and peeled

Preheat an oven to 350°F.

Grease a 10-inch springform pan. Sprinkle the graham cracker crumbs over the bottom of the pan.

In a large bowl, combine the cream cheese, honey, sugar, eggs, and vanilla and beat until smooth. Grind the hazelnuts in a nut mill, blender, or food processor, being careful not to overprocess to a paste. Add to the cream cheese mixture and pour into the prepared pan. Place the springform pan in a baking pan and add hot water to the baking pan to a depth of 1 inch.

Bake for 2 hours, or until the cake is firm. Turn off the oven, but leave the cheesecake in it for 1 hour longer. Then leave at room temperature for 1 hour before serving, then release the pan sides and remove to a serving plate.

Pineapple-Coconut Cheesecake

Serves: 12

Zwieback Crust:
1 cup fine zwieback crumbs
1 tablespoon sugar
$^1/_4$ cup butter, melted

Filling:
1 can (8$^1/_4$ ounces) crushed pineapple
2 packages (8 ounces each) cream
  cheese, softened
$^1/_4$ cup sugar
3 large eggs
6 tablespoons canned coconut milk (stir
  well before measuring)

1 teaspoon vanilla extract
1 teaspoon lemon juice
1 teaspoon grated lemon rind
$^1/_3$ cup shredded dried coconut
1 can (8$^1/_4$ ounces) sliced pineapple, well
  drained

Preheat an oven to 350°F.

To make the crust, in a small bowl, combine the zwieback crumbs, sugar, and melted butter and mix well. Turn into an 8-inch springform pan and press over the bottom and about three-fourths up the sides of the pan. Bake for 10 minutes, or until the top edge browns very lightly. Remove from the oven and let stand until the filling is ready to bake. Reduce the oven temperature to 300°F.

To make the filling, turn the crushed pineapple into a strainer; set aside and let drain while preparing the cheese mixture. In a large bowl, beat the cream cheese until soft and fluffy. Gradually beat in the sugar. Add the eggs one at a time, beating well after each addition. Beat in the coconut milk 1 tablespoon at a time. Add the vanilla and lemon juice and rind. Press the crushed pineapple lightly with the back of a spoon to drain off any excess syrup, then add to the cheese mixture, mixing well. Turn the filling into the baked crust.

Bake for 35 minutes, or just until barely set in the center. Turn off the oven, leave the oven door ajar, and let stand for about 30

(continued)

minutes. Cover and refrigerate for 2 hours. At serving time, sprinkle the shredded coconut around the edges of the cake. Release the pan sides. Remove to a serving plate. Arrange the sliced pineapple on top.

Mocha Nut Cheesecake

Makes: 24 mini cakes

2 cups hazelnuts, toasted and skinned
3 tablespoons packed light brown sugar
$^1/_4$ cup unsalted butter, melted
8 ounces cream cheese, at room temperature
$^3/_4$ cup granulated sugar
1 egg
$^1/_4$ cup boiling water
1 tablespoon instant coffee powder
$1^1/_2$ teaspoons unsweetened cocoa powder
$^1/_2$ cup sour cream

Preheat an oven to 325°F. Lightly grease 24 mini-muffin-tin-cups.

In a food processor, process the hazelnuts until finely chopped. Transfer to a bowl and add the brown sugar and melted butter. Mix well. Put 1 tablespoon into each prepared cup, spreading the mixture over the entire surface with the back of a teaspoon. Bake for 15 minutes and remove from the oven.

In a bowl, combine the cream cheese and granulated sugar. Using an electric mixer set on medium speed, beat together until well blended. Beat in the egg. In a small bowl, combine the boiling water, coffee powder, and cocoa powder, and stir to dissolve the coffee and cocoa. Beat the sour cream into the cream cheese mixture at medium speed, then beat in the coffee mixture. Fill the hazelnut-lined cups with the mixture, dividing evenly.

Bake for about 20 minutes, or until the mini cheesecakes puff up. Let cool on a rack for 1 hour. Chill for at least 3 hours before serving.

Pumpkin Marble Cheesecake

Serves: 8

$1^1/_2$ cups graham cracker crumbs
$^1/_2$ cup finely chopped pecans
$^1/_3$ cup butter, melted

2 packages (8 ounces each) cream cheese, softened
$^3/_4$ cup sugar
1 teaspoon vanilla extract
3 eggs
1 cup pumpkin pie filling
$^3/_4$ teaspoon ground cinnamon
$^1/_4$ teaspoon ground nutmeg

Preheat an oven to 350°F. Grease a 9-inch springform pan.

To make the crust, in a bowl, combine the crumbs and pecans. Add the butter and stir until the mixture is evenly moistened.

Bake for 10 minutes, or until set. Let cool on a rack for 15 minutes.

To make the cheesecake, combine the cream cheese, $1/2$ cup of the sugar, and the vanilla in a bowl and beat, using a mixer, for about 4 minutes until smooth. Add the eggs one at a time and mix. Reserve 1 cup of the batter and place in a separate bowl. Add the remaining sugar, pumpkin, and spices to the remaining batter and mix well. Spoon the pumpkin batter and the reserved batter alternately over the crust. Cut through the batter with a knife for a marbling effect.

Bake for 55 minutes. Let cool on a rack. Chill well before serving.

Cookies and Cream Cheesecake

Serves: 12

> $3^1/4$ cups Oreo cookie crumbs
> 6 tablespoons unsalted butter, melted
> 1 envelope unflavored gelatin
> $1/4$ cup water
> 1 package (8 ounces) cream cheese, softened
> $1/2$ cup sugar
> $3/4$ cup milk
> 1 cup whipping cream, whipped

In a bowl, mix 2 cups of the crumbs and the melted butter. Toss with a fork until evenly moistened. Lightly grease a 9-inch springform pan. Press the crumb-butter mixture over the bottom of the pan, forming an even layer.

In a small saucepan, sprinkle the gelatin over the water; let stand for about 5 minutes, then stir over low heat until dissolved. Remove from the heat. In a large bowl, using an electric mixer set on medium speed, beat together the cream cheese and sugar until blended and smooth. Gradually add the gelatin mixture and milk and beat until blended. Cover and chill until thickened but not set, for up to 1 hour.

Remove from the refrigerator and fold in the whipped cream. Reserve $1^1/2$ cups of the mixture. Pour the remaining mixture evenly over the crust. Top evenly with the remaining $1^1/4$ cups Oreo crumbs. Top with the reserved mixture. Cover and chill for at least 2 hours before serving.

Chapter 12: Tortes

T ortes are the ultimate fancy cake. In fact, in American usage, a torte is by dictionary definition a rich cake made with many eggs and usually containing nuts. Tortes are usually garnished with whipped cream, ice cream or fresh fruit. Whatever your choice, serving a torte is the ultimate, extravagant cake dessert.

Peach Blueberry Torte

Serves: 12

6 egg whites
1 teaspoon distilled white vinegar
$^1/_2$ teaspoon vanilla extract
pinch of salt
1$^3/_4$ cups sugar
$^1/_4$ cup maraschino cherries, chopped
8 cooked or canned peach halves, chilled
*   and drained*
blueberries
1 pint peach ice cream

Preheat an oven to 250°F. Cover a baking sheet with a piece of heavy brown paper. Draw an 11-by-8-inch rectangle in the center of the paper.

In a large bowl, beat together the egg whites, vinegar, vanilla, and salt until very soft peaks form. Gradually add the sugar, beating until stiff peaks form and all the sugar has dissolved. Fold in the maraschino cherries. Spread the mixture within the rectangle, hollowing out the center and building up the sides.

Bake for 1 hour. Turn off the heat and leave in the oven with the door closed until cool. Peel off the paper from the bottom of the meringue shell and place the shell on a serving plate. Fill the shell with 2 rows of peach halves, hollow sides up. Spoon blueberries between the rows and top with ice cream. Sprinkle with more blueberries, then pass a bowl of blueberries for guests to add as desired.

Chocolate-Apricot Torte

Serves: 10

$^1/_3$ cup butter or margarine, softened
1 cup sugar
$^1/_2$ teaspoon salt
5 eggs, separated
1 whole egg
3 squares (3 ounces) unsweetened
*   chocolate, melted and cooled*
$^3/_4$ cup almonds, ground
1 cup apricot jam
1 container (8 ounces) frozen whipped
*   topping, thawed*
1 to 2 tablespoons milk
additional whipped topping (optional)

Preheat an oven to 350°F. Line the bottoms of three 8-inch round cake pans with wax paper.

In a bowl, cream together the butter, sugar, and salt, beating until light and fluffy. Add the egg yolks and the whole egg and beat well. Add the chocolate and mix well. Stir in the ground almonds. Beat the egg whites until stiff but not dry. Fold carefully into the chocolate mixture. Pour into the prepared pans.

Bake for 15 to 20 minutes, or until a cake tester inserted into the center comes out clean. Let cool in the pans on racks for 15 minutes, then turn out onto the racks and peel off the paper. Let cool completely.

Stir the jam to break up its fruit. Fold the jam into the whipped topping. Stir in the milk. Stack the layers, spreading the filling between them and on the top of the torte. Garnish with additional whipped topping, if desired. Chill for at least 2 hours before serving.

Chocolate Almond Torte

Serves: 12

1 quart chocolate almond ice cream
1 quart almond fudge ice cream
2 cups whipping cream
2 teaspoons chocolate extract
¼ cup sugar
1 cup toasted almonds, sliced

10 maraschino cherries, halved
2 bars (1.2 ounces each) chocolate (optional)

Line the bottoms of two 8-inch roun cake pans with wax paper. Slightly soften both ice creams. Fill each pan (level with the top) with an ice cream flavor. Freeze for 1 hour. Place a serving plate in the refrigerator to chill.

In a bowl, beat together the cream and chocolate flavoring until the mixture begins to thicken. Gradually add the sugar, beating until the cream holds its shape.

Invert the 2 pans to remove the ice cream layers and peel off the wax paper. Put the chocolate almond layer on the chilled serving plate. Spread the top lightly with some of the chocolate whipped cream. Top with the second ice cream layer and press into place. Working quickly, frost the sides with more chocolate whipped cream. Freeze for 30 minutes.

Remove from the freezer and press the sliced almonds onto the sides of the torte. Frost and swirl the top with the remaining whipped cream. Garnish with the cherries. If desired, cut the chocolate bars into strips and press sideways into the top of the torte. Freeze for at least 2 hours, then let mellow in the refrigerator for 10 minutes before cutting into wedges.

Cappuccino Torte

Serves: 12

Crust:

4 graham crackers

$1/2$ cup chopped walnuts

$1/2$ cup blanched slivered almonds

$1/4$ cup sugar

5 tablespoons unsalted butter, melted
and cooled

Fudge Cream:

2 cups whipping cream

1 pound semisweet chocolate, finely
chopped

2 tablespoons light corn syrup

$1/2$ cup unsalted butter, cut into 8 pieces,
at room temperature

Buttercream:

$2^1/2$ cups packed brown sugar

$1/2$ cup water

6 egg yolks

$1^1/2$ cup unsalted butter, at room
temperature, cut into 1 tablespoon
pieces

1 tablespoon instant espresso powder
dissolved in 1 teaspoon water

4 squares (4 ounces) unsweetened
chocolate, chopped, melted, and cooled

Coffee Whipped Cream:

$1^1/4$ cups whipping cream

2 teaspoons instant espresso powder

$1/2$ teaspoon vanilla extract

2 tablespoons confectioners' sugar

1 cup chocolate shavings

1 package (8 ounces) coffee bean candies
(optional)

Preheat an oven to 350°F. Butter a 10-inch springform pan.

To make the crust, in a food processor, process the graham crackers until coarsely ground. Add all the nuts, the granulated sugar, and the salt and process until coarsely chopped. Add the melted butter and process until evenly distributed.

Press the crumb mixture into the bottom of the prepared pan. Bake for 15 minutes, or until the edges start to brown. Let cool on a rack.

To make the fudge layer, in a heavy saucepan, bring the cream to a boil. Reduce the heat to low, then stir in the chocolate until melted. Remove from the heat and stir in the corn syrup. Stir in the butter, a piece at a time, until the mixture is smooth. Let cool, stirring now and then, until lukewarm.

Pour the fudge into the cooled crust. Cover and place in the refrigerator for 2 hours, or until the fudge is firm.

To make the buttercream, in a heavy saucepan over very low heat, combine the brown sugar and water, stirring until the sugar dissolves. Bring the mixture to a boil and cook for 2 more minutes.

In the meantime, in a bowl, using an electric mixer set on high speed, beat the egg

yolks until thick. With the mixer running, gradually add the boiling syrup to the yolks, taking care not to scrape the sides of the saucepan. Continue beating for another 15 minutes, or until the yolk mixture is cool. Reduce the speed to medium and beat in the butter, 1 tablespoon at a time. Beat in the dissolved espresso mixture and the melted chocolate.

Spread the buttercream over the chilled fudge layer. Loosely cover the pan with wax paper and chill overnight.

To make the coffee whipped cream, in a small bowl, stir together 1 tablespoon of the whipping cream, the espresso powder, and the vanilla until the powder dissolves. In a larger bowl, using an electric mixer, whip the remaining cream until it starts to thicken. Add the coffee mixture and the confectioners' sugar and continue beating until the mixture forms firm peaks.

Loosen the torte by running a small knife around the edges of the pan. Remove the pan sides. Spread some of the coffee whipped cream on the top and sides of the torte, reserving some for decorating the top of the dessert. Press the grated chocolate around the sides of the torte. Place the torte on a serving platter. Pack the remaining whipped cream into a pastry bag fitted with a medium star tip and pipe rosettes around the perimeter of the top of the torte. Garnish with the chocolate shavings and the coffee bean candies, if desired. Let stand for 1 hour at room temperature before serving.

A Coffee Bar in Your Home

Get that jar of instant coffee out of your house! Just as you use the highest-quality flour and freshest eggs for your cakes and cookies, you need great coffee to start with, too. If you don't already have a coffee grinder, invest in one. Buy a pound of whole beans—hazelnut is a favorite for flavored coffees—and then invite your guests to help out, from grinding to brewing, in putting together these recipes.

The Everything
Dessert Cookbook

Chapter 13: Crusts

Pies, tarts, and pastries have an ill-earned reputation for being suitable mostly for special occasions, like Christmas and Thanksgiving. We should take a lesson from our Colonial ancestors, who were in the habit of eating pie for breakfast every morning. Sometimes it was a savory rather than a sweet pie, but our forefathers needed the dense nutrition and satisfaction that comes from eating a good-sized hunk of pie.

Many of the pie and tart recipes given here have a lighter side to them than our ancestors would have chosen, but given the much wider variety of ingredients we have to pour into a pie shell these days, as well as our increased focus on desserts that fall on the lighter side, I think they'd forgive us.

Pastry for 2 or 4 Pies

Makes: 2 double-crust or 4 one-crust pies

> *5 1/2 cups flour*
> *1 teaspoon salt*
> *3 tablespoons packed brown sugar*
> *1 pound (2 cups) vegetable shortening*
> *1 egg*
> *1 tablespoon white distilled vinegar*
> *cold water*

In a large bowl, sift together the flour, salt, and brown sugar. Add the shortening and, using a pastry blender, cut in until the mixture forms crumbs the size of peas. Put the egg in a measuring cup and blend with a fork. Add the vinegar, and then enough cold water to measure 3/4 cup. Add to the flour mixture and mix until incorporated. Chill for at least 30 minutes, preferably for 2 or more hours.

Divide the dough into 4 equal pieces to make 4 one-crust 9-inch pies or 2 double-crust 9-inch pies. Roll out the dough and line pie pans as needed. Freeze any unused dough for up to 24 hours.

Perfect Pie Crust

Makes: Pastry for a double-crust 9-inch pie

> *2 1/4 cups flour*
> *1 teaspoon salt*

$^3/_4$ *cup vegetable shortening*
$^1/_4$ *cup cold water*

In a bowl, sift together 2 cups of the flour and the salt. Add the shortening and, using a pastry blender, cut in until the mixture is the consistency of coarse sand. In a small bowl, combine the remaining $^1/_4$ cup flour with the water to make a paste. Add quickly to the flour-shortening mixture and lightly mix with a fork. Shape the dough into a ball. Cover and chill thoroughly.

Divide the dough into 2 portions, one slightly larger than the other. The larger portion will be for the bottom crust, and the smaller portion for the top crust. Roll out on a lightly floured work surface.

Crumble Crust

Makes: 1 9-inch pie crust

> *2 cups sifted flour*
> *2 teaspoons sugar*
> *1 teaspoon salt*
> $^2/_3$ *cup vegetable oil*
> $^1/_4$ *cup cold milk*

Preheat an oven to 400°F.
Sift together the sifted flour, sugar, and salt into a 9-inch pie plate. Combine the oil and milk in a measuring cup. Beat with a fork until creamy. Pour, all at once, into the center of the flour mixture. Mix with the fork until the flour is completely moistened. Set aside one-third of the dough for the top. Push and

press the dough with your fingers to a uniform thickness to line the bottom and sides of the plate. Shape and press to even the edges. Pinch lightly to flute the edges. Fill the lined pie plate with a filling. Using your fingers, crumble the remaining dough and sprinkle over the filling.

Bake for 15 minutes. Reduce the heat to 350°F and bake for 30 to 40 minutes longer, or until the filling is done.

Coconut Rum Tarts

Makes: 8 tartlets

> *pastry for a double-crust, 9-inch pie*
> $^1/_4$ *cup toasted dried coconut*
> *1 can (8$^1/_4$ ounces) crushed pineapple, undrained*
> *1 package (3$^3/_4$ ounces) instant vanilla pudding and pie filling mix*
> *2 cups whipping cream*
> *2 tablespoons dark rum*
> *1 tablespoon candied ginger, finely chopped*

Preheat an oven to 425°F.
Prepare the pastry as directed, folding the toasted coconut into the flour. Roll out on a lightly floured work surface. Cut the dough into 8 rounds each 4 inches in diameter. Press into fluted 3-inch tart pans. Bake for 15 minutes, or until lightly browned. Let cool.

Remove the pastry shells from the pans. Drain the pineapple well, reserving $^1/_3$ cup syrup. Combine the pudding mix and cream

(continued)

in a large bowl. Beat until well blended and slightly thickened. Beat in the reserved $^1/_3$ cup pineapple syrup and the rum. Fold in the drained pineapple and ginger. Spoon into the tart shells. Chill for about 1 hour before serving.

Mini Cheese Tarts

Makes: 74 tarts

1 pound (two 8-ounce packages) cream cheese, softened
$^1/_2$ cup sugar
2 eggs
2 teaspoons vanilla extract
74 vanilla wafers
74 mini foil baking cups

Preheat an oven to 350°F.

In a bowl, beat together the cream cheese, sugar, eggs, and vanilla until smooth. Place a vanilla wafer in each baking cup, round side down. Place the foil cups on 1 or more baking sheets, and spoon the cream cheese mixture into the baking cups.

Bake for 20 minutes, or until the filling is cooked through. Cool on a rack. Top with blueberries, cherries, pineapple, or strawberries. For pineapple, use a can of crushed pineapple, add 1 drop of yellow food coloring, 2 tablespoons sugar and 1 heaping tablespoon of cornstarch. Mix until the cornstarch dissolves. Cook until mixture thickens. Stir while cooking. Cool tarts and then top with the fruit.

Lime Divine Tarts

Makes: 36 tartlets

Tart Shells:
2 cups flour
1 cup confectioners' sugar
$^3/_4$ cup unsalted butter or margarine
2 tablespoons ice water

Filling:
4 eggs
1 cup sugar
$^1/_2$ cup lime juice
1 teaspoon grated lime rind
$^1/_2$ cup unsalted butter or margarine

tiny mint sprigs or small lime slices

Preheat an oven to 400°F.

To make the tart shells, in a bowl, combine the flour and confectioners' sugar. Add the butter and, using a pastry blender, cut in until the mixture is crumbly. Stir in the water with a fork, mixing until fine crumbs form. Gather up the dough and pat into a ball. (If using a food processor, slowly combine the first 3 ingredients, then add the water while the machine is spinning.) On a lightly floured work surface, roll out the dough $^1/_{16}$ inch thick. Cut out 36 rounds to fit tartlet tins $1^7/_8$ inches in diameter. Bake for 12 minutes. Let cool.

To make the filling, in a bowl, beat the eggs until light. Add the sugar and lime juice and rind and stir well. Pour into the top pan

of a double boiler. Add the butter and place over (not touching) simmering water. Cook, stirring constantly, until thickened. Remove from the heat, pour into a bowl, let cool, and chill.

Fill the tart shells to the brim with the cooled filling. Garnish with tiny mint sprigs or small lime slices.

Honeybee Tarts

Makes: 4 to 6 tartlets

2 eggs
$1/2$ cup honey
$1/4$ cup sugar
$1/4$ teaspoon salt
1 teaspoon vanilla extract
$2/3$ cup pecans, broken into pieces
4 to 6 unbaked 4-inch pastry tartlet shells

Preheat an oven to 400°F.

In a bowl, beat together the honey, sugar, salt, vanilla, and pecans. Pour into the pastry shells.

Bake for 15 to 18 minutes, or until the filling is set. Let cool.

Maple Butter Tarts

Makes: 12 tartlets or 6 tarts

pastry for double-crust pie
$1/3$ cup butter, melted and cooled
$1/2$ cup maple syrup
$1/4$ teaspoon salt
$1/4$ teaspoon ground nutmeg

$1/2$ cup packed brown sugar
$1/2$ cup raisins
2 eggs, lightly beaten

Prepare the pastry dough and use to line twelve 2-inch tartlet pans or 6 cups of a muffin tin. Combine all the remaining ingredients in a bowl and mix well.

Preheat an oven to 450°F. Fill the pastry-lined pans two-thirds full.

Bake for 15 to 20 minutes. Let cool for 10 minutes before removing from the pans.

Strawberry Pie

Serves: 8 to 10

1 pound (two 8-ounce packages) cream
 cheese, softened
$1/4$ cup sugar
1 to 2 teaspoons grated lemon rind
4 tablespoons lemon juice
1 fully baked 9-inch pie shell
2 pints strawberries, hulled and sliced
2 tablespoons cornstarch
$1/4$ cup water
1 jar (12 ounces) strawberry preserves
whipped cream (optional)

In a bowl, combine the cream cheese, sugar, lemon rind to taste, and 2 tablespoons of the lemon juice and mix well. Spread in the bottom of the prebaked shell. Top with the strawberries. In a small saucepan, combine the cornstarch and water. Stir well to dissolve the cornstarch, then stir in the

(continued)

preserves. Bring to a boil, stirring constantly. Cook and stir for about 5 minutes, or until thick and clear. Remove from the heat and stir in the remaining 2 tablespoons lemon juice. Let cool to room temperature. Pour the cooled preserves over the berries. Chill well. If you like, garnish with whipped cream before serving.

Strawberries and Cream Pie

Serves: 10

> 2 pints strawberries, hulled
> $^3/_4$ cup sugar
> 2 tablespoons cornstarch
> $^1/_2$ cup water
> 1 teaspoon lemon juice
> few drops of red food coloring
> 1 cup whipping cream
> 2 tablespoons confectioners' sugar
> $^1/_2$ teaspoon vanilla extract
> 1 9-inch graham cracker pie crust, prebaked
> ground nutmeg

Crush enough of the strawberries to measure 1 cup. Reserve the remaining berries. In a saucepan, combine the sugar and cornstarch and stir to dissolve the cornstarch. Add the crushed berries and water and place over medium heat. Cook, stirring constantly, until the mixture thickens and comes to a boil. Boil for 1 minute. Remove from the heat and stir in the lemon juice.

Add enough red food coloring to turn the mixture an attractive color. Cover and let cool to lukewarm.

In a bowl, beat together the cream and confectioners' sugar until stiff peaks form. Fold in the vanilla. Layer half of the whipped cream on the bottom of the crust. Sprinkle lightly with nutmeg. Top with the reserved berries and then with the cooled glaze. Top with the remaining whipped cream, placing several tablespoonfuls of it in a circle. Chill for at least 2 hours before serving.

Strawberry–White Chocolate Mousse Tart

Serves: 6

Pastry:
> $1^3/_4$ cups flour
> $^1/_4$ cup packed light brown sugar
> $2^1/_2$ teaspoons grated orange rind
> $^1/_8$ teaspoon salt
> $^7/_8$ cup unsalted butter, cut into chunks
> $1^1/_2$ tablespoons orange juice
> 1 egg yolk
> 1 teaspoon vanilla extract
> 2 squares (2 ounces) white chocolate, chopped

Mousse:
> 6 squares (6 ounces) white chocolate
> $^1/_4$ cup whipping cream
> 1 egg white, at room temperature
> 1 tablespoon sugar

½ cup whipping cream, whipped
2 tablespoons Grand Marnier or other
 orange-flavored liqueur
½ cup strawberry jam
1 pint strawberries, stemmed and cut into
 half lengthwise

To make the pastry, in a large bowl, stir together the flour, brown sugar, orange rind, and salt. Add the butter and, using a pastry blender, cut it in until the mixture resembles fine meal. In a separate bowl, stir together the orange juice, egg yolk, and vanilla. Add enough of the juice mixture to the flour-butter mixture to form a ball that comes together easily. Gather the dough into a ball and flatten into a 12-inch round.

Preheat an oven to 375°F. Place the dough round between sheets of plastic wrap, and roll out ⅛ inch thick. Trim to an 11-inch round. Remove the top sheet of plastic wrap and invert the pastry into a 10-inch springform pan. Peel off the plastic wrap and gently press the pastry into the bottom and up the sides of the pan. Crimp the top edges. Freeze for 15 minutes.

Line the tart shell with aluminum foil and fill with pie weights or dried beans. Bake for about 10 minutes, or until the sides are set. Remove the weights and foil. Return the tart shell to the oven and bake for 15 to 20 minutes, or until golden brown. Sprinkle the 2 ounces of white chocolate over the hot crust. Let stand for 1 minute. Using the back of a spoon, spread the chocolate over the bottom and up the sides of the pastry. Transfer to a rack to cool completely.

To make the mousse, in a small, heavy sauce pan over very low heat, melt the white chocolate with ¼ cup of the heavy cream, stirring constantly. Pour into a bowl. Let stand until just cool. In another small bowl, beat the egg white until soft peaks form. Gradually add the sugar and beat until stiff peaks form. Fold the whipped cream, 1 tablespoon of the liqueur, and the egg white into the chocolate mixture just until combined. Spoon the mousse into the prepared pan, spreading evenly. Refrigerate the mousse until set, 2 hours or as long as overnight.

To assemble, in a small, heavy saucepan, bring the jam and the remaining 1 tablespoon liqueur to a boil, stirring constantly. Transfer to a processor and purée. Brush a thin layer of the jam over the mousse. Place the strawberries on top of the mousse.

Fresh Peach Pie

Serves: 10

pastry for double-crust, 9-inch pie (page 196)
8 peaches
⅔ cup packed light brown sugar
½ teaspoon ground nutmeg
¾ cup flour
½ teaspoon ground cinnamon
¼ teaspoon ground ginger

Preheat an oven to 400°F.

(continued)

Line a 9-inch pie plate with half of the pastry. Peel, quarter, and pit the peaches and place in a bowl. In another bowl, combine the brown sugar, flour, cinnamon, nutmeg, and ginger and mix until well blended. Add the sugar-flour mixture to the peaches, tossing gently. Pour the filling into the lined pie shell. Cover with the top crust and prick with a fork.

Bake for 10 minutes. Reduce the heat to 375°F and continue baking for 50 to 55 minutes, or until the crust is golden.

Apple Pie

Serves: 10

$^1\!/_2$ cup sugar
1 teaspoon ground cinnamon
$^1\!/_4$ teaspoon ground nutmeg
pinch of salt
$^3\!/_4$ cup water
1 tablespoon lemon juice
3 cups peeled and thinly sliced tart
    cooking apples (5 to 6 medium apples)
2 tablespoons cornstarch
1 tablespoon butter
1 prepared 9-inch graham cracker pie crust
ice cream or whipped cream (optional)

Preheat an oven to 350°F.
Combine the sugar, cinnamon, nutmeg, and salt in a saucepan. Stir in $^1\!/_2$ cup of the water, lemon juice, and apples. Place over medium heat and stir gently until the mixture comes to a boil. Cover and simmer for 13 to

20 minutes, or until the apples are almost tender, stirring occasionally. Meanwhile, in a small bowl, dissolve the cornstarch in the remaining $^1\!/_4$ cup water. When the apples are ready, stir in the cornstarch until thickened and clear. Stir in the butter. Pour the apple filling into the pie crust.

Bake for 30 minutes, or until bubbling hot and the apples are tender. Top the pie with ice cream or whipped cream, if desired.

Honey Apple Pie

Serves: 10

pastry for double-crust, 9-inch pie (page 196)
$^3\!/_4$ cup sugar
1 teaspoon ground nutmeg
6 cups peeled and sliced apples
2 tablespoons butter, cut into bits
$^1\!/_2$ cup honey
1 tablespoon grated orange rind
confectioners' sugar

Preheat an oven to 425°F.
Line a 9-inch pie pan with half of the pastry, leaving 1 inch of pastry hanging over the edge of the pan. In a large bowl, stir together the sugar and nutmeg. Add the apple slices and mix lightly. Transfer the apple mixture to the prepared pan. Dot with the butter. On a lightly floured work surface, roll out the remaining pastry into a thin round and cut into $^1\!/_2$-inch-wide strips. Moisten the edge of the bottom pastry with water. Arrange the pastry strips on top of the pie, forming a

lattice top. Trim the ends of the strips as necessary and press the ends to the bottom crust. Turn the edge of the bottom crust and strips under and flute to make a high rim. Cover the edge carefully with a 1 1/2-inch-wide strip of aluminum foil to keep it from getting too brown.

Bake for 50 to 60 minutes, or until the apples are tender and the pastry is well browned. In a small bowl, stir together the honey and orange rind and pour the mixture through the openings in the lattice. Return to the oven for 5 minutes. Let cool to lukewarm and sift confectioners' sugar over the top.

Easy Apple Pie

Serves: 10

Pastry:
1 3/4 cups sifted flour
1/4 cup sugar
1/4 teaspoon salt
1 teaspoon ground cinnamon
2/3 cup butter, softened
about 1/4 cup water

Filling:
1 egg, lightly beaten
1 1/2 cups sour cream
1 cup sugar
1/4 cup flour
1/2 teaspoon salt
2 teaspoons vanilla extract
4 large McIntosh apples, peeled, cored,
    and sliced

(continued)

Apple Pie Surprise

When making a double-crust apple pie, sprinkle a light layer of grated Cheddar cheese over the apples before adding the top crust. Bake as usual.

Topping:

$^1/_2$ cup butter, softened
$^1/_2$ cup flour
$^1/_2$ cup sugar
$^1/_2$ cup packed brown sugar
$^1/_2$ cup oatmeal

To make the pastry, combine the flour, sugar, salt, and cinnamon in a bowl. Add the butter and cut in with a pastry blender until the mixture has the consistency of coarse meal. While tossing and stirring with a fork, sprinkle in just enough of the water to moisten. Gather the dough into a ball. On a lightly floured work surface, roll out the dough into a 12-inch round. Transfer the round to a 9-inch pie plate. Chill.

Preheat an oven to 450°F.

To make the filling, in a large bowl, combine the egg, sour cream, sugar, flour, salt, and vanilla. Beat until smooth. Add the apples to the sour cream mixture and toss gently to mix. Spoon into the chilled pastry shell.

Bake for 10 minutes. Reduce the oven temperature to 350°F and bake for 35 minutes longer, or until the apples are tender.

Meanwhile, make the topping: In a bowl, combine all the ingredients and, using a fork, mix thoroughly until crumbly. Sprinkle evenly over the baked pie. Return to the oven and bake for 15 minutes longer, or until lightly browned. Let cool and store in the refrigerator.

Gingery Apple Pie

Serves: 8

1 recipe double-crust pie dough, (page 196) with 2 teaspoons finely chopped candied ginger mixed in with the butter pieces

Filling:

3 pounds (9 or 10 medium) Granny Smith apples, peeled, cored, and sliced $^1/_4$ inch thick
1 tablespoon lemon juice
$^1/_2$ cup granulated sugar, plus extra for sprinkling
$^1/_4$ cup packed light brown sugar
3 tablespoons flour
1 teaspoon grated lemon zest
$^1/_2$ teaspoon ground cinnamon
$^1/_4$ teaspoon ground cloves
2 tablespoons raisins
3 tablespoons unsalted butter, cut into small pieces
1 egg
1 tablespoon water

Prepare the pie dough as directed and chill.

In a large bowl, combine the apple slices and the lemon juice and toss to coat. In a bowl, stir together the $^1/_2$ cup granulated sugar, the brown sugar, flour, lemon zest, cinnamon, cloves, and raisins. Sprinkle the mixture over the apples, and toss well to combine.

To assemble the pie, divide the pie dough in half. Wrap one-half in plastic wrap and refrigerate. On a lightly floured work surface, roll out the other half into a 12-inch round. Drape around the rolling pin and carefully transfer to a 9-inch pie plate. Gently ease the round into the bottom and sides of the pie plate. Trim the edges so they are even with the edge of the plate. Spoon the filling into the pie shell, spreading it evenly. Refrigerate while you prepare the top crust.

Take the remaining dough from the refrigerator and prepare a lightly floured work surface Shape the dough into a rough square by pressing the sides of the dough onto the work surface. Roll out the dough into a 9-by-12-inch rectangle. Using a fluted pastry wheel or chef's knife, cut the dough the short way into 24 strips, each measuring $1/2$ inch wide and 9 inches long. Arrange 12 of the strips, $1/4$ inch apart, on a floured baking sheet.

Beginning from the top left strip, fold every other strip in half, back toward you. Place one of the reserved strips of dough horizontally across the unfolded strips, just above the fold. Unfold the strips away from you, back to their original position, over the horizontal strip. Now beginning with the top strip, second from the left, fold back every other strip again. Insert another horizontal strip and unfold the vertical strips again. Repeat this process until you have inserted 6 horizontal strips to the top of the pan. Rotate the pan 180 degrees and repeat the process

on the other side. Place the sheet with the lattice top on it in the refrigerator for at least 30 minutes.

In the meantime, make the egg wash: in a small bowl or cup, whisk together the egg and water. Set aside.

Preheat an oven to 375°F. Remove the pie and the lattice top from the refrigerator. Brush the rim of the bottom crust with the egg wash. Gently slide the lattice top over the apple filling. Press the edge of the lattice against the edge of the bottom crust and cut away excess dough. Flute the edge of the crust as desired. Brush the lattice with egg wash and sprinkle with the granulated sugar.

Bake for 40 to 45 minutes, or until the crust is golden and the filling is bubbling. Let cool on a rack before cutting.

Wild Blackberry Pie

Serves: 12

pastry for a double-crust, 9-inch pie
4 cups blackberries
$1/2$ cup chopped black walnuts
1 tablespoon lemon juice
$1/2$ cup granulated sugar
$1/2$ cup packed brown sugar
$1/2$ teaspoon ground cinnamon
3 tablespoons flour
3 tablespoons butter, cut into bits
melted butter
ground cinnamon and sugar for dusting

(continued)

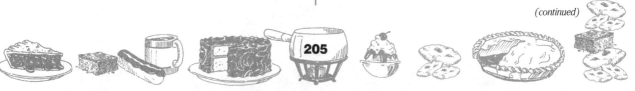

Preheat an oven to 350°F.

Line a deep-dish 9-inch pie plate with half of the pastry, leaving 1 inch of the pastry hanging over the edge of the plate. In a large bowl, combine the blackberries, nuts, lemon juice, sugars, cinnamon, and flour. Mix lightly. Spoon into the prepared pastry shell. Dot with the butter. On a lightly floured work surface, roll out the remaining pastry into a thin round and cut into $1/2$-inch-wide strips. Moisten the edge of the bottom pastry with water. Arrange the pastry strips on top of the pie, forming a lattice top. Trim the ends of the strips as necessary and press the ends to the bottom crust. Turn the edge of the bottom crust and strips under and flute to make an attractive rim. Brush the lattice and the edges with the melted butter. Sprinkle lightly with cinnamon and sugar.

Bake for 45 minutes, or until the top crust is golden.

Wild Blueberry Angel Pie

Serves: 8

4 eggs, separated
$1/8$ teaspoon salt
$1 1/3$ cups sugar
$1/4$ cup cornstarch
1 cup fresh orange juice
2 cups dry-pack frozen blueberries, thawed and drained

l cup whipping cream, whipped additional blueberries (optional)

Preheat an oven to 250°F. Grease a 9-inch pie pan.

In a bowl, beat together the egg whites and salt until stiff peaks form. Gradually beat in 1 cup of the sugar 1 tablespoon at a time until the mixture is stiff and glossy. Spread a 1-inch layer of the egg whites in the prepared pan. Place the remaining egg whites in a pastry bag fitted with a large star tip; press out rosettes, positioning them around the outer edge of the pie.

Bake for 1 hour.

Turn off the heat but leave in the oven for another hour. Remove from the oven and let cool.

In a small saucepan, combine the cornstarch and the remaining $1/3$ cup sugar. Stir in the orange juice. Place over medium heat and cook, stirring, until the sauce bubbles and thickens. Meanwhile, in a bowl, beat the egg yolks until blended. Gradually beat the hot sauce into the yolks. Let cool. Fold in the blueberries and then the whipped cream. Spread the mixture into the cooled meringue shell. Decorate the top, if you like, with additional thawed and drained wild blueberries. Chill for 12 hours before serving.

Macaroon Pie

Serves: 8

1/4 cup chopped pecans
1 unbaked 9-inch pastry shell
2 eggs
1/2 cup water
1 1/2 cups sugar
1/4 cup flour
1/4 teaspoon salt
1 1/3 cups shredded dried coconut
1/2 cup butter, melted

Preheat an oven to 325°F.

Sprinkle the pecans in the bottom of the pastry shell. In a bowl, combine the eggs, water, sugar, flour, salt, coconut, and butter, mixing well. Pour the mixture over the nuts—do not stir.

Bake for 45 minutes, or until golden brown.

Coconut-Citrus Frozen Pie
(Courtesy of Godiva Chocolates)

Serves: 10

Coconut pie pastry:
1 cup plus 2 tablespoons flour
1 tablespoon sugar
pinch of salt
6 tablespoons unsalted butter, chilled and
    cut into 1/2-inch cubes
3 to 3 1/2 tablespoons ice water
3/4 cup lightly packed sweetened shredded
    coconut

Toasted coconut topping:
1 cup sweetened shredded coconut

Coconut sorbet filling:
2 pints lemon sorbet, slightly softened
1/2 cup cream of coconut

To make the pie shell, in a food processor, combine the flour, sugar, and salt and pulse 3 or 4 times to mix well. Scatter the butter cubes over the flour mixture and pulse 10 to 15 times until the mixture resembles coarse meal. Add 3 tablespoons of the ice water and pulse 15 times until the dough starts to pull away from the sides of the bowl. If the dough is still dry, add the remaining ice water 1 teaspoon at a time and pulse 2 or 3 times. Add the coconut and pulse just to combine.

Scrape the dough out onto a work surface and form it into a ball. Flatten it into a 5-inch disk and wrap in plastic wrap. Refrigerate for 20 to 30 minutes, or until firm enough to roll.

Lightly dust a work surface and a rolling pin with flour. Place the dough on the surface and roll out into a 12-inch round, lifting and rotating the dough after each turn. Dust underneath the dough with more flour if necessary to roll.

Carefully roll up the dough around the rolling pin and transfer it to a 9-inch glass pie plate. Gently ease the dough into the bottom and up the sides of the pie plate without stretching it.

(continued)

Trim the edge of the pastry to a ¹/₂-inch overhang. Tuck the edge of the dough underneath itself and flute the edge to form a decorative border. Refrigerate until firm, 20 to 30 minutes.

Position 1 rack in the bottom third of an oven and another in the top third. Preheat to 350°F.

Line the pie shell with a piece of aluminum foil, leaving a 1-inch overhang. Fill with pie weights or dried beans. Place the pie shell on the lower rack and bake for 15 minutes. Using the aluminum foil overhang as handles, remove the foil and weights. Continue to bake the pie shell for 12 to 15 minutes longer, or until lightly browned. Let cool completely on a rack.

To prepare the coconut topping, spread the coconut on a baking sheet. Place the baking sheet on the upper oven rack and bake, stirring frequently, for 7 to 10 minutes, or until lightly toasted. Let cool, then transfer to an airtight container until ready to serve.

Cover the cooled pie shell with plastic wrap and refrigerate for 20 to 30 minutes, or until cold.

To make the filling, in a large bowl, combine the sorbet and cream of coconut and stir until well blended. Cover and freeze for about 10 minutes, to firm slightly.

Spoon the sorbet mixture into the chilled pie shell. Using a large rubber spatula, spread the mixture evenly, mounding it slightly in the center. Cover the pie with plastic wrap and freeze for at least 2 hours, or until frozen.

To serve, sprinkle the toasted coconut evenly over the top of the pie. Using a large heavy knife, cut the pie into wedges and place on individual dessert plates. Serve immediately.

Mincemeat Pie

Serves: 10

> 1 package (9 ounces) mincemeat
> 1 ¹/₄ cups water
> 1 cup sugar
> 2 heaping tablespoons flour
> 2 eggs, beaten
> pinch of salt
> ¹/₂ teaspoon vanilla extract
> 1 fully baked 9-inch pastry shell

Crumble the mincemeat into a bowl, add the water, and let soak for 30 minutes, or until swollen. Transfer the mincemeat to a saucepan and add the sugar, flour, eggs, salt, and vanilla. Place over low heat, bring to a simmer, and simmer, stirring constantly, for about 10 minutes, or until thick. Spread the mixture in the pastry shell. Let cool before serving.

Peanut Butter Pie

Serves: 12

Pastry:

$1/2$ cup margarine, softened
$1/2$ cup packed brown sugar
$1 1/4$ cups flour
$1/4$ teaspoon baking soda
$1/2$ teaspoon vanilla extract
$1/2$ cup chopped peanuts

Filling:

2 cups smooth peanut butter
1 package (8 ounces) cream cheese
8 cups whipped cream
chocolate curls or chocolate syrup

Preheat an oven to 350°F.

To make the pastry, in a bowl, combine the margarine and brown sugar and cream it together. Add the flour, baking soda, vanilla, and peanuts and stir until crumbly. Press the mixture into the bottom and sides of an ungreased 9-inch pie plate. Bake for 15 minutes, or until golden brown. Let cool completely before filling.

To make the filling, combine the peanut butter and cream cheese in a bowl and beat together until smooth. Fold in 4 cups of the whipped cream. Spread the mixture in the cooled pastry shell. Spread the remaining 4 cups whipped cream over the filling. Garnish with chocolate curls or a thin drizzle of chocolate syrup. Chill for 30 minutes before serving.

Pear Cheese Pie

Serves: 8

1 can (1 pound) pear halves, well drained
1 prepared 9-inch graham cracker crust
2 egg yolks, well beaten
1 package (8 ounces) cream cheese, softened
1 cup sour cream
$1/2$ teaspoon grated lemon rind
1 teaspoon lemon juice
$3/4$ cup sugar
1 tablespoon flour
$1/2$ teaspoon salt
$1/2$ teaspoon ground nutmeg
2 egg whites
$1/4$ teaspoon cream of tartar

Preheat an oven to 375°F.

Arrange the pear halves into the graham cracker crust. In a bowl, combine the egg yolks and cream cheese and beat until smooth. Blend in the sour cream, lemon rind, and juice. In another bowl, combine $1/2$ cup of the sugar, the flour, salt, and nutmeg and mix well. Add the sugar mixture to the cheese mixture and mix well. Pour over the pears.

Bake for 25 minutes, or until set. Meanwhile, beat the egg whites with the cream of tartar until frothy. Gradually add the remaining $1/4$ cup sugar, beating until stiff peaks form. When the pie is ready, remove from the oven and spread the meringue over the filling, sealing to the edges of the pastry.

(continued)

Pretty Neat Custard Pies

To pour a custard filling into a pie crust without making a mess, fill your pie shell at the oven. Mix the filling in a bowl and then transfer to a pitcher or a bowl with a pouring spout. Place the pie shell on the oven rack and then carefully pour in the custard.

Continue to bake for 10 minutes longer, or until the meringue is golden brown.

Rhubarb Cream Pie

Serves: 8

> *pastry for double-crust, 9-inch pie (page 196)*
> $^1/_2$ *cup sugar*
> $^1/_4$ *cup flour*
> $^3/_4$ *teaspoon ground nutmeg*
> *3 eggs, lightly beaten*
> *4 cups sliced rhubarb (1-inch thick slices)*
> *1 tablespoon butter or margarine, cut*
> *   into bits*

Preheat an oven to 400°F.

Line a 9-inch pie plate with half of the pastry, leaving 1 inch of the pastry hanging over the edges of the pan. In a large bowl, combine the sugar, flour, and nutmeg. Add the eggs and beat well to blend. Add the rhubarb and stir and toss to combine. Spoon into the prepared pastry shell. Dot with the butter. On a lightly floured work surface, roll out the remaining pastry into a thin round and cut into 1-inch-wide strips. Moisten the edge of the bottom pastry in the water. Arrange the pastry strips on top of the pie, forming a lattice top. Trim the ends of the strips as necessary and press the ends to the bottom crust. Turn the edge of the bottom crust and strips under and flute to make an attractive rim.

Bake for 50 to 60 minutes, or until filling bubbles.

Serve warm or cooled.

Custard Pie

Serves: 8

1 unbaked 9-inch pastry shell (page 196)
4 eggs, lightly beaten
$\frac{1}{2}$ cup sugar
$\frac{1}{4}$ teaspoon salt
$\frac{1}{2}$ teaspoon vanilla extract
$\frac{1}{8}$ teaspoon almond extract
$\frac{1}{2}$ cup milk, scalded
ground nutmeg

Chill the pie shell while you make the filling.

Preheat an oven to 400°F.

In a bowl, beat together the eggs, sugar, salt, and vanilla and almond extracts. Gradually add the hot milk, stirring constantly. Pour into the pie shell. Sprinkle with nutmeg. Bake for 25 to 30 minutes, or until a knife inserted halfway between the edge and the center of the custard comes out clean. Let cool on a rack for 15 to 30 minutes, then chill before serving.

Chocolate Coconut Pie
(Courtesy of Godiva Chocolates)

Serves: 10

Chocolate coconut crust:
14 ounces semisweet chocolate, coarsely chopped
2 tablespoons unsalted butter
$1\frac{1}{2}$ cups crisped rice cereal
$\frac{1}{2}$ cup shredded sweetened coconut

Filling:
8 squares (8 ounces) bittersweet chocolate, coarsely chopped
2 tablespoons water
1 tablespoon unsalted butter
$\frac{1}{8}$ teaspoon salt
$1\frac{1}{4}$ cups whipping cream
$\frac{1}{2}$ cup cream of sweetened coconut
2 teaspoons vanilla extract

To make the crust, spray the bottom and sides of a 9-inch pie pan well with nonstick cooking spray. In the top of a double boiler or in a heatproof bowl, melt the chocolate with the butter over simmering water. Stir until smooth.

In a large bowl, combine the chocolate mixture, cereal, and coconut, mixing well. Scrape the mixture into the prepared pan. Using a small flexible metal spatula, spread the mixture evenly onto the bottom and up the sides of the pan, covering completely. Refrigerate while preparing the filling.

To make the filling, melt the chocolate with the water and butter over simmering water. Stir in the salt. Let cool for 15 minutes.

In a large, chilled bowl, combine the cream, cream of coconut, and vanilla. Using a handheld electric mixer set on high speed, beat until soft peaks begin to form. Using a large rubber spatula, fold one-third of the whipped cream mixture into the chocolate mixture to lighten it. Fold in the remaining cream mixture.

(continued)

Scrape the filling into the prepared crust, smoothing the top with a cake spatula. Cover and refrigerate for at least 2 hours, or until the filling is set.

Let stand at room temperature for at least 30 minutes before serving.

Coconut Custard Pie

Serves: 10

> 1 unbaked 9-inch pastry shell (page 196)
> 4 eggs
> $\frac{1}{2}$ cup granulated sugar
> $\frac{1}{4}$ teaspoon salt
> 1 teaspoon vanilla extract
> $2\frac{1}{2}$ cups milk, scalded
> $1\frac{1}{2}$ cups flaked dried coconut
> $\frac{1}{4}$ cup packed brown sugar
> 2 tablespoons butter or margarine, softened

Chill the pie shell while you make the filling. Preheat an oven to 400°F.

In a bowl, beat the eggs slightly and stir in the granulated sugar, salt, and vanilla. Gradually stir in the hot milk. Reserve $\frac{1}{2}$ cup of the coconut. Add the remaining 1 cup coconut to the milk mixture and mix well. Pour into the pie shell.

Bake for 25 to 30 minutes, or until a knife inserted halfway between the edge and the center of the custard comes out clean. Let cool on a rack. At serving time, preheat a broiler. Combine the reserved $\frac{1}{2}$ cup coconut, the brown sugar, and the butter together and mix with a fork.

Sprinkle on top of the pie. Broiler 3 to 4 inches from the heat for 2 to 4 minutes, or until lightly browned. Serve at once.

Pumpkin Pie

Serves: 8

> 1 unbaked 9-inch pastry shell
> $1\frac{1}{2}$ cups canned or mashed cooked pumpkin
> $\frac{3}{4}$ cup sugar
> $\frac{1}{2}$ teaspoon salt
> 1 to $1\frac{1}{4}$ teaspoons ground cinnamon
> $\frac{1}{2}$ to 1 teaspoon ground ginger
> $\frac{1}{4}$ to $\frac{1}{2}$ teaspoon ground nutmeg
> $\frac{1}{4}$ to $\frac{1}{2}$ teaspoon ground cloves
> 3 eggs, lightly beaten
> $\frac{1}{4}$ cup milk
> $\frac{3}{4}$ cup evaporated milk

Preheat an oven to 400°F.

When lining the pie pan, be sure to crimp the edges high, as this recipe fills the pastry shell generously. In a large bowl, combine the pumpkin, sugar, salt, and spices to taste. Mix well. Stir in the eggs, milk, and evaporated milk until well blended. Pour into the pastry shell.

Bake for 50 minutes, or until a knife inserted halfway between the edge and the center of the filling comes out clean. Let cool completely on a rack.

Classic Pecan Pie

Serves: 10

3 eggs
²/₃ cup sugar
pinch of salt
1 cup dark corn syrup
¹/₃ cup butter or margarine, melted
1 cup pecan halves
1 unbaked 9-inch pastry shell (page 196)

Preheat an oven to 350°F.

In a bowl, combine the eggs, sugar, salt, corn syrup, and melted butter. Beat thoroughly. Stir in the pecans. Pour into the pastry shell.

Bake for 50 minutes, or until a knife inserted halfway between the edge and the center of the filling comes out clean. Let cool completely on a rack before serving.

Old South Pecan Pie

Serves: 10

pastry for a single-crust, 9-inch pie (page 196)
flour
¹/₃ cup butter or margarine, melted
¹/₂ cup light corn syrup
¹/₂ cup dark corn syrup
1 cup packed brown sugar
¹/₂ teaspoon vanilla extract
¹/₄ teaspoon salt
3 eggs, beaten
1 heaping cup pecan halves

Preheat an oven to 400°F. Sprinkle a small amount of flour over the bottom of a 9-inch pie plate, then line the plate with the pastry.

In a bowl, combine the melted butter, corn syrups, brown sugar, vanilla, salt, eggs, and nuts. Beat until well blended. Pour the pecan mixture into the pastry shell.

Bake for 10 minutes. Reduce the oven temperature to 375°F and bake for 45 to 50 minutes longer. To test for doneness, shake the pie gently; it should be firm near the edges but slightly jiggly in the center. Let cool on a rack before serving.

Quick and Easy Cranberry Apple Pie

Serves: 10

1 package frozen pie-crust shells (2 shells)
1 can (1 pound 5 ounces) apple pie filling
1 cup whole berry cranberry sauce
¹/₂ cup walnuts, chopped
1 egg, beaten

Preheat an oven to 400°F.

Separate the 2 pie shells in the package; let thaw at room temperature for about 30 minutes, or until the dough becomes soft. In a bowl, combine the pie filling, cranberry sauce, and nuts and mix well. Pour into 1 pie shell. Brush the edge of the pie shell with water. Carefully remove the second pie shell from its pan and turn it upside down on top of the apple filling. Press the edges

(continued)

of the 2 pastry layers together with the tines of a fork. Trim the edges with a sharp knife and cut vents in the top crust. Brush with the egg.

Bake for 35 to 40 minutes, or until the pie is brown and bubbly. Let cool completely on a rack before serving.

Classic Key Lime Pie

Serves: 10

> 1 envelope unflavored gelatin
> 1 cup sugar
> $1/4$ teaspoon salt
> 4 eggs, separated
> $1/2$ cup lime juice
> $1/4$ cup water
> 1 teaspoon grated lime rind
> few drops of green food coloring
> 1 cup whipping cream, whipped stiff
> 1 fully baked 9-inch pastry shell, cooled
> grated lime rind for garnish
> grated pistachio nuts and thin lime slices
>   for garnish (optional)

In a saucepan, combine the gelatin, $1/2$ cup of the sugar, and the salt. Mix well. In a bowl, beat together the egg yolks, lime juice, and water until well blended and stir into the gelatin mixture. Place over medium heat and cook, stirring, just until the mixture comes to a boil. Remove from the heat. Stir in the 1 teaspoon grated rind. Add the food coloring

sparingly to tint pale green. Chill, stirring occasionally, until the mixture mounds slightly when dropped from a spoon.

In a large bowl, beat the egg whites until soft peaks form. Gradually add the remaining $1/2$ cup sugar, beating until stiff peaks form. Fold the gelatin mixture into the egg whites. Fold in half of the whipped cream. Pile into the pastry shell and chill until firm. To serve, spread with the remaining whipped cream and sprinkle grated lime rind around the edge. If desired, sprinkle the center with pistachio nuts and decorate the top with lime slices.

Cranberry Velvet Pie

Serves: 8 to 10

> 1 envelope unflavored gelatin
> $1/4$ cup cold water
> 1 cup boiling water
> $1/4$ cup sugar
> 1 can (6 ounces) frozen cranberry or
>   cranberry-grape juice cocktail
>   concentrate, thawed and diluted
> 2 teaspoons lemon juice
> 1 package (3 ounces) cream cheese,
>   softened
> $1/3$ cup confectioners' sugar
> 1 teaspoon vanilla extract
> pinch of salt
> 1 cup whipping cream
> 1 fully baked 9-inch pastry shell
>   (page 196)

additional whipped cream (optional)
shaved sweet chocolate (optional)

In a bowl, soften the gelatin in the cold water. Pour the boiling water over the softened gelatin and stir until dissolved. Add the sugar, cranberry juice cocktail concentrate, and lemon juice. Refrigerate, stirring often, for about an hour, or until the mixture mounds when dropped from a spoon.

In a large bowl, combine the cream cheese, confectioners' sugar, vanilla, and salt and beat with an electric mixer until smooth. Gradually blend in the cream, then beat on high speed until thick and creamy. Fold the cranberry mixture into the cheese mixture, mixing until evenly blended. Turn into the pastry shell and refrigerate until set. Decorate with whipped cream and grated chocolate, if desired.

Candy Bar Pie

Serves: 12

1 1/2 cups graham cracker crumbs
1 tablespoon plus 1/2 cup plus 1/3 cup sugar
6 tablespoons unsalted butter, melted
6 tablespoons flour
1/2 teaspoon baking powder
1/2 teaspoon salt
1/2 cup unsalted butter, cut into 8 pieces
4 squares (4 ounces) semisweet chocolate, chopped

1 square (1 ounce) unsweetened chocolate, chopped
2 whole eggs
1 egg yolk
2 teaspoons vanilla extract
2 cups chopped assorted chocolate, caramel, and nut candy bars (1/2-inch pieces)
1 package (10 ounces) cream cheese, at room temperature
2 squares (2 ounces) milk chocolate, chopped
2 tablespoons whipping cream

Preheat an oven to 350°F. Butter a 9-inch deep-dish glass pie plate.

In a bowl, combine the graham cracker crumbs and 1 tablespoon sugar. Add the melted butter and stir until the crumbs are evenly moistened. Press the graham cracker mixture evenly over the bottom and up the sides of the prepared dish. Bake for about 5 minutes, or until crust is set. Let cool on a rack. Leave the oven set at 350°F.

In a bowl, sift together the flour, baking powder, and salt.

In the top of a double boiler, combine the 1/2 cup butter, semisweet chocolate, and unsweetened chocolate. Place over simmering water and stir until melted and smooth. Remove from over the water and let cool slightly.

(continued)

Pie Crust Secrets

As in many other areas of baking, patience helps make many recipes turn out better, including pie crusts. One time-worn way to ensure that your pie crust turns out flaky and tender is to chill the dough for at least 12 hours before you plan to roll it out; overnight is even better. Be sure to take the dough out of the refrigerator about 1 hour before starting. Your reward will be a wonderful pie crust.

In a bowl, using an electric mixer, beat together the $\frac{1}{2}$ cup sugar, 1 whole egg, and egg yolk until slightly thickened, about 1 minute. Add 1 teaspoon of the vanilla and the cooled chocolate mixture and mix until well blended. Add the flour mixture and mix just until combined. Pour into the prepared crust.

Bake for about 17 minutes, or until almost set and a tester inserted into the center comes out with moist batter still attached. Cover the crust with foil if it is browning too quickly. Let cool on a rack for 10 minutes, then arrange the candy bar pieces evenly over the fudge layer. Leave the oven set at 350°F.

In a bowl, using an electric mixer, beat together the cream cheese and $\frac{1}{3}$ cup sugar until smooth. Add the remaining whole egg and 1 teaspoon vanilla and beat just until smooth. Carefully spread the mixture over the surface of the pie.

Bake for about 15 minutes, or until the cream cheese layer is set. Let cool on a rack.

In the top of a double boiler, combine the milk chocolate and cream and place over simmering water. Stir until melted and smooth. Remove from the heat. Dip a spoon into the chocolate mixture and drizzle it over the top of the pie. Refrigerate until well chilled before serving.

Peppermint-Crisp Ice Cream Pie

Serves: 12

*1 package (9 ounces) chocolate
   wafer cookies (about 2 cups),
   crushed*

6 tablespoons unsalted butter, melted

*7 ounces (7 squares) semisweet chocolate,
   chopped, or 1 cup plus 3 tablespoons
   semisweet chocolate chips*

2 tablespoons vegetable oil

*1 quart chocolate ice cream, softened for
   30 minutes in the refrigerator*

*1 cup peppermint candy (about 5$\frac{1}{2}$
   ounces), coarsely chopped*

*1 quart peppermint ice cream, softened for
   30 minutes in the refrigerator*

Preheat an oven to 325°F. Butter a 9-inch springform pan.

In a bowl, combine the chocolate cookie crumbs and melted butter and stir until the crumbs are moistened evenly. Press the crumb mixture evenly over the bottom and 1 inch up the sides of the prepared pan. Bake until the crust is set, about 6 minutes. Let cool on a rack completely.

In the top of a double boiler, combine the semisweet chocolate and vegetable oil and place over simmering water. Stir until melted and smooth.

Using a flexible metal spatula, spread the softened chocolate ice cream over the crumb crust. Sprinkle half of the peppermint candy evenly over the ice cream. Using a teaspoon, drizzle 3 tablespoons of the chocolate sauce evenly over the peppermint topping. Spread the peppermint ice cream, cover it as well. Sprinkle the remaining peppermint candy evenly over the peppermint ice cream. Drizzle 2 tablespoons of the chocolate coating in thin, crisscrossing lines over the peppermint candy.

Place the remaining chocolate sauce in a heatproof container. Cover and refrigerate to serve with the pie. Cover the pie tightly with plastic wrap, then aluminum foil. Freeze for at least 6 hours or up to 2 weeks.

To serve, remove the chocolate sauce from the refrigerator and warm in a microwave or in the top of a double boiler over barely simmering water. Stir until the mixture is melted and pourable. Remove the ice cream pie from the freezer 10 to 15 minutes before serving. Dip a dish towel in hot water and wring it dry. Hold the hot towel around the sides of the springform pan for 15 seconds. Release the sides of the pan.

Using a sharp knife, cut the ice cream pie into wedges. Pass around the pitcher of warm chocolate sauce.

Nutmeg Custard Apple Pie

Serves: 10

1 package (11 ounces) pie crust mix
1¹⁄₂ pounds tart cooking apples
4 eggs
1¹⁄₂ cups light cream
1¹⁄₂ cups packed light brown sugar
1 teaspoon ground nutmeg

Following the package directions, make the pastry for a 9-inch pie shell. On a lightly floured work surface, roll out into an 11-inch round. Use to line a 9-inch pie plate. Fold under the edges of pastry and press into an upright rim, about 1 inch high, to make a substantial edge. Flute attractively and refrigerate.

Preheat an oven to 350°F.

Peel and core the apples, then slice thinly. Arrange half of the apple slices over the bottom of the pie shell, to cover completely. Arrange the remaining apple slices in an attractive pattern on top. Sprinkle with ¹⁄₂ cup brown sugar.

In a small bowl, beat together the eggs, cream, the remaining 1 cup brown sugar, and the nutmeg. Pour half of the egg mixture over the apples.

Bake for 20 to 25 minutes. Remove the pie from the oven and pour the remaining egg mixture over the apple slices. Return to the oven. Bake for 30 minutes longer, or until the apples are tender when pierced. Let cool on a rack, then cover and chill. Serve lightly chilled.

Raisin Pie

Serves: 10

³⁄₄ cup sugar
1 tablespoon cornstarch
¹⁄₄ teaspoon salt
1 teaspoon ground cinnamon
¹⁄₂ teaspoon ground nutmeg
¹⁄₄ teaspoon ground cloves
1 cup sour cream
1 tablespoon lemon juice
1 cup raisins
2 egg yolks, lightly beaten
¹⁄₂ cup walnut pieces
1 fully baked 8-inch pastry shell (page 196)

Meringue:
2 egg whites
¹⁄₄ teaspoon cream of tartar
¹⁄₄ cup sugar

In a heavy saucepan, combine the sugar, cornstarch, salt, and all the spices and stir well. Stir in the sour cream and lemon juice. Add the raisins and stir to incorporate. Place over medium heat and bring to a boil, stirring constantly. Cook, continuing to stir, for 10 minutes, until thick. Remove from the heat. Stir a small amount of the hot mixture into the egg yolks, then stir the egg yolks into the hot mixture. Return to medium heat and cook, stirring, for 1 minute. Let cool to lukewarm. Add the nuts and stir well. Pour into the cooled shell.

Preheat an oven to 350°F.

To make the meringue, in a bowl, combine the egg whites and cream of tartar and beat until soft peaks form. Gradually add the sugar, beating until stiff peaks form. Spread the meringue over the pie filling, sealing to the edges of the pastry. Bake for 12 to 15 minutes, or until meringue peaks are lightly browned. Let cool on a rack.

Lemon Meringue Pie

Serves: 6

1 1/2 cups sugar
3 tablespoons cornstarch
3 tablespoons flour
pinch of salt
1/2 cup hot water
3 egg yolks, lightly beaten
1/2 teaspoon grated lemon rind
2 tablespoons butter or margarine
1/3 cup lemon juice
1 fully baked 9-inch pastry shell
   (page 196)

Meringue:
3 egg whites
1 teaspoon lemon juice
6 tablespoons sugar

In a saucepan, combine the sugar, cornstarch, flour, and salt and stir well. Stir in the hot water. Bring to a boil over high heat,

Happy Meringue

When I was growing up and watched my mother make lemon meringue pie, I always thought that the meringue part of the process—beating the egg whites and then spooning them onto the lemon filling—was fascinating. Especially after the peaks of meringue began to lean gently to one side, under their own weight. After the pie was baked and cooled, I always ate the meringue, never the lemon custard, which was not sweet enough for me.

For your own happy meringue, make sure that you use a copper bowl to beat the whites, and don't even bother when the humidity is above 80 percent.

(continued)

stirring constantly. Reduce the heat to medium and cook and stir for 8 minutes longer or until fully thickened. Remove from the heat. Stir a small amount of the hot mixture into the egg yolks, then stir the egg yolks into the hot mixture. Return to high heat and bring to a boil, stirring constantly. Reduce the heat to low and cook and stir for 4 minutes longer. Remove from the heat. Add the lemon rind and butter. Stir in the lemon juice. Cover with plastic wrap, pressing it directly onto the surface, and let cool for 10 minutes. Pour into the pastry shell. Let cool.

Preheat an oven to 350°F.

To make the meringue, in a bowl, combine the egg whites and lemon juice and beat until soft peaks form. Gradually add the sugar, beating until stiff peaks form. Spread the meringue over the pie filling, sealing to the edges of the pastry. Bake for 12 to 15 minutes, or until the meringue is lightly browned. Let cool.

Pumpkin Meringue Pie

Serves: 8

$3/4$ cup sugar
3 tablespoons cornstarch
1 teaspoon ground cinnamon
$1/2$ teaspoon salt
$1/2$ teaspoon ground nutmeg
$1/2$ teaspoon ground ginger
$1/4$ teaspoon ground cloves

1 cup canned or cooked, mashed pumpkin
2 cups milk
3 egg yolks, lightly beaten
1 prebaked 9-inch pie shell

Meringue:

$1/2$ cup egg whites (from about 4 eggs)
1 teaspoon vanilla
$1/2$ teaspoon cream of tartar
1 cup sugar

In a saucepan, combine the sugar, cornstarch, cinnamon, salt, nutmeg, ginger, and cloves and stir well. Stir in the pumpkin and milk until well blended. Place over medium heat and bring to a boil, stirring constantly. Cook and stir for 10 to 12 minutes, or until the mixture thickens. Cook for 2 minutes longer; remove from the heat. Stir a small amount of the hot mixture into the egg yolks, then stir the egg yolks into the hot mixture. Return to medium heat and cook and stir for 2 minutes. Remove from the heat and let cool. Pour into the pastry shell.

Preheat an oven to 350°F.

To make the meringue, in a bowl, combine the egg whites, vanilla, and cream of tartar. Beat until soft peaks form. Gradually add the sugar, beating until stiff peaks form. Spread the meringue over the pie filling, sealing to the edges of the pastry. Bake for 12 to 15 minutes, or until the meringue is slightly browned. Let cool completely on a rack.

Lemon Orange Chiffon Pie

Serves: 8

1 envelope unflavored gelatin
$^1/_2$ cup plus $^1/_3$ cup sugar
pinch of salt
4 eggs, separated
$^1/_2$ cup lemon juice
$^1/_2$ cup orange juice
$^1/_4$ cup water
$^1/_2$ teaspoon grated lemon rind
$^1/_2$ teaspoon grated orange rind
4 egg whites
1 fully baked 9-inch pastry shell, cooled
whipped cream and thin orange slices

In a saucepan, combine the gelatin, $^1/_2$ cup sugar, and salt and mix well. In a bowl, beat together the egg yolks, fruit juices, and water and stir into the gelatin mixture. Place over medium heat and cook, stirring, just until the mixture comes to a boil. Remove from the heat and stir in the citrus rinds. Chill, stirring occasionally, until the mixture mounds slightly when dropped from a spoon.

In a bowl, beat the egg whites until soft peaks form. Gradually add the $^1/_3$ cup sugar, beating until stiff peaks form. Fold the gelatin mixture into the egg whites. Pile into the baked pastry shell. Chill until firm. Decorate with whipped cream and thin slices of orange.

Pumpkin Chiffon Pie

Serves: 8

$^3/_4$ cup packed brown sugar
1 envelope unflavored gelatin
$^1/_2$ teaspoon salt
1 teaspoon ground cinnamon
$^1/_2$ teaspoon ground nutmeg
$^1/_4$ teaspoon ground ginger
3 egg yolks, lightly beaten
$^3/_4$ cup milk
$1^1/_4$ cups canned or mashed cooked
    pumpkin
3 egg whites
$^1/_3$ cup granulated sugar
1 prepared 9-inch graham cracker crust
whipped cream

In a saucepan, combine the brown sugar, gelatin, salt, and all the spices and stir well. Combine the egg yolks and milk in a small bowl and mix until blended. Stir the yolk mixture into the sugar mixture. Place over high heat and bring to a boil, stirring constantly. Remove from the heat and stir in the pumpkin. Chill, stirring occasionally, for about 1 hour, or until the mixture mounds slightly when dropped from a spoon. (Test every now and then, and don't let it get too stiff.)

In a bowl, beat the egg whites until soft peaks form. Gradually add the granulated sugar, beating until stiff peaks form. Fold the pumpkin mixture into the egg whites. Pile into the crust. Chill until firm. Garnish with whipped cream.

Airy Chiffon

Readers who grew up in the 1960s and 1970s as I did remember those margarine commercials where Chiffon brand was a guarantee of airiness and delicious taste. We've learned to expect nothing less from any chiffon pie that passes before us. To make sure that your chiffon pie fits the bill, don't overbeat the egg whites. Also, a light touch when folding the egg whites into the other ingredients will help to ensure a chiffon pie that honors your memories.

Peanut Butter Chiffon Pie

Serves: 10

1 envelope unflavored gelatin
1 cup water
$\frac{1}{2}$ cup sugar
$\frac{1}{2}$ teaspoon salt
$\frac{3}{4}$ cup creamy peanut butter
1 teaspoon vanilla extract
3 egg whites
1 cup whipping cream, whipped stiff
1 fully baked 9-inch pastry shell
    (page 196) or crumb crust (page 197)
chopped peanuts

In the top pan of a double boiler, soften the gelatin in the water. Add $\frac{1}{4}$ cup of the sugar and the salt and place over (not touching) boiling water. Stir until the gelatin and sugar are dissolved. Remove from the heat and stir in the peanut butter and vanilla, mixing well. Whip until slightly thickened.

In a bowl, beat the egg whites until frothy. Gradually add the remaining $\frac{1}{4}$ cup sugar, beating until stiff peaks form. Fold the whites and the whipped cream into the peanut butter mixture. Pile into the pie shell. Sprinkle with the peanuts. Chill for at least 3 hours before serving.

Strawberry Chiffon Pie

Serves: 8

1 pint strawberries
$\frac{3}{4}$ cup sugar
1 envelope unflavored gelatin
$\frac{1}{4}$ cup cold water

^{1}/$_2$ cup hot water
1 tablespoon lemon juice
^{1}/$_2$ cup whipping cream, whipped
dash of salt
2 egg whites
1 prepared 9-inch graham cracker crust

whipped cream and strawberries

In a bowl, crush the strawberries. There should be 1 ^{1}/$_4$ cups. Cover with ^{1}/$_2$ cup of the sugar and let stand for 30 minutes. In a large bowl, soften the gelatin in the cold water. Add the hot water and stir to dissolve. Let cool. Add the crushed strawberries, lemon juice, and salt. Chill an hour. Stir occasionally, or until the mixture mounds slightly when dropped from a spoon. Fold in the whipped cream.

In a bowl, beat the egg whites until soft peaks form. Gradually add the remaining ^{1}/$_4$ cup sugar, beating until stiff peaks form. Fold the egg whites into the strawberry mixture. Pour into the crust. Chill until firm. Top with more whipped cream and berries before serving.

Vanilla Cream Pie

Serves: 8

^{3}/$_4$ cup sugar
^{1}/$_3$ cup flour or 3 tablespoons cornstarch
^{1}/$_4$ teaspoon salt
2 cups milk
3 egg yolks, lightly beaten
2 tablespoons butter or margarine

1 teaspoon vanilla extract
1 fully baked 9-inch pastry shell, cooled (page 196)

Meringue:
3 egg whites
^{1}/$_2$ teaspoon vanilla extract
^{1}/$_4$ teaspoon cream of tartar
6 tablespoons sugar

In a saucepan, combine the sugar, flour, and salt and stir well. Gradually stir in the milk. Place over medium heat and cook, stirring, until the mixture comes to a boil. Cook, stirring, for 2 minutes longer. Remove from the heat. Stir a small amount of the hot mixture into the egg yolks, then stir the egg yolks into the hot mixture. Return to medium heat and cook and stir for 2 minutes. Remove from the heat. Add the butter and vanilla and let cool to room temperature. Pour into the pastry shell.

Preheat an oven to 350°F.

To make the meringue, beat together the egg whites, vanilla, and cream of tartar until soft peaks form. Gradually add the sugar, beating until stiff peaks form. Spread over the pie filling, sealing to the edges of the pastry. Bake for 12 to 15 minutes, or until the meringue is lightly browned. Let cool completely on a rack.

Chocolate Coconut Cream Pie

Serves: 10

^{2}/$_3$ cup plus 9 tablespoons sugar
^{1}/$_2$ cup cornstarch

(continued)

  **223**

Cream Pies and Super Crust

One of the secrets to a perfectly baked cream pie is to bake the crust *before* you fill it. For a smooth, creamy filling, make sure that both the crust and the pan are cool to the touch before you pour in the filling.

$^1/_4$ teaspoon salt
3 cups plus 2 tablespoons milk
3 eggs, separated
1 tablespoon butter
2 teaspoons vanilla extract
$^1/_2$ cup flaked dried coconut
3 tablespoons unsweetened cocoa powder
1 fully baked 9-inch pastry shell or crumb crust, cooled
$^1/_4$ teaspoon cream of tartar

Preheat an oven to 350°F.

In a saucepan, combine the $^2/_3$ cup sugar, cornstarch, salt, and 3 cups milk and mix well. In a small bowl, lightly beat the egg yolks. Add to the milk mixture and blend well. Place the pan over medium heat and bring to a boil, stirring constantly. Cook and stir 1 minute. Remove from the heat and stir in the butter and vanilla. Pour $1^1/_2$ cups of the cooked mixture into a small bowl. Stir in the coconut and set aside. In a small cup, stir together the cocoa, 3 tablespoons of the sugar, and the 2 tablespoons milk. Blend into the cooked mixture remaining in the saucepan. Return the pan to medium heat and cook, stirring constantly, until the mixture begins to boil. Remove from the heat.

Pour 1 cup of the chocolate mixture into the pie shell. Spread the coconut mixture over the chocolate. Top with the remaining chocolate mixture, spreading evenly.

In a bowl, beat together the egg whites and cream of tartar until foamy. Gradually add the

remaining 6 tablespoons sugar, beating until stiff peaks form. Spread the meringue over the hot pie filling, sealing to the edges of the pastry.

Bake for 8 to 10 minutes, or until lightly browned. Let cool on a rack to room temperature, then chill for several hours before serving.

Coconut Custard Pie

Serves: 8

1 unbaked 9-inch pie shell
1 egg white
5 whole eggs
$^{1}/_{2}$ cup plus 2 tablespoons confectioners' sugar
2 teaspoons vanilla extract
$^{1}/_{2}$ teaspoon salt
2 cups milk
$^{1}/_{2}$ cup whipping cream
1 $^{3}/_{4}$ cups flaked dried coconut

Preheat an oven to 450°F.

Brush the bottom of the unbaked pie shell with the unbeaten egg white. Chill while you make the filling. Break the whole eggs into a mixing bowl and stir lightly. Do not beat. Add the confectioners' sugar, vanilla, and salt, then pour in the milk and cream. Stir together lightly. Place the coconut in the pie shell and pour the egg mixture through a fine-mesh strainer into the shell.

Bake for 10 minutes. Reduce the oven temperature to 350°F and bake for 20 minutes longer, or until the filling is set. Let cool on a rack completely before serving.

Sour Cream Apricot Pie

Serves: 8

Pastry:
2 cups sifted flour
1 tablespoon baking powder
1 teaspoon salt
$^{1}/_{2}$ cup vegetable shortening
1 egg
milk, as needed
melted butter

Filling:
1 package (3 ounces) cream cheese, softened
1 $^{1}/_{2}$ cups sour cream
1 can (12 ounces) apricot halves, drained
1 tablespoon ground cinnamon stirred into $^{1}/_{2}$ cup sugar

Preheat an oven to 450°F.

To make the pastry, in a bowl, sift together the sifted flour, baking powder, and salt. Add the shortening and, using a pastry blender, cut in until the mixture resembles meal. Beat the egg and pour into a measuring cup. Add enough milk to measure $^{2}/_{3}$ cup. Add to the flour mixture and stir and toss with a fork until a dough forms. Gather into a ball. On a lightly floured work surface, roll out the dough into an 11-inch round. Transfer to a 9-inch pie plate, turn under the edges, and flute to form a high, attractive rim. Bake for 10 minutes. Brush the shell with melted butter. Let cool before filling.

(continued)

To make the filling, combine the cream cheese and sour cream and beat until light. Pour into the baked pie shell. Place the apricot halves close together on top to cover completely. Sprinkle with the cinnamon-sugar mixture. Chill well before serving.

Warm Pineapple Tart with Coconut Sauce

Serves: 10

Coconut Sauce:

8 egg yolks
1 cup granulated sugar
1 cup coconut milk
$^1/_2$ pineapple, cored and puréed (about 1 cup)
2 tablespoons dark rum

Pineapple Tart:

1 sheet frozen puff pastry, about 8$^1/_2$
    ounces
$^1/_4$ cup confectioners' sugar
2 egg yolks
4 tablespoons granulated sugar
1 pineapple, cored, thinly sliced, and cut
    into $^1/_2$-inch wedges
mint sprigs (optional)

To make the sauce, in a saucepan, whisk together the yolks and sugar until pale. Slowly whisk in the coconut milk and pineapple purée. Place the saucepan over medium-low heat and continue stirring constantly with a flat-edged wooden spatula. Do not allow to boil. The mixture is ready when you can run your finger

down the back of the coated spatula and a path remains in the sauce for several seconds.

Remove from the heat and immediately strain the sauce through a fine-mesh strainer into a metal bowl that is set into a larger bowl filled with ice water. Stir the sauce for 5 minutes, or until cool. Add the rum. Cover with plastic wrap and refrigerate until ready to assemble.

Preheat an oven to 325°. Line a baking sheet with wax paper.

To make the tart, thaw the sheet of puff pastry according to the package directions. Lay the sheet on a lightly floured work surface and roll out into a 16-inch square. Using a 7-inch round plate as a guide, cut out 4 rounds with a paring knife. Using a fork, prick the rounds well. Transfer the rounds to the prepared baking sheet. Place the baking sheet in the freezer for 10 minutes.

In a small bowl, stir together the confectioners' sugar and yolks until smooth. Remove the prepared rounds from the freezer and brush with the egg mixture. Bake for 16 to 18 minutes, or until golden brown.

In a large nonstick pan, without using any fat, sauté the pineapple wedges over high heat. Sauté one side only, until golden brown. Remove from the pan and let cool.

Preheat a broiler.

To assemble the tart, arrange one-fourth of the pineapple wedges on each pastry round, fanning them from the rim to the center. Sprinkle each pineapple tart with 1 tablespoon

of the granulated sugar. Place in the broiler 5 inches from the heat and broil for 5 minutes, or until golden brown.

Ladle some of the coconut sauce on a 10-inch dessert plate. Place the tart on top. Garnish with mint.

Chocolate Cannoli
(Courtesy of Godiva Chocolates)

Serves: 4

$^1/_3$ *cup plus 1 tablespoon granulated sugar*
2 tablespoons Dutch-process unsweetened cocoa powder
$^1/_2$ *cup water*
3$^1/_2$ squares (3$^1/_2$ ounces) semisweet chocolate, finely chopped
1$^1/_3$ cups ricotta cheese
1$^1/_3$ cups granulated sugar
$^1/_2$ *cup unsweetened non-alkalized cocoa powder*
3 cups whipping cream
8 ready-made cannoli shells
confectioners' sugar, for dusting

In a small saucepan, combine the $^1/_3$ cup plus 1 tablespoon granulated sugar and the Dutch-process cocoa powder. Slowly whisk in the water, stirring until blended. Place over medium-low heat and cook, stirring constantly, for 3 to 4 minutes, or until the sugar dissolves. Stop stirring, raise the heat to medium-high, and bring the mixture to a boil. Remove from the heat and add the chopped

chocolate. Let the mixture stand for 1 to 2 minutes to melt the chocolate. Using a wire whisk, stir the chocolate until smooth. Strain the chocolate sauce through a fine-mesh sieve into a small bowl; let cool. Cover with plastic wrap, pressing it directly onto the surface of the sauce, and keep at room temperature.

In a large bowl, using an electric mixer set at medium-high speed, beat the ricotta, sugar, and the $^1/_2$ cup cocoa powder for 3 to 5 minutes, or until smooth; set aside.

In a chilled large bowl, using an electric mixer set on medium-high speed, beat the cream until stiff peaks just start to form. Do not overbeat.

Using a large rubber spatula, fold one-third of the whipped cream into the ricotta mixture to lighten it. Gently fold in the remaining whipped cream until just combined.

Fill a pastry bag fitted with a large closed star tip with the ricotta filling. Pipe the filling into the two ends of each cannoli shell. Refrigerate until serving, up to 1 hour.

To serve, carefully place 2 chocolate cannoli on each of 4 dessert plates. Using a rubber spatula or a spoon, drizzle some chocolate sauce over each chocolate cannoli. Dust with confectioners' sugar, if desired.

The Everything
Dessert Cookbook

Chapter 14: Fruit Desserts

Even though I am a serious chocoholic—for years, when I was living in Manhattan, after a spicy meal at a Chinese restaurant, I'd head straight for the nearest fresh-baked cookie shop for a bag full of warm, chewy chocolate chip cookies—today there are times when only a fresh fruit dessert will do.

Either it's summertime and I feel guilty not taking advantage of all of the fresh produce, or I've eaten way too much chocolate recently—yes, even I can admit I overdo it on chocolate occasionally. In any case, the fruit desserts listed here require little effort to spice up a bowl of fresh strawberries, peaches or blueberries, and they're perfect on the days when you crave fruit for dessert, but want something a little fancier than just eating plain fruit.

Strawberries in Butterscotch Sauce

Serves: 4 to 6

> 1 cup packed brown sugar
> 1 cup dark corn syrup
> $^1/_2$ cup whipping cream
> 3 or 4 drops of vanilla extract
> 1 pint strawberries

Combine the sugar and corn syrup in a saucepan. Stir over low heat until the sugar dissolves. Cook for 5 minutes, or until slightly thickened. Remove from the heat. Stir in the cream and vanilla and beat for about 2 minutes, or until the sauce is smooth. Pour the warm sauce over the strawberries, divided among individual bowls.

Fresh Strawberries Devonshire

Serves: 6

> $^1/_2$ cup whipping cream
> $^1/_2$ cup sour cream
> 2 to 3 tablespoons orange-flavored liqueur
> 2 pints strawberries, hulled
> brown sugar
> mint sprigs

In a bowl, beat the cream until stiff peaks form. Fold in the sour cream and the liqueur. Place the strawberries in individual bowls and spoon the cream mixture over the top. Sprinkle with brown sugar to taste. Garnish with mint sprigs.

Rich Strawberry Shortcake

Serves: 6

2 cups sifted flour
2 tablespoons sugar
1 tablespoon baking powder
$1/2$ teaspoon salt
$1/2$ cup butter or margarine
1 egg, lightly beaten
$2/3$ cup light cream
*butter or margarine, softened, for
    spreading*
*3 to 4 cups sliced strawberries, sweetened
    with sugar*
1 cup whipping cream, whipped stiff

In a bowl, sift together the flour, sugar, baking powder, and salt. Add the butter and, using a pastry blender, cut in until the mixture resembles coarse crumbs. Combine the egg and cream in a small bowl and stir to combine. Add all at once to the flour mixture and stir only to moisten.

Preheat an oven to 450°F.

To make a large shortcake, grease an 8-inch round cake pan and spread the dough in it, slightly building up the dough around the edges. Bake for 15 to 18 minutes, or until golden brown. Remove from the pan to a rack and let cool for about 3 minutes. Using a serrated knife, split horizontally into 2 layers and lift off the top carefully. Spread butter on the bottom layer. Spoon some of the berries onto the bottom layer and top with some of the whipped cream. Replace the top layer and spoon the remaining berries and whipped cream over the top. Cut into 6 wedges and serve warm.

To make individual shortcakes, turn out the dough onto a floured work surface. Knead gently for 1 minute. Pat or roll out the dough $1/2$-inch thick. Using a floured $2 1/2$-inch round or fluted cutter, cut out 6 biscuits. Place on an ungreased baking sheet. Bake for about 10 minutes, or until golden brown. Remove to a rack to cool for about 3 minutes, then split horizontally into 2 layers. Spread butter on the bottom layers. Fill and top with the berries and whipped cream. Serve warm.

Plain Strawberry Shortcake

Serves: 6

2 cups sifted flour
1 tablespoon sugar
1 tablespoon baking powder
$1/2$ teaspoon salt
$1/3$ cup vegetable shortening
1 egg, beaten
$2/3$ cup milk
*butter or margarine, softened, for
    spreading*
*3 to 4 cups sliced strawberries, sweetened
    with sugar*
1 cup whipping cream, whipped stiff

In a bowl, sift together the flour, sugar, baking powder, and salt. Add the shortening

(continued)

Canned Versus Fresh Fruit

Fruit-and-cake-type desserts are among the few kinds of desserts in which canned fruits can be easily substituted for fresh fruits, creating wonderful surprise desserts during colder weather. Just be sure to drain the fruit thoroughly—if specified—before using it in the recipe, or else you might end up with a mushy mess. You can even mix two different fruits in the same recipe with ease.

and, using a pastry blender, cut in until the mixture resembles coarse crumbs. Combine the egg and milk in a small bowl and stir to combine. Add all at once to the flour mixture and stir only to moisten.

Preheat an oven to 450°F.

To make a large shortcake, follow the directions in Rich Strawberry Shortcake, increasing the baking time to 18 to 20 minutes. Cool, split, and fill as directed. To make individual shortcakes, follow the directions for the rich shortcake, then cool, split, and fill as directed.

Strawberry Whip

Serves: 4

>1 egg white
>1 1/4 cups strawberries, crushed
>1/4 cup sugar
>few drops of lemon juice

In a bowl, whip together the egg white and strawberries. When the mixture begins to thicken, gradually add the sugar. Continue to beat until the mixture holds soft peaks. Stir in the lemon juice. Chill well before serving.

Peach Shortcake

Serves: 8

>1 1/2 cups sifted flour
>2 teaspoons baking powder
>2 teaspoons sugar
>1/2 teaspoon salt

6 tablespoons vegetable shortening
1 egg, well beaten
1/2 cup milk
butter slices
3 cups peeled and sliced peaches
1 cup whipping cream, whipped

Preheat an oven to 400°F. Grease a 10-inch tube pan.

In a bowl, sift together the sifted flour, baking powder, sugar, and salt. Add the shortening and, using a pastry blender, cut in until the mixture resembles coarse meal. Combine the egg and cream in a small bowl and stir to combine. Add all at once to the flour mixture and stir only to moisten. Spread in the prepared tube pan. Bake for 25 minutes, or until a knife comes out clean. Immediately turn out onto a serving plate. Using 2 forks, tear slits 1 inch apart into the surface of the shortcake. Insert butter into the slits. Fill the center of the cake with the peaches. Serve with the whipped cream.

Blueberry Buckle

Serves: 8 to 10

1/2 cup vegetable shortening
1 cup sugar
1 egg, well beaten
2 1/2 cups sifted flour
1 1/2 teaspoons baking powder
1/4 teaspoon salt
1/2 cup milk

1 pint blueberries
1/2 teaspoon ground cinnamon
1/4 cup butter or margarine, softened

Preheat an oven to 350°F. Grease an 11 1/2-by-7 1/2-by-1 1/2-inch baking pan.

In a bowl, cream together the shortening and 1/2 cup of the sugar. Add the egg and mix well. Sift together 2 cups of the sifted flour, the baking powder, and the salt and add to the creamed mixture alternately with the milk. Pour into the prepared pan. Sprinkle the blueberries evenly over the batter. In a bowl, combine the remaining 1/2 cup sugar and 1/2 cup flour and the cinnamon. Add the butter and cut in with a pastry blender until crumbly. Sprinkle over the blueberries.

Bake for 45 to 50 minutes, or until blueberry mixture bubbles. Let cool slightly on a rack. Cut into 8 to 10 squares. Serve warm.

Apple Crisp with Variations

Serves: 8

4 or 5 tart cooking apples (about 4 medium), cored, peeled, and sliced
2/3 to 3/4 cup packed light brown sugar
1/2 cup flour
3/4 teaspoon ground nutmeg
3/4 teaspoon ground cinnamon
1/2 cup quick-cooking rolled oats
3/4 cup margarine or butter, softened
cream or ice cream (optional)

(continued)

Preheat an oven to 375°F. Grease an 8-inch square baking pan.

Arrange the apples in the prepared pan. In a bowl, combine the sugar, flour, nutmeg, cinnamon, and oats and stir well. Add the butter and cut in with a pastry blender until crumbly. Sprinkle over the apples.

Bake for about 30 minutes, or until the topping is golden brown and the apples are tender. Let cool slightly on a rack. Serve warm. Accompany with cream or ice cream, if desired.

Apricot Crisp: Substitute 2 cans (16 ounces each) apricot halves, drained, for the apples. Use the lesser amount of brown sugar.

Cherry Crisp: Substitute 1 can (21 ounces) cherry pie filling for the apples. Use the lesser amount of brown sugar.

Peach Crisp: Substitute 1 can (29 ounces) sliced peaches, drained. Use the lesser amount of brown sugar.

Fresh Apple Cream

Serves: 6

2 pounds tart apples, peeled, cored, and sliced
$^1/_2$ cup water
1 tablespoon lemon juice
1 teaspoon grated lemon rind
1 cup sugar

$^1/_2$ cup whipping cream, whipped
$^1/_2$ cup macaroon crumbs (see note)

In a saucepan, combine the apples and water and place over medium heat. Cover and cook for about 15 to 20 minutes, or until the apples fall apart. Remove from the heat and push through a strainer into a bowl. Add the lemon juice, lemon rind, and sugar and mix well. Fold in the whipped cream. Sprinkle with macaroon crumbs.

Note: To make the macaroon crumbs, heat 6 or 7 macaroons in a 350°F oven for 15 minutes. Let cool, then place between sheets of wax paper and crush with a rolling pin to make crumbs.

Lime-Pineapple Fluff

Serves: 6 to 8

1 can (12 ounces) crushed pineapple
1 envelope unflavored gelatin
$^1/_3$ cup sugar
pinch of salt
$^1/_4$ cup lime juice
1 cup whipping cream, whipped
few drops of green food coloring
whipped cream and sweetened fresh raspberries or thawed dry-pack frozen raspberries for serving

Drain the pineapple, reserving the syrup. Add enough water to the syrup to measure 1 $^1/_2$ cups. In a saucepan, combine the

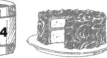

gelatin, sugar, and salt and stir well. Add the syrup mixture, place over low heat, and stir until the gelatin dissolves. Remove from the heat and add the lime juice. Chill for about 1 hour, or until partially set. Beat with an electric mixer until light and fluffy. Fold in the drained pineapple and the whipped cream. Add food coloring to tint pale green. Pour into a 1-quart mold. Chill until firm.

Unmold onto a serving plate. Top with additional whipped cream and sweetened red raspberries, or pass a bowl of thawed frozen berries (a few crystals remaining) for a sauce.

Baked Pears

Serves: 6

2 tablespoons lemon juice
6 pears, peeled and cored
2 to 4 tablespoons sugar
whipped cream (optional)

Preheat an oven to 375°F.
In a 2-quart baking dish, combine the lemon juice and enough water to cover the bottom. Add the pears, cover, and bake for 20 to 25 minutes, or until tender.

Remove from the oven. Uncover and sprinkle each pear with 1 to 2 teaspoons sugar. Bake, uncovered, for 10 minutes longer to glaze. Serve warm or chilled. Top with whipped cream, if desired.

Pears In Kirsch

Serves: 8

1 cup packed brown sugar
1 cup water
8 firm pears, peeled with stems intact
¹/₂ cup kirsch

In a wide saucepan, combine the sugar and water. Heat, stirring, until the sugar is dissolved. Add the pears to the syrup and cook over low heat about 10 minutes, basting frequently. Turn the pears over when they are about half done. When the pears are soft but are still holding their shape, remove from the syrup with a slotted spoon. Pour the kirsch into a shallow bowl and dip each pear into the liqueur. Set aside to cool in a serving dish. Add the remaining kirsch to the syrup and continue cooking over low heat for about 10 minutes longer, or until slightly reduced. Pour the syrup over the pears. Serve very cold.

Poached Pears

Serves: 4

4 firm Bosc pears
juice of 1 lemon
1¹/₂ cups dry red wine
³/₄ cup packed brown sugar
vanilla ice cream

Preheat an oven to 350°F.

(continued)

In a heavy saucepan, combine the lemon juice, wine, and sugar and bring to a simmer. Cook 7 to 8 minutes, or until the sugar is dissolved. Lay the pears next to one another in a baking pan. (Use a pan that will hold the pears snugly.) Pour the simmering liquid over the pears and cover tightly with aluminum foil. Make slits in the foil.

Bake for about 10 minutes. Uncover and turn the pears over. Re-cover and cook for 10 to 15 minutes longer, or until the pears are tender and the liquid is slightly reduced. Serve warm over vanilla ice cream.

Pears à la Compote

Serves: 4

> 1 cup sugar
> 3 cups water
> 1/3 cup lemon or lime juice
> pinch of salt
> 4 pears
> 2 cups grapes

In a saucepan, combine the sugar, water, lime juice, and salt. Bring to a boil. Meanwhile, halve the pears lengthwise, leaving the stems intact, and core but do not peel. Add the pears to the syrup. Cover and cook over low heat for 20 minutes, or until tender.

Arrange the grapes and pears in a serving dish. Pour the hot syrup over the fruit. Chill before serving.

Ginger Pear Crumble

Serves: 6

> 1 1/2 cups fine gingersnap crumbs
> 1/2 cup packed brown sugar
> 1/2 teaspoon salt
> 1/4 cup butter or margarine, melted and
>   cooled
> 3 fresh pears, halved, peeled, and cored,
>   or 1 can (16 ounces) pear halves,
>   drained
> 1 tablespoon lemon juice
> 6 maraschino cherries
> vanilla ice cream or whipped cream

Preheat an oven to 350°F.

Grease an 8 1/4-inch round baking dish with 1 1/4-inch sides.

In a bowl, combine the crumbs, brown sugar, salt, and butter. Place half of the mixture in the bottom of the prepared dish. Top with pear halves, cut sides up. Sprinkle with the lemon juice and the remaining crumbs.

Bake for 25 to 30 minutes, or until the pears are tender and the top is crisp. To serve, place a maraschino cherry in the hollow of each pear half. Serve warm topped with ice cream or whipped cream.

Blueberry Flummery

Serves: 6

> 2 tablespoons cornstarch
> $^1/_2$ cup sugar
> 1$^1/_2$ cups water
> 2$^1/_4$ cups dry-pack frozen blueberries,
>   rinsed and drained
> grated rind and juice of 1 lemon
> lemon rind strips
> whipping cream (optional)

In a saucepan, combine the cornstarch and sugar and stir well. Stir in the water, blueberries, grated rind, and lemon juice. Place over low heat and cook, stirring, for about 10 to 15 minutes, or until the flummery bubbles and thickens. Spoon into sherbet glasses. Let cool and chill well.

Garnish each serving with a twist of lemon rind and accompany with cream, if desired.

Brown Betty

Serves: 8

> 2 cups bread crumbs or graham cracker
>   crumbs
> $^3/_4$ cup butter, melted and cooled
> 3 or 4 apples, peeled, cored, and sliced
> $^1/_2$ cup packed brown or granulated sugar
> 1 tablespoon lemon juice
> $^1/_2$ teaspoon grated lemon rind
> $^1/_3$ cup hot water

(continued)

Grunts, Crumbles, Slumps, and Buckles

I love eating these kinds of desserts simply because their names are so much fun. It's said that these dishes took their names from the types of sounds they made while baking, as well as what happened after they cooled: the hot fruit filling would "grunt" while baking, and then the pastry topping would "buckle" before serving. Here's an idea: make one of these dishes and ask your family or guests to describe it as a grunt, crumble, slump, or buckle, then have them defend their choices.

Preheat an oven to 375°F. Grease an 8-inch square baking pan.

In a skillet, combine the crumbs and butter. Place over low heat and stir until lightly browned. Place one-third of the crumb mixture in the prepared pan. Arrange half of the apples over the crumbs. Sprinkle with half of the sugar, lemon juice, and rind. Top with half of the remaining crumbs and all the remaining apples, sugar, lemon juice, and lemon rind. Cover with the remaining crumbs. Pour the water evenly over the top. Bake for 30 to 40 minutes.

Serve warm with whipped cream or ice cream.

Apple Dumplings

Serves: 6

> 1 1/2 cups sugar
> 1 1/2 cups water
> 1/4 teaspoon ground cinnamon
> 1/4 teaspoon ground nutmeg
> 6 to 10 drops red food coloring
> 3 tablespoons butter or margarine
> 2 cups sifted flour
> 2 teaspoons baking powder
> 1 teaspoon salt
> 2/3 cup vegetable shortening
> 1/2 cup milk
> 6 medium apples, peeled and cored
> whipping cream

In a saucepan, combine 1 cup of the sugar, the water, cinnamon, nutmeg, and food coloring. Bring to a boil. Remove from the heat and add the butter. In a bowl, sift together the flour, baking powder, and salt. Add the shortening and, using a pastry blender, cut in until the mixture resembles coarse crumbs. Add the milk all at once and stir just until the flour is moistened. Gather into a ball and place on a lightly floured work surface. Roll out the dough into an 18-by-12-inch rectangle between 1/8 and 1/4 inch thick. Cut into six 6-inch squares. Place a whole apple in the center of each square. Sprinkle each apple generously with the remaining sugar and the remaining cinnamon and nutmeg; dot with the remaining butter. Moisten the edges of the squares. Bring up the corners to the center and pinch the edges together to seal. Place 1 inch apart in an ungreased 11 1/2-by-7 1/2-by-1 1/2-inch baking pan. Pour the syrup over the dumplings; sprinkle with the remaining sugar.

Bake for 35 minutes, or until the apples are tender. Serve warm with cream.

Note: If you wish, you may use 1/2 apple, sliced, in each square of pastry.

Baked Apples

Serves: 6

> 6 large baking apples
> 6 to 12 tablespoons brown or white sugar
> 2 tablespoons butter
> 1 cup water

Preheat an oven to 350°F.

Core the apples. Peel a strip from the top of each apple. Place in a baking dish. In the center of each apple, place 1 to 2 tablespoons brown or white sugar and $1/2$ teaspoon butter. Pour the water around the apples. Bake, uncovered, for 45 to 60 minutes, or until the apples are tender, basting several times during baking. Serve hot.

Variations: The apple centers may also be filled with chopped dates, raisins, or mincemeat. Or mix $1/4$ teaspoon aniseeds and 1 tablespoon chopped nuts with the sugar for each apple.

Peach Crumble

Serves: 4

> 1 can sliced peaches, drained
> $1/4$ cup pie crust mix
> 1 teaspoon grated lemon rind (optional)
> $3/4$ cup packed brown sugar
> butter or margarine, cut into bits
> whipped dessert topping or light cream

Preheat an oven to 325°F.

Place the peaches in a medium-sized baking dish. Add the lemon rind, if using. Crumble the pie crust mix into a bowl; add the sugar and mix well. Dust the peaches with the pie crust mixture and dot liberally with the butter or margarine. Bake for 45 minutes, or until top is crusty. Serve warm with dessert topping or cream.

French Apple Cobbler

Serves: 8 to 10

Filling:

> 5 cups peeled and sliced tart apples
> $3/4$ cup sugar
> 2 tablespoons flour
> $1/4$ teaspoon salt
> $1/2$ teaspoon ground cinnamon
> 1 teaspoon vanilla extract
> $1/4$ cup water
> 1 tablespoon butter or margarine, cut into bits

Batter:

> $1/2$ cup sifted flour
> $1/2$ cup sugar
> $1/2$ teaspoon baking powder
> $1/4$ teaspoon salt
> 2 tablespoons butter or margarine, softened
> 1 egg, lightly beaten

> whipped cream (optional)

Preheat an oven to 375°F.

To make the filling, combine the apples, sugar, flour, salt, cinnamon, vanilla, and water. Turn into a 9-inch baking pan and dot the apples with the butter.

To make the batter, in a bowl, combine the sifted flour, sugar, baking powder, butter, and egg. Beat with a spoon until smooth. Drop the batter in 9 portions onto the apples,

(continued)

spacing evenly. (The batter will spread during baking.)

Bake for 35 to 40 minutes, or until the apples are fork tender and the crust is golden brown. Serve warm with whipped cream.

Toffee Apples and Bananas

Serves: 4

> 2 large Granny Smith apples
> 2 large ripe bananas
> $\frac{1}{4}$ cup flour
> $\frac{1}{4}$ cup cornstarch
> 1 egg
> 3 teaspoons sesame oil
> 1$\frac{1}{3}$ cups peanut oil
> $\frac{3}{4}$ cup granulated sugar
> 2 tablespoons sesame seeds, toasted

Peel and core the apples, then cut each into 8 large wedges. Peel the bananas and cut them into 1$\frac{1}{2}$-inch chunks. In a small bowl, stir together the flour, cornstarch, egg, and 1 teaspoon of the sesame oil until a smooth, very thick batter forms.

In a deep-fat fryer or a wok, combine the peanut oil and the remaining 2 teaspoons sesame oil. Heat until medium-hot. Slip the fruit pieces, a few at a time, into the batter. Then, using a slotted spoon, lift out the pieces, draining off excess batter. Slip the pieces into the hot oil and deep-fry for about 2 minutes, or until golden. Again using a

slotted spoon, transfer to paper towels to drain. Repeat the process until you have deep-fried all the fruit.

Just before serving, ready a bowl of ice water filled with ice cubes. Reheat the oil over medium heat and deep-fry the fruit a second time for about 2 minutes. Drain again on paper towels. Put the sugar, sesame seeds, and 2 tablespoons of the deep-frying oil into a saucepan. Place over medium heat and cook until the sugar melts and begins to caramelize.

When the caramel is light brown, add the fruit pieces. Stir gently to coat them with the caramel syrup. Then, using a slotted spoon or tongs, remove the pieces a few at a time and drop them into the ice water to harden. Do them only a few at a time to prevent them from sticking together. Remove them from the water and place on a serving platter. Serve at once.

Sweet Banana Risotto

Serves: 4

> 1 cup raw Arborio rice
> 3 ripe bananas peeled and sliced
> $\frac{1}{4}$ cup packed brown sugar
> 3 cups milk
> $\frac{1}{4}$ cup crème de cacao liqueur
> $\frac{1}{2}$ teaspoon ground cinnamon

Preheat an oven to 375°F.

Sprinkle about one-third of the rice in the bottom of a 2-quart baking dish. Then sprinkle

on one-third of the banana slices and one-third of the sugar. Repeat the layers twice. Slowly pour in the milk, being careful not to disturb the layers, and then pour in the crème de cacao. Sprinkle with the cinnamon. Cover and bake until the liquid has been absorbed and the rice is tender, about 1 hour. Serve warm.

Country Rhubarb Dessert

Serves: 8

2 cups cut-up rhubarb ($^1/_2$-inch chunks)
1$^1/_4$ cups flour
$^1/_2$ cup butter, softened
$^1/_3$ cup confectioners' sugar
3 eggs
1$^1/_4$ cups granulated sugar
1 teaspoon baking powder
1 teaspoon vanilla extract
$^1/_4$ teaspoon salt
whipped cream
1 pint strawberries, stemmed

Preheat an oven to 350°F. Grease a 9-inch square pan.

In a bowl, combine 1 cup of the flour and the butter. Using a pastry blender, blend together until the mixture resembles coarse crumbs. Add the confectioners' sugar and press into the prepared pan. Bake for 15 minutes, or until golden.

While the crust is baking, in a bowl, using an electric mixer set on medium speed, beat the eggs until frothy. Gradually add the granulated sugar and beat on high speed until very

(continued)

Roll That Jelly Roll

Most people opt for store-bought jelly rolls—even when they feel like making one themselves—because the rolling process makes them nervous. Here's a hint: you have to roll up the cake while it is still warm, so be sure to have all of your ingredients ready to go once you take it out of the oven.

Customized Fruitcakes

If you prefer, you can create your own mix of candied fruits and peels for fruitcake. I think they are much tastier and healthier than the store-bought mix, and they are easy to put together, too. I like 4 ounces each of candied citron, orange peel, lemon peel, and cherries with 12 ounces candied pineapple. You can buy the fruits and peels already chopped or dice them yourself.

light and fluffy, about 5 minutes. Reduce the speed to low and add the remaining $1/4$ cup flour, the baking powder, vanilla, and salt. Using a rubber spatula, fold in the rhubarb. Pour over the baked crust, spreading evenly. Bake for 40 minutes, or until light brown and the top feels dry. Let cool on a rack. Serve with whipped cream and strawberries.

Apple Turnovers

Makes: 8 turnovers

Pastry:
2 cups flour
1 teaspoon salt
$1/2$ pound (1 cup) butter, chilled
$1/2$ cup ice water

Filling:
4 large apples, peeled and sliced
1 cup granulated sugar
1 tablespoon cornstarch
1 teaspoon lemon juice
$1/4$ teaspoon ground cinnamon

1 egg
2 tablespoons water
$1/2$ cup confectioners' sugar

To make the pastry, in a bowl, stir together the flour and salt. Add half of the butter and cut in with a pastry blender until the mixture resembles coarse crumbs. Sprinkle with the

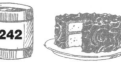

ice water and, using a fork, mix well. Shape the dough into a ball and place on a lightly floured work surface. Using a lightly floured rolling pin, roll out the dough into an 18-by-8-inch rectangle. Cut $\frac{1}{4}$ cup of the remaining butter into thin slices. Starting at one of the 8-inch sides, place the butter slices over two-thirds of the rectangle to within $\frac{1}{2}$ inch of the edges. Fold the unbuttered one-third of the pastry over the middle third. Then fold the opposite end over to make an 8-by-6-inch rectangle. Roll out the dough into an 18-by-8-inch rectangle. Slice the remaining $\frac{1}{4}$ cup butter. Place the slices on the dough and fold as before. Wrap in plastic wrap and chill for 30 minutes. Remove from the refrigerator and roll again to an 18-by-8-inch rectangle. Fold lengthwise then crosswise. Wrap again and chill for 1 hour.

To make the filling, in a saucepan, combine the apples, granulated sugar, cornstarch, lemon juice, and cinnamon. Place over low heat and cook, stirring frequently, until the apples are tender. Remove from the heat, let cool, cover, and chill.

Preheat an oven to 450°F. Remove the pastry dough from the refrigerator and cut in half crosswise. On a lightly floured work surface, roll out half of the dough into a 12-inch square; keep the other half chilled. Cut into quarters to make four 6-inch squares. Beat the egg in a cup with 1 tablespoon of the water; brush over the squares. (This

prevents the juice from the filling from soaking into the pastry.) Spoon one-eighth of the apple mixture in the center of each square; fold in half and press the edges to seal. Place the turnovers on an ungreased baking sheet. Chill while preparing the other half of the dough. Brush all the turnovers with the remaining egg mixture. With a knife, cut 2 small slashes on each turnover.

Bake for 20 minutes, or until golden. Let cool completely on a wire rack. In a bowl, beat together the confectioners' sugar and the remaining 1 tablespoon water. Drizzle over the turnovers.

The Everything
Dessert Cookbook

Chapter 15: Pasta Desserts

P asta for dessert? Sure, in fact, the next time you have guests over and serve an easy-to-prepare meal like roast chicken or pork roast, prepare one of the following pasta desserts to open their eyes. After they take one bite, you'll be lauded as an innovative genius!

Orange Almond Pastina Soufflé

Serves: 4

2 cups milk
$^1/_3$ cup pastina
$^3/_4$ cup sugar
3 tablespoons butter
2 tablespoons grated orange rind
1 teaspoon almond extract
4 eggs, separated, at room temperature

Preheat an oven to 350°F.

Pour the milk into a large saucepan and bring to just below a boil over high heat. Stir in the pastina. Reduce the heat to medium and cook, stirring constantly, for about 5 minutes, or until the pastina is softened and the mixture has thickened. Add $^1/_4$ cup of the sugar and stir until it dissolves. Stir in the butter, orange rind, and almond extract. Remove from the heat.

In a bowl, beat the egg yolks until blended. Add $^1/_4$ cup of the sugar and beat until foamy. In another bowl, beat the egg whites, adding the remaining $^1/_4$ cup sugar as they become foamy. Then continue to beat until shiny but not too stiff. Fold the yolks into the pastina mixture, mixing well. Then carefully fold in the egg whites just until no white streaks remain. Pour into a 2-quart baking dish set in a baking pan. Add hot water to the pan to a depth of 1 inch.

Bake for about 35 minutes, or until the contents are set and the top is golden. Serve warm or at room temperature.

Berry Medley with Noodles

Serves: 6

juice of 1 lemon
3 tablespoons fruit-flavored brandy
2 cups mixed berries such as blueberries, strawberries, and raspberries
$^1/_3$ cup confectioners' sugar
3 quarts water
1 teaspoon salt
8 ounces medium egg noodles
$^3/_4$ cup half-and-half
$^1/_4$ cup walnuts, coarsely chopped and toasted

Combine the lemon juice and brandy in a cup. Place the berries in shallow bowl and sprinkle with the sugar and the brandy mixture. Chill for 2 hours.

In a large pot, bring the water to a rolling boil. Add the salt and the noodles and stir to prevent sticking. Cook until al dente. Drain.

Pour the half-and-half into a wide saucepan large enough to hold the noodles. Add the noodles and toss over low heat. Transfer to a warmed serving dish and top with the berries. Sprinkle with the nuts and serve.

Festive Farfalline

Serves: 4

> juice of 2 oranges
> grated rind of 1 orange
> $1/4$ cup unsalted butter
> $1/4$ cup sugar
> $1/4$ cup light cream
> 2 kiwifruits, peeled and each cut into
>   eighths
> 3 quarts water
> 1 teaspoon salt
> 8 ounces farfalline
> 2 tablespoons flaked dried coconut,
>   toasted
> vanilla ice cream (optional)

In a wide saucepan, combine the orange juice and rind, butter, sugar, and cream. Place over low heat and stir until the sugar has dissolved and the mixture is heated through. Add the kiwifruits; keep warm.

Meanwhile, in a large pot, bring the water to a rolling boil. Add the salt and farfalline, stirring to prevent sticking. Cook until al dente. Drain.

Add the pasta to the saucepan holding the sauce and toss over low heat until well combined. Pour into a warmed serving dish. Sprinkle with the coconut. Serve alone or with ice cream.

Tagliatelle with Peaches

Serves: 4

> juice of 1 orange
> grated rind of 1 orange
> $1/4$ cup plus 1 tablespoon unsalted butter
> 2 tablespoons plus 1 teaspoon sugar
> 1 tablespoon Cointreau or other orange-
>   flavored liqueur
> 2 peaches, peeled, pitted, and sliced
> $1/2$ teaspoon ground cinnamon
> 3 quarts water
> 1 teaspoon salt
> 8 ounces tagliatelle
> 2 tablespoons chopped pecans, toasted

In a wide saucepan, combine the orange juice and rind, $1/4$ cup butter, and 2 tablespoons sugar. Place over low heat and stir until the sugar has dissolved and the mixture is heated through. Add the Cointreau, stir well, and heat through; keep warm. In a small saucepan, melt the 1 tablespoon butter over low heat. Add the peach slices and sprinkle with the 1 teaspoon sugar and cinnamon. Heat through, but do not cook; keep warm.

Meanwhile, in a large pot, bring the water to a rolling boil. Add the salt and tagliatelle, stirring to prevent sticking. Cook until al

(continued)

Pasta Desserts

In one short decade, the American pasta lexicon has gone from spaghetti and macaroni to such wonderfully trilling words as radiatori, farfalle, and tagliatelle, plus pasta is even turning up in desserts. And why not? After all, cooks have used rice as an important dessert ingredient for centuries. Use my pasta recipes as a springboard for your own imaginative pasta desserts.

dente. Drain. Add the pasta to the orange juice mixture and toss over low heat until well combined. Pour into a warmed serving dish and top with the peaches. Sprinkle with the pecans and serve.

Honeyed Noodles With Bananas

Serves: 4

$3/4$ cup honey
juice of 2 lemons
grated rind of 1 lemon
$1/2$ cup unsalted butter
2 bananas, peeled and sliced
3 quarts water
1 teaspoon salt
8 ounces wide egg noodles
2 tablespoons almonds, coarsely chopped
    and toasted

In a small saucepan, combine the honey, lemon juice and rind, and raisins. Set aside. Melt the butter in a small skillet over medium heat. Add the bananas and brown on both sides.

Meanwhile, in a large pot, bring the water to a rolling boil. Add the salt and noodles, stirring to prevent sticking. Cook until al dente. Drain.

Place the pasta in a warmed serving dish. Carefully toss with the honey mixture and the bananas. Top with the nuts and serve.

Magic Cookie Wontons

Makes: 30 cookies

3 dozen wonton skins
2 squares (2 ounces) semisweet chocolate
$\frac{1}{2}$ cup butter, melted
$\frac{1}{2}$ cup confectioners' sugar
$\frac{1}{4}$ cup walnuts, chopped
2 tablespoons flaked dried coconut
1 egg white
vegetable oil for deep-frying
confectioners' sugar for dusting

In a saucepan, melt the chocolate over low heat, stirring frequently. Remove from the heat and let cool. Whisk in the melted butter. Add the confectioners' sugar and whisk or beat with a wooden spoon until well combined. Stir in the nuts and coconut.

Lay out about 10 wonton skins on a work surface. Keep the remainder covered to prevent drying. Brush each wonton skin very lightly with the beaten egg white. In the center of each, place 1 teaspoon of the chocolate filling. Fold to form a triangle, sealing the edges. With the center point at the top, fold back the two other corners so that the right corner overlaps the left corner. Press the ends together to seal, using additional egg white to hold if necessary. Place on a lightly oiled baking sheet and cover with a towel. Continue until all the wonton skins are filled.

In a 5-quart saucepan or a deep fryer, pour in oil to a depth of 2 inches and heat to 370°F. When the oil is hot, add the wontons a few at a time and fry, turning as necessary, for about 5 minutes, or until golden brown. Using tongs or a slotted spoon, remove to paper towels to drain. Keep warm while frying the remaining filled wontons. Sprinkle with confectioners' sugar and serve hot.

Couscous with Yogurt and Fruit

Serves: 4

1 cup milk
1 tablespoon butter
$\frac{1}{4}$ teaspoon salt
$\frac{2}{3}$ cup quick-cooking couscous
$\frac{1}{2}$ cup vanilla yogurt
2 tablespoons sugar
$\frac{1}{2}$ cup diced fresh fruit or whole berries
sugar for sprinkling

In a saucepan, combine the milk, butter, and salt and bring to a boil. Stir in the couscous. Cover and remove from the heat. Let stand for 5 minutes.

Fluff the couscous with a fork to separate the grains. Stir in the yogurt and sugar and fold in the fruit. Sprinkle with additional sugar and serve hot.

Noodle Pudding with Nut Topping

Serves: 8

3 quarts water
$1\frac{1}{2}$ teaspoons salt

(continued)

8 ounces medium egg noodles
3 tablespoons unsalted butter
3 eggs
1 cup cottage cheese
1 cup sour cream
1/2 cup sugar
1/2 teaspoon salt
juice of 1/2 lemon
1/2 teaspoon ground cinnamon
1/2 cup raisins

Topping:
2/3 cup sugar
6 tablespoons butter, softened, cut up
1/2 cup flour
1 cup walnuts, finely chopped
1/2 teaspoon ground cinnamon

Preheat an oven to 350°F.

In a large pot, bring the water to a rolling boil. Add 1 teaspoon of the salt and the noodles, stirring to prevent sticking. Cook until al dente. Transfer to a large bowl and toss with the butter.

Meanwhile, in a large bowl, combine the cottage cheese and sour cream and beat with an electric mixer until smooth. Beat in the sugar, the remaining 1/2 teaspoon salt, the lemon juice, and cinnamon. Fold in the raisins. In a separate bowl, beat the eggs until frothy.

To make the topping, combine all the ingredients in another bowl and crumble together with your fingers to form a pebblelike consistency.

Combine the noodles with the cottage cheese mixture, mixing well. Transfer to a 9-by-13-inch baking dish. Pour the eggs over the top, then spread the topping evenly over the surface.

Bake for 1 hour, or until set and top is golden brown. Serve warm.

Fruit Kugel

Serves: 8

4 quarts water
1 teaspoon salt
1 1/2 pounds flat noodles
1/2 cup margarine or corn oil
3 apples, peeled, cored, and chopped
1/2 cup raisins
3 eggs, beaten
1 tablespoon sugar (optional)
ground cinnamon and sugar

Preheat an oven to 375°F. Grease an 8-by-10-inch baking dish.

In a large pot, bring the water to a boil. Add the salt and noodles, stirring to prevent sticking. Cook until al dente. Drain.

Place the noodles in a large bowl and add the margarine, apples, and raisins. Toss to combine. Add the eggs and the sugar, if using, and mix thoroughly. Spoon into the prepared baking dish. Sprinkle generously with cinnamon and sugar.

Bake for 30 minutes, or until top is brown and crisp. Serve hot.

Fruit-Filled Lasagna

Serves: 8

2 quarts water

4 lasagna noodles

*1 pound (two 8-ounce packages) cream
cheese, softened*

½ cup sugar

½ cup half-and-half

2 eggs

*1 can (21 ounces) apple or other fruit pie
filling*

Topping:

¼ cup sugar

¼ cup packed brown sugar

*½ cup old-fashioned or quick-cooking
rolled oats*

2 tablespoons flour

2 tablespoons butter, softened, cut up

¼ teaspoon ground nutmeg

pinch of salt

Preheat an oven to 325°F.

In a pot, bring the water to a boil. Add
the salt and the noodles, stirring to prevent
sticking. Cook until al dente. Do not pour the
noodles directly into a colander or they will
stick together. Bring the pot to the sink and
position it over a colander. Run cold water
into the pot as you pour the noodles out.
Grab each noodle with your fingers, gently
shake, and place on a paper towel or cloth to
blot excess water. Keep moist under a lightly
dampened towel until ready to fill.

(continued)

Coffee as the Final Touch

Sometimes, when you serve a
wonderfully satisfying meal,
everyone is completely
stuffed and not even thinking
about dessert. However,
something is missing; you
need a sweet taste, but you
can't eat another bite.

Serving coffee is the
perfect answer. Not only will
the caffeine help to perk up
you and your guests, but the
sweet tooth that everyone
lays claim to—whether they
admit it or not—will be
satisfied by adding sugar,
creme, or your favorite
liqueur.

Meanwhile, in a bowl, combine the cream cheese and sugar and beat with an electric mixer until light and airy. Beat in the half-and-half and eggs briefly, just until the mixture is smooth. Have the pie filling ready. To make the topping, in a bowl, combine all the ingredients and crumble together with your fingers to form a pebblelike consistency.

To assemble the lasagna, spread about one-third of the pie filling on the bottom of a 9-by-12-inch baking dish. Lay 2 noodles on top. Spread half of the cream cheese mixture over the noodles. Spread another third of the pie filling over the cream cheese mixture. Top with the remaining 2 noodles. Spread the remaining cream cheese mixture over the top and then the remaining pie filling. Spread the topping evenly over the surface.

Bake for about 50 minutes, or until a knife inserted in the center comes out clean. Let stand for 15 minutes before cutting. Serve warm or at room temperature.

Chocolate Lasagna

Serves: 8

1 3/4 cups flour
2 tablespoons unsweetened cocoa powder
2 pinches of salt
2 eggs
2 teaspoons corn oil
4 cups part-skim ricotta cheese
2 cups whipping cream
6 tablespoons sugar
1 tablespoons grated orange rind
2 tablespoons Grand Marnier or other
*   orange-flavored liqueur*

12 squares (12 ounces) bittersweet
*   chocolate, chopped*

In a bowl, stir together the flour, cocoa, and 1 pinch of salt. Make a well in the center. Add the eggs and oil to the well and mix with a fork to form a dough. Turn out onto a floured work surface and knead the dough until smooth and shiny, about 15 minutes, adding more flour if necessary to keep the dough from sticking. Wrap well with plastic wrap and let it rest for 30 minutes.

Roll out the pasta dough by hand on a lightly floured work surface (or on a pasta machine) into a thin sheet. Cut into eight 4 1/2-by-11-inch strips. Bring a saucepan filled with salted water to a boil. Add 2 strips of the dough and cook for just 20 seconds after the water returns to a boil. Remove with a slotted spoon or skimmer and plunge into cold water to stop the cooking. Drain in a colander. Repeat with the remaining dough strips, cooking only 2 strips at a time.

In a bowl, combine the ricotta cheese, cream, sugar, orange rind, Grand Marnier, and the remaining pinch of salt. Stir until very smooth.

Preheat an oven to 425°F. Grease a 9-by-13-inch baking dish.

Form a layer with 2 of the noodles in the bottom of the prepared dish. Top with one-fourth of the cheese filling and then one-third of the chocolate. Repeat the layers, ending with the cheese filling.

Bake for 20 to 25 minutes, or until the top is lightly colored. Let the lasagna stand for 10 minutes before cutting. Serve warm.

INDEX

254